Born in France in 1909, Robert Charroux was a civil servant in the Department of Posts and Telegraphs from 1930 to 1943, and then served as the Minister for Cultural Affairs in the French Government for the following two years. After 1945 he worked as a journalist, but from 1960 onwards he has become increasingly well known as a writer on archaeology and prehistory, and his reinterpretation of ancient civilizations and his enthusiasm for discovering and explaining strange phenomena have gained him a large following both in Europe and America. His books have been widely translated, and both *Lost Worlds* and *The Mysterious Unknown* (1969) have become international best-sellers. Robert Charroux is at present working on a book which will reveal his discovery of remarkable prehistoric cave paintings in the Andes.

Robert Charroux

LOST WORLDS

Scientific Secrets of the Ancients

Translated by Lowell Blair

FONTANA/COLLINS

First published by Éditions Robert Laffont in 1971
under the title *Le Livre des Mondes Oubliés*

First English language edition published in the U.S.A.
by Walker Publishing Company Inc.

First British edition published in 1973 by Souvenir Press Ltd.
Published in Fontana 1974
© Éditions Robert Laffont 1971
English translation © Walker & Co. 1973

Made and printed in Great Britain by
William Collins Sons & Co. Ltd., Glasgow

Contents

Illustrations

Acknowledgements

Those photographs not supplied by the author are reproduced
be permission of the following: *Plate 1*, Paul Popper Ltd.;
Plate 7, Horst V. Irmer; *Plate 18*, Francis Mazière; *Plate 19*,
'Cl. X' from *Kama Kala* by Mulk Raj Anand; *Plate 21*, Roger
Viollet Agency.

'He who builds, sows, plants, and launches ideas is inhabited by the Creator.
'He who destroys, cuts down, and criticizes is under the dominion of the devil.'

PREFACE

The Pyramid in France

There is a pyramid as big as a cathedral at Plouézoch, in the department of Finistère, France.

The radiant rock of Ylo, north of Arequipa, Peru, bears an indecipherable inscription which, according to tradition, tells how to reach the entrance to the 'Ancient Lost World.'

An explorer in the Brazilian wilderness found an electric lamp, composed of a column surmounted by a sphere, that had been shining since time immemorial.

A hundred thousand years ago, our Superior Ancestors successfully performed heart transplants. Proof of this is in the University of Leningrad.

Soviet scientists have just discovered the second half of the secret of the Philosopher's Stone and are already making the mother water of immortality.

These revelations and a score of others like them make up the strange and mysterious content of this book – the content that you expect. Whenever possible, the assertions are supported by photographs.

In short, it is unlikely that the book will disappoint you in the parts devoted to forgotten continents, archaeology, the bizarre, and the Mysterious Unknown.

But afterward . . .

The Mystery of Jesus

Afterward, there is the problem of Jesus. He will be laid bare, dissected, examined from the most heretical viewpoints in a smell of fire and brimstone – exposed, that is, in his most convincing probable reality, the one that is accepted by the five to ten thousand people in the world who *know but cannot speak*. It will be a harsh, irritating investigation, but not at all sacrilegious. The Jesus of the Gospels will not be spared, but the real, authentic Jesus, the Essenian Teacher of Righteousness, stern and incorruptible, will emerge alive.

Foreseeing certain reactions, I want to assure the reader of my good faith. It is as a historian, an exegetist – not as a Christian, an atheist, or a man who has made up his mind in advance and owes allegiance to a conspiracy – that I have studied the pseudo-Holy Scriptures, others that you probably do not know, and finally the Dead Sea Scrolls. Moreover, what I express is only the most acceptable hypothesis. I grant the possibility that it may be false or only partially accurate. At any rate I am obliged to present things from this viewpoint to avoid going beyond the narrow bounds of permitted freedom.

I am a Heretic

Have I not already been banished from television, radio, and the mass-circulation press?

We must grope our way toward truth, with successive errors and empirical discoveries. The seeker wanders in a labyrinth without ever reaching the Centre.

Mea culpa, mea culpa; I have made many mistakes: the Candlestick of the Andes is not carved in rock, but dug in sand; the 'round stones of Guatemala' are not vestiges of an ancient civilization, but are of volcanic origin . . . I have been misled by false statements, but in this book I will humbly correct my errors.

A more serious charge is brought against me: students in high schools and universities too often use my books as justification for disputing some of the conventional doctrines taught to them.

I sincerely deplore this and I ask my young friends to understand that although some of the views I present – in prehistory, for example – are based on conclusive evidence, most of them are only exercises, intellectual games that are subject to improvement, useful in sharpening the mind and *perhaps* capable of being confirmed some day. But this work, this game, presupposes knowledge of classical theories in chemistry, physics, biology, and mathematics.

Robert Charroux Clubs have been formed in France and abroad, spontaneously. They are composed of students and other young people interested in unconventional knowledge, the unusual and the supranormal. These clubs periodically receive subjects for study, discussion, and reflection, but I notify my friends *beforehand* that these are only working hypotheses. I do not wish to lead them away from their scholastic education in any way. Quite the contrary.

Initiation and Science

In this book, initiation and the Mysterious Unknown are treated more in depth than in my previous works. I have made a greater effort to eliminate superstitions and blind, deceptive beliefs. Here, too, I may offend a few readers devoted to loose and easy ways of thinking, but the initiation I am proposing is not meant for the great majority, or to be pleasing and reassuring. It is meant only to be a means of seeking knowledge.

'He who seeks truth and demands it impatiently must ask it of someone who knows. Any impostor will do.'

Everything he says will be as sweet as honey, as comforting as a balm, as empty as his brain.

Ultimately, the tragic history of civilizations has always been characterized by a long struggle between the two great human breeds: the oppressors and the oppressed, the evil, always victorious, and the good, always vanquished. Perhaps the initiate belongs to a third breed. This is only a supposition, however; the truth must be sought, but woe to him who finds it.

R. C.

Part 1

THE FANTASTIC

The Candlestick of the Andes and the Mystery of Nazca

When people discover unusual things on their planet, such as drawings or writing that they can neither date nor decipher, they are invariably tempted to ascribe them to unknown and sometimes even extraterrestrial civilizations. Furthermore, these mysteries are always regarded as having the nature of a message.

On two hills called Gog and Magog, near Cambridge, England, one can see from an aeroplane immense drawings that escape observation on the ground. Victor Kernbach reports that in Somerset there is a map of the sky as seen from our hemisphere, reproduced by the dry land and the canals bordering a pond several miles long. In the United States there are earth embankments shaped to represent enormous snakes, the work of a mysterious ancient people.

These symbols seem to have been intended for observers coming from the sky or capable of rising above the earth, either in machines or by the power of their astral bodies.

Mysterious Grooves

The Paracas Peninsula is a hundred and ninety miles south of Lima, Peru. It is here that the enigmatic Candlestick of the Andes is dug into the side of a small, purple, crescent-shaped mountain. The soil of the mountainside is sandy, with a thin surface layer of purple gravel over a thick layer of fine, compact, yellow sand without a trace of impurity.

The Candlestick, or Los Tres Cruces, as it is called in the region, is across the bay from Pisco, ten miles away. Since the Peruvians are not very curious by nature, I believe that we – Yvette Charroux, my friend Edmond Wartenschlag, and I – were the first people to set foot on the sands of Paracas in this century.

On April 26, 1969, we rented a small yacht at our hotel, crossed the bay and, after a difficult approach to the steep cliffs, went ashore less than a mile from the Candlestick. Our captain anchored two hundred yards offshore because he was unfamiliar with the bottom. He had never had any desire to land and see the Candlestick from close up!

We found that the ground was completely clear of human footprints. We saw only the tracks of a puma.

'He must have been here last night,' remarked Yvette Charroux, because the tracks appeared to be quite fresh.

'Or last week,' replied Edmond Wartenschlag, who knew about the phenomena of Paracas.

Or it might have been ten years ago! For this is the miraculous property of the Paracas dunes that has enabled the Candlestick to survive the hazards of time and weather: once an imprint is made in the sand, it is preserved indefinitely.

On our way to the Candlestick from the point where we landed, we walked parallel to the shore on a little plateau of rather hard sand. The dunes rose on our left at an angle of forty degrees, to an altitude of about twelve hundred feet. We soon made our first discovery: three grooves running from the top of a dune to the edge of the cliff. They were less than an inch deep and looked like three tracks made by a wheel ten inches wide – as though a wheel had rolled down the slope three times *all by itself*. Explain it if you can!

The Miracle of the Golden Sand

As we approached the Candlestick, the sand became increasingly softer and Yvette's bare feet sank into it up to her ankles, leaving deep yellow tracks that contrasted sharply with the purple surface around them.

Before us, only the Incas or their ancestors had passed over this ground, on their way to dig the mysterious monument. I carefully stepped in Yvette's footprints, out of an obscure respect for the virginity of the sand. We were all filled with deep emotion.

The Candlestick – but is it really a candlestick? – is formed by trenches dug into the slope. They are generally though not always bordered by friable, striated, calcareous rocks, with what I believe to be quartz protruding from between their layers.

The centre axis of the Candlestick looks as if it might be the furrow left by a gigantic toboggan or boat that had been dragged along the slope. It is about fifteen feet wide, two feet deep, and fifteen hundred feet long. The two side branches, and the designs that seem to represent either persons or animals, are narrower and shallower. The rocks beside the grooves are half buried in the sand. They do not appear to have been cemented and are merely strewn along the edges of the grooves, rather than being precisely aligned.

In some places the slope is so steep that Yvette had to climb it on all fours and even then she felt uneasy because the wind blows very hard in the Pisco region. The winds of Paracas are as famous in Peru as the tramontana in the Mediterranean.

These details are extremely important because *in spite of the strong wind and the steepness of the slope, there was not one grain of sand in the air, not even a speck of dust.* The forces of dispersion are overcome by the density of the sand. It is an established fact that very fine sand resists wind and that a microscopic powder will not move in the midst of a hurricane.

It is incredible but true: in the sands of Paracas, traces that would be effaced in an hour anywhere else remain intact *for hundreds and probably even thousands of years.*

The Candlestick of the Andes

It is likely that the Candlestick of the Andes goes back to the time of the Incas, or perhaps to that of the Aymaras. The Christians, of course, have taken it over by baptizing it the 'Three Crosses.' The Indians usually called it the 'Trident.'

It has the shape of a three-branched candlestick, with the centre branch resting on a rectangular base. In the middle of this base is an excavation in the sand, presumably made much later than the Candlestick itself.

At the top of the centre branch is a kind of totem with what seems to be a head and two upraised arms. A little farther down, on either side, are two projecting lines that end in spirals. The two side branches extend horizontally from just below the centre of the main branch, then turn upwards at right angles. Their tops are lower than that of the centre branch and they have the shape of a lizard or a salamander. The 'braces' (actually two trenches) fictitiously support these side branches.

The Candlestick has been said to be a 'tree of life,' but Eduardo Garcia Montero writes that it was 'a signal left by pirates to mark the vicinity of hidden treasure.' According to others, the 'Three Crosses' were made in about 1835 by a priest, Father Guatemala, 'between Pejerrez Point and San Gallán Island, so that the fishermen of Pisco Bay could contemplate them in that place lashed by furious winds.' This is unquestionably a pious falsehood, since the Candlestick was seen and described more than a century earlier.

The truth is that we cannot say with certainty when or by whom it was made. The miraculous preservation of the trenches that compose it has never been studied by Peruvian archaeologists; as for those of other countries, they are not even aware of its existence.

The only observation I will venture to make on the subject is that, apart from the natural resistance that the fine sand offers to the forces of dispersion, the orientation of the slope shelters it from the prevailing winds of Paracas, which usually blow from the west.

The Ker Lan of Paracas

What is the meaning of that great drawing which, lacking a better description, we are obliged to call the Candlestick of the Andes?

I have personally seen another 'candlestick,' larger and more beautiful, in the Nazca pampa. This one resembles a shrine.

It is undeniable that the Nazca drawings are closely related to the Candlestick of the Andes, and an explanation of one would provide essential data for solving the enigma of the other.

One thing is certain: the Paracas region (Pisco Bay) is rich in archaeological remains, to which its name has been given. The pottery of Paracas is famous in Peru. It was also at Paracas that a large number of Incan mummies were found in caves. There are surely others that have not been discovered and it seems reasonable to believe that this region was primarily a holy place, a burial ground: what the Celts called a *ker lan,* that is, 'city of the holy place.'

On the inner side of the peninsula, which I know well, and on the side facing the open sea, which I have not explored, there are many steep cliffs with deep caves in them. Some of these caves extend far underground, others are labyrinths with jagged pillars in which waves break and are multiplied in an array of shifting colours.

It was in these caves that the famous 'Paracas mummies' were discovered; it was in them – according to conjectures that are probably true – that pirates and privateers once hid their treasures.

Did pirates make the Candlestick of the Andes so they could easily recognize the place where their booty was hidden?

Certainly not. The Candlestick dates from before the sixteenth century. Furthermore, the design of the Candlestick – a trident with salamanders – seems much more closely related to the style of the Incas than to that of pirates!

The Sign of a Taboo

As is commonly believed in Peru, and as my friend Kerlam has conjectured, the Candlestick must be given the value of a sign. I am surely not far from the truth in maintaining that the Paracas Peninsula is placed under the sign of a taboo.

At the foot of the mountain: tombs, mummies, perhaps treasures, surely gold. At the top: the Candlestick keeping watch and proclaiming the taboo. It is forbidden to violate this place!

Here is an explanation that would be satisfactory if it could also be applied to the Nazca pampa.

On this hypothesis, the mysterious lines spread over an immense area, some of them nearly forty miles long, mark

and cover an enormous necropolis containing thousands and
thousands of mummies, each with a provision of gold for
the next world. All the gold of Peru . . . the most fantastic
treasure on the globe!

In this case, the geometrical lines and the drawings of
persons, flowers, animals (llamas, condors, spiders, snakes),
and objects such as the 'Shrine of Nazca' would constitute
either epitaphs that have become incomprehensible or bound-
aries for tribes, races, peoples, or generations.

Perhaps the prodigious treasure of the Incas, which Pizarro
and Almagro failed to find, is sleeping in the golden sands
of Paracas and Nazca. Both history and legend speak of
this treasure. According to the chroniclers Cieza de León and
Garcilaso de la Vaga, it was hidden 'by the Orejones before
the arrival of the Spaniards, as soon as the Incas realized
that the conquerors were interested only in their wealth.'

Hidden where? History does not say!

Till now it has been thought that the hiding place must
be situated in the highlands between Cuzco and Machu
Picchu, where we saw several Incan tombs unknown to
prehistorians, but it would be advisable to search in the
vicinity of the Shrine of Nazca, which is like an unexpected
jewel in the pampa amid a veritable maze of crossed or
parallel lines. Yet there is only a slender hope of identifying Nazca as a necropolis, for the lines are cut by a long
modern road, the Pan-American Highway, whose construction, to the best of my knowledge, gave rise to no edifying
discoveries.

The Nazca Pampa

On the fifteenth parallel between seventy-three and seventy-
five degrees of west longitude there are desert plateaux
cut by valleys. It is in this desert, improperly called a
pampa, that one can see from the air the mysterious lines
of Nazca, spread over thousands and thousands of acres.

To anyone who would like to examine them, I recom-
mend going first to Lima and then, by taxiplane, either to
Paracas, near the Candlestick of the Andes, or to Nazca,
within easy reach of the desert pampa. The Pan-American
Highway that runs from Lima to Valparaiso, by way of

Pisco and Nazca, passes through the lines and nearly touches the edge of the famous Spider. A close examination of them requires a trip by taxi, from Nazca to Rio Grande, for example, or from Nazca to Palpa.

But there are *pistas* (as the lines are called in Peru) everywhere, from Paracas to Chile. The best way to see them is to fly back and forth over the region; it is then possible to sight dozens of previously undiscovered designs.

There is one important precaution: these reconnaissance flights must be made *in the morning* because the winds of Paracas usually become violent in the afternoon and make aerial prospecting dangerous.

On Sunday, April 27, our pilot, Luis Astengo Alvizuri, famous in Peru under the name of Golden Arrow, crashed his Cessna at Molina, on his way to pick us up at Pizco. On that same day at the same time, the president of the Bolivian Republic, Rene Barrientos, was in a helicopter crash near Cochabamba, and eighteen people were killed in the crash of a scheduled airliner. The Andes were bloodthirsty that day. We ourselves escaped only by a miracle.

Taxiplanes can be rented at Lima, but there is also a chance of finding one at Pisco, where there is a military airfield.

Work of a People from Beyond the Earth

At eleven o'clock on the morning of Sunday, April 27, our little Piper Cub, piloted by a young lieutenant from the air base, took off from Pisco and headed southeast. We were accompanied by our friend and guide, Edmond Wartenschlag.

The lieutenant was thoroughly familiar with the region, since he flew over it nearly every day (which saved our lives on the way back). He told me that when we were about twelve miles from Pisco we would see designs whose existence was known to very few people. They are among the most beautiful of all those on the pampa. They represent, among other things, a condor with its wings spread and a man with his llama. We took movies of them but no still photographs, having foolishly reserved our film for the Nazca lines.

When we had been in the air for about an hour, we flew over a green valley which I assume to have been the valley of the Rio Grande. It is here that the area of the lines begins. The valley winds like a green snake, contrasting with the aridity of that whole region of Peru, which is dominated by 'pampas' that are actually deserts of sand and stone. There is desert everywhere, in fact, as on the Paracas Peninsula with its Candlestick.

It is the immense 'runways' that most forcibly strike the imagination when one flies over Nazca. Why are they called 'runways'? Simply because that is what immediately comes to mind when one sees the great rectangles or trapezoids hundreds of yards to several miles in length, and the clusters of triangles in the shape of wings which form vast light areas against the darker background of the soil.

This whole desert is filled with dense writing that leaves no blank spaces. From one horizon to the other, the lines – sometimes parallel, more often divergent, but always rigorously straight – follow rises in the ground, plunge into ravines, cross each other, and form a profusion of rectangles, trapezoids, and triangles.

What was the purpose of these lines? The mind vainly tries to find a meaning for them, but the first and irresistible impression always returns: runways, like those on the great airports of Paris, New York, London, or Tokyo.

Precise and geometrical, the *pistas* seem to have come from the blueprints of a gigantic architect belonging to a powerful scientific civilization from beyond the earth. It is as though they had been inscribed on the sandy desert of Nazca from a distance, perhaps by means of a laser beam.

Or are they a message written by earthlings, intended for extraterrestrial readers? Were they meant to serve as a beacon or a system of signals for space travellers? Our conscious mind is hesitant and puzzled, but our unconscious receives contradictory impressions from which certain ideas emerge: 'spaceports,' inscriptions by laser beams, a message from an extraterrestrial civilization . . .

No rationalist can accept these impressions as literal truths, but neither can any rationalist escape the images I have just suggested if he goes to Nazca to see for himself.

Logically, we must assume that these geometrical lines, interspersed with drawings of flowers, birds, insects, gods, and surrealistic objects, can only be the work of an ancient people, perhaps the Incas, who lived in this part of Peru. But it is equally logical to assume that no ancient South American people had enough technical and scientific knowledge to carry out that colossal work. It is not on a human scale; it suggests, rather, a civilization of titans.

And how were the lines and drawings laid out? From what distance in space? If we continue listening to the voice of logic, we must assume that only an eye and a brain at a considerable distance from the earth could have laid out the designs with such precision, which amounts to saying that *the architect worked from a helicopter, an aeroplane, or some other kind of aircraft.*

Incoherence, contradiction, extraterrestrial science ... How are we to make sense of this puzzle?

The Straight Lines Are Older than the Drawings

The Nazca designs are not entirely geometrical: they also represent many animals and objects. Near the Pan-American Highway, for example, about a mile from the valley, there is a spider whose length we estimated at about thirty yards. In this same area there are also mysterious designs, 'targets' with seven circles, spirals, and a bird with a long beak and outspread wings and tail.

Elsewhere – in the Palpa region (Pampa de Huayuri), in the ravines between Chesica and Lima, along the Canta road, in the Puquio ravines – there are, besides the inevitable 'runways,' birds, haloed gods, three-headed snakes, and flowers with six petals.

These drawings are all amazingly sharp; they were stylized by highly developed minds and show an artistic maturity comparable to that of the greatest period in French painting: from the late nineteenth century to the early twentieth.

The geometrical designs have given rise to fascinating hypotheses, but I do not believe that their enigma has yet been solved.

Examination reveals one important detail: the drawings are sometimes superimposed on 'runways,' which means that the latter are older.

Incredible but True

Like that of Paracas, the soil of Nazca is light yellow sand covered by a darker granitic film. The designs are therefore astonishingly clear, since the yellow sand of the lines stands out sharply against the dark purple background of the unmarked soil.

As at Paracas, the lines are shallow grooves, usually with a raised border of sand and stone. Sometimes there is no border, however, and the lines, like the parallel grooves near the Candlestick of the Andes, are only mysterious imprints. But imprints of what? Made how?

And how can the yellow sand of the lines continue to be exposed without becoming covered by the purple granitic film that lies over the rest of the ground? Professor Kosok believes that the darkened stones of the *pistas* were removed to expose the lighter-coloured soil, but I cannot accept this explanation. It is not stones (which are very rare) that make the desert dark: it is the layer of purple gravel that covers the yellow sand.

And how have the *pistas* continued to exist in spite of the frequent winds and occasional rains in the region? As at Paracas, we are forced to acknowledge that it is incredible but true, for the winds of Nazca are as violent as those at the site of the Candlestick.

This was the case, for example, on April 27, 1969, when our little plane had to interrupt its reconnaissance flight because of whirlwinds and turbulence. For an anxious hour or two, we were jolted and tumbled in the air. The airfields at Nazca and Pisco would not allow us to land because of the terrible wind. Yvette, who had stayed behind at the Pisco field, later told us that the dust picked up from the ground by the wind had reduced visibility to three hundred feet, and that she had to stand with her back against the wall of a hangar to keep from being knocked down by the gusts.

But while the dust of the airfield was blowing in the wind, at the same time, despite an equally strong wind, the yellow sand of Nazca remained motionless and underwent no detectable change, as we later saw for ourselves.

Is the Key on Venus

Historians and archaeologists have shown little interest in the Nazca designs. Only Paul Kosok, a professor at New York University, has investigated the matter, with the collaboration of Maria Reiche, an astronomer and mathematician in Lima. Their study has led them to the following conclusions:

1) Some of the designs resemble the decorations on old Nazca pottery.
2) The designs show evidence of an overall organization. Many of them radiate from centres located on hillocks where the ruins of small stone structures can still be seen.
3) Some lines form an agrarian, zodiacal, and astronomical calendar. They indicate times for sowing, the rising and setting of constellations and stars, and the courses of certain heavenly bodies. Professor Kosok has described them as the world's greatest astronomy book.
4) The designs are totemic symbols of various tribes.

Unfortunately these conclusions are not very satisfactory. The designs are unquestionably 'organized' in the sense that they were obviously not produced by pure chance. They have a certain geometrical rigour, but they form no distinguishable overall pattern. Very few of them radiate from geometrical centres, and I personally saw no signs of a structure at any of those centres.

It is futile to read astronomical meaning into the designs because, with thousands of lines going in all possible directions, anyone can easily find whatever directions he chooses to look for!

Nor can the designs be regarded as totemic symbols, since only a minute fraction of them lend themselves to such an interpretation.

They were apparently made after the worldwide Deluge (twelve thousand years ago), for otherwise they would have been effaced.

Perhaps they can be dated from about 3000 B.C., when the Great Teachers, known by the names of Orejona and

Viracocha to the pre-Incas, came 'from the sky.' According to tradition these teachers, deified by the people, were from the planet Venus.

Did Venus hold the key to Nazca and the Candlestick before it was changed into a fiery comet, then again became a planet stabilized by our solar system? I am rather tempted by that hypothesis.

An Extraterrestrial Brain

It is hard to believe that the sparse, poverty-stricken, and primitive population of southern Peru could have conceived the Nazca designs, whether they be regarded as a page of writing or an astronomical table. The plan of the designs does not seem to belong to the imagination of earthlings. Earthlings may have done the physical work, but it seems to me that the concept must have come from a brain that was alien to our planet.

To my correspondent and friend Robert Carras, the Nazca designs suggest that the earth may have been *marked* by or for interplanetary travellers. 'Are they the signature of Orejona?' he asks. (See Chapter III of my book *One Hundred Thousand Years of Man's Unknown History*, Berkeley, 1970.)

It is odd that Professor Kosok neglected to establish a connection between what happened at Nazca in the past and what still happens today. On many mountains in what was once the empire of the Incas, twentieth-century Peruvians and Bolivians inscribe slogans such as *'Viva el Peru'* or *'Viva X y Y.'* They do this either by forming the letters with certain plants or by removing stones from the sand to make the letters stand out as light-coloured lines against a darker background. The stones are placed along the edges of the letters, which then appear as *Pistas.*

2 The Mystery of the Thirty-Fifth Parallel

The occult mystery that surrounds and inhabits us has its favourite places where it seems to amuse itself by disconcerting us.

We know that there are telluric currents which condition the people who live in a given region, and places where 'the spirit breathes,' but it seems that there are also areas subject to strange and often sinister influences.

Roger de Lafforest studies this subject in his engaging book *Ces Maisons qui tuent,* particularly with regard to houses whose inhabitants may be 'conditioned by forces that arise from the ground beneath the house, or immaterial deluges that fall from the cosmos, or the materials of which the house is made, or lines invented by an irresponsible architect, or things inside or outside the house whose geometry may cause radiation of more or less violent "shape waves." '

All these phenomena are related to electromagnetic or psychic factors, and to radiations that are often harmful if they emanate from places where unhealthy thoughts have accumulated.

But what are we to say of those vast areas that seem to be in the grip of evil spells cast by the demons of mythology?

Disappearing Sailors

Two portions of the globe are under the influence of those awesome forces: the Azores and the segment of the western Atlantic that has entered occult history under the name of the Bermuda Triangle.

If we believe tradition, the Azores, eight hundred miles west of Portugal, were the cultural centre of the antediluvian world. This was the heart of happy Atlantis, this was where

she had built her capital of glittering orichalcum: Poseidonis.
Then came the Deluge, and since then the place has been
the scene of strange and sometimes tragic events.

Here is a summary of some of the elements that make
up the mystery of the Azores:

- It is here that the phantom island of San Brandan
  periodically appears.
- This is the birthplace of the anticyclones that determine the weather of Europe.
- It was here that Atlantis was engulfed twelve thousand
  years ago.
- Five hundred miles west of the Azores, petrels fly in
  circles until their strength is exhausted.
- On the island of Sao Miguel, in the eastern Azores,
  water boils in craters that still spew out lava.
- In 1954 an island emerged from the ocean and became
  part of Fayal Island.
- It is here, finally, that ships lose their crews as though
  they had mysteriously vanished from the earth.

Since 1969, five yachts have been found in this region
during periods of calm weather, most of them in excellent
condition, but without a single person aboard.

No valid explanation has yet been put forward. Among
sailors, the region of the Azores has a reputation of sinister
mystery.

The Mary Celeste, a Ghost Ship

In November, 1872, the brigantine *Mary Celeste* left New
York for Genoa with a crew of twelve aboard. On December 2 it was seen off the coast of Europe, apparently
proceeding normally on its way. On December 4 it was
sighted by the British ship *Dei Gracia*. The *Mary Celeste* was
sailing briskly before the wind, but the captain of the
Dei Gracia was surprised to receive no answer to his signals.
Moving closer, the British crewmen saw that there was no
one at the helm or on deck, and one of them said jokingly,
'Here's a ghost ship at last!'

His words were truer than he knew, for when some of
the British sailors rowed to the *Mary Celeste* and boarded
it, they found it completely empty. And yet, except for

the heavy silence, there was nothing to give the impression that a tragedy had occurred. Everything was in order. Breakfast was on the table, the deck had been washed, the lines were correctly coiled, the lifeboat was in its davits in perfect condition. Recently washed clothes had been hung out to dry. There was plenty of food in the storeroom.

The British sailors searched the ship from stem to stern without finding a living soul.

This was the first time within memory that such a thing had ever happened at sea. There seemed to be no possible explanation. The Atlantic is always rather rough near the Azores at that time of year, but there had been neither a storm nor unusually high waves, and a two-masted brigantine with a crew of twelve would have been able to cope with almost any kind of weather.

It may not be quite true to say that there was not a living soul aboard the *Mary Celeste*: a placid grey cat was found. Disturbingly, sailors regard their pets as bringing them good luck and always try to save them even if they abandon ship.

A Strange Thing

There was no solution to the enigma. If the crew members had been forced to leave the ship, they would have used the lifeboat; if there had been a mutiny, signs of struggle or disorder would have been found; if a storm had endangered the ship, it would have been damaged and the sails would have been taken in.

The British sailors made one discovery that might be regarded as a clue, although it served only to direct their conjectures into the realm of the unknown. In the ship's log, the captain of the *Mary Celeste* had noted only routine details, such as weather conditions, until the last sentence, which was unfinished and contained these cryptic words: 'A strange thing is happening to us . . .'

Look, It's Atlantis!

A group of American spiritualists organized a séance in San Diego, California, during which a medium supposedly received a message from the spirit of Mrs Briggs, wife of the captain of the *Mary Celeste*.

During the voyage, said the message from Mrs Briggs, she played the piano every day. When the ship had passed the Azores, a strange phenomenon began occurring: each time she played the piano, faraway music seemed to answer her own. It was like the echo that can sometimes be heard in the mountains, yet it came from the open sea. The whole crew heard it and were obviously frightened by it. Some of them asked Mrs Briggs not to play the piano any more. There was even the beginning of a mutiny, which her husband, the captain, succeeded in quelling only with considerable difficulty.

He had read a great deal and he believed that the ship was now sailing over the sunken continent of Atlantis. One day as he was looking down into the sea, he saw a kind of floating meadow covered with plants that did not seem to be seaweed. Another time, he excitedly brought his wife up on deck to show her what appeared to be the ruins of marble houses. She saw them, but assumed that the sight was an optical illusion.

That night, the ship was shaken by strange impacts against its hull. At dawn it came to a standstill. It had run aground on an unknown shore. The captain shouted, 'Look, it's Atlantis!' The continent had miraculously risen above the surface of the ocean.

The captain, his wife, and the whole crew went ashore. The first thing they noticed was the extraordinary nature of the plant life. As they were approaching what seemed to be the ruins of a temple, the ground sank beneath them and Atlantis returned to the depths of the sea. They were all drowned. The *Mary Celeste*, no longer held prisoner by the beach on which it had run aground, continued on its way, empty.

Optical Illusion or Newborn Island?

For those who believe in revelations from the Great Beyond, this story would be plausible if it did not contain certain inadmissible details.

The beginning of a mutiny is incompatible with the perfect order that was found aboard the *Mary Celeste*. If a vessel of that tonnage runs aground, it is always at a certain distance from dry land, and it is hard to imagine the crew abandoning it without first dropping the anchor. And finally, the description of Atlantis given by the medium is childish and unconvincing.

It is not impossible, however, that something like the events related in the story may have happened, either as the result of a collective hallucination or a kind of contagious madness, or because a body of dry land actually did rise from the ocean.

Such a body of land could not have plant life and ruins, but, because of underwater volcanic activity, portions of the ocean floor do sometimes rise above the surface in the vicinity of the Azores, as is shown by the recent appearance of the land that became part of Fayal Island.

It is conceivable that the *Mary Celeste* may have run aground on a newly emerged island that sank a short time later, but it is worth noting that in the case of Fayal the soil was so hot that it had to cool for several months before anyone could walk on it, and it still has no plant life. It therefore seems reasonable to conclude that if the *Mary Celeste* had encountered such an island the crew would have been unable to go ashore.

Exaggerated Coincidences

Since the beginning of this century a number of boats without crews have been found on the thirty-fifth parallel, but the phenomenon did not attract any great public attention until 1969, when there were five new cases that can be described, at the very least, as exaggerated coincidences.

On June 30 the British ship *Maple Bank* discovered a sixty-foot unidentified yacht floating upside down. There was nothing particularly extraordinary about this, but on July 4 another British ship, the *Cotopaxi*, sighted another unidentified yacht under way with its automatic rudder in operation and no one aboard.

Two days later, the Liberian ship *Golar Frost* found the *Vagabond*, a yacht belonging to the solitary sailor William Wallin; again there was no one aboard.

On July 8, still on the thirty-fifth parallel, between the Azores and Portugal, the British tanker *Helisoma* encountered an abandoned forty-foot yacht.

On July 10 the press devoted long articles to the discovery of the *Teignmouth Electron,* belonging to another solitary sailor, Donald C. Crowhurst.

Five empty yachts sighted near the Azores in eleven days, in clear summer weather – even the most optimistic statistician would find it hard to call this a coincidence.

Crowhurst was a Victim of Occult Forces

William Wallin and Donald C. Crowhurst were both experienced sailors, but Crowhurst's case can be dissociated from the others because his logbook was recovered and it contains information which at first sight – but only at first sight – gives a solution to the mystery.

Crowhurst was a contestant in a race around the world sponsored by the London *Sunday Times.* He was one of the favourites, but his need to win was apparently so great that he could not bear the thought of losing. This must have been what gave him the idea of a hoax that deceived the press for a long time.

He sailed to a point seven hundred miles west of the Azores, near the thirty-fifth parallel, and stayed there. He then sent periodic messages to the BBC describing his fictitious progress. He announced that he had rounded Cape Horn, then the Cape of Good Hope, and finally that he was heading back toward England. He was thought to be in first place!

On June 24, 1969, Crowhurst received a message from the *Sunday Times* telling him that he would be met at the Scilly Islands, interviewed by the BBC and given a triumphal welcome. Panic-stricken, he decided not to send any more messages. He then wrote the truth in his logbook.

He admitted that his boat, a trimaran, had not moved from the thirty-fifth parallel, but he added comments that gave evidence of mental derangement. He spoke of God and a 'world system' in which he was under control of a cosmic brain.

Did he stay in the Azores region of his own free will?

His confession, obviously sincere, would seem to indicate that he was kept there by occult forces.

On June 30 he wrote that he had made up his mind to die, that his soul was at peace and that the truth had at last been revealed. On July 10 the British ship *Picardy* sighted his trimaran and took it in tow. Crowhurst was not aboard it, and his body was never found.

According to some reports he is still alive and has been recognized in England, but the fact is that his disappearance remains shrouded in mystery.

The 'Strange Thing' that Drives Men Mad

Such are the strange events that have taken place on the thirty-fifth parallel, particularly during the month of July, 1969.

In the case of Crowhurst, everything would be clear if it were not for certain lines in his logbook. What did he mean, exactly, by his 'world system' in which he was under the control of a cosmic brain? Was it only a meaningless remark by a man whose mind had been deranged? Perhaps, but it seems that a 'strange thing' caused a similar derangement in the captain of the *Mary Celeste,* and we will see later that it was also a 'strange thing' which caused pilots to lose their reason in the Bermuda Triangle.

Since there is no logical explanation of the mystery of the thirty-fifth parallel, we are forced to fall back on the irrational.

Of all those who have disappeared, not one body has ever been found, which leads us to believe that they did not fall into the sea – unless their bodies were weighted with lead or there was a school of sharks nearby.

Were they abducted? It is hard to believe!

All that can be said with certainty is that the disappearances took place under *strange conditions.* Something happened which had its origin in either the sky or the water. In the first case, we cannot help thinking of stories about extraterrestrials taking samples of the earth's animal and plant life. These stories are, of course, unsubstantiated; but what if this were the 'strange thing' mentioned by the captain of the *Mary Celeste*?

If the strangeness came from the sea, how are we not to think of Atlantis, sudden appearances of volcanic islands, or the mirage of San Brandan? These are not very satisfactory explanations either; can it be that they are not irrational enough?

The Magic of Scientists

Are we to seek the explanation in the miraculous? In magic? If so, we are more at ease in our speculations, more in harmony with the atmosphere of the dramatic and the mysterious.

Twentieth-century magic has abandoned the incantations and spells of the older magic, and has become the fantastic science of our time, just as the enchanted land of the Other World has become the parallel universe. Modern men would be ashamed to believe in witches, spirits, and ghosts, but they are willing to accept the hypothesis of another world governed by unknown dimensions.

If we look closely, we soon see what a narrow margin separates superstition from belief, the Other World of the Holy Grail from the universe of four or five dimensions, inspired novelists from advanced physicists.

If there has been magic in the Azores, therefore, the explanation must be sought by introducing new scientific notions into a problem that is insoluble by means of conventional mathematics.

Does a 'cosmic brain,' to use Crowhurst's expression, exercise power over human beings? That is the view of religion and it is tending to become the view of science also, but on a higher (or apparently higher) level.

The mystery of the Azores becomes less impenetrable if we accept the idea that sailors have disappeared from our tangible world and entered a parallel universe governed by dimensions unknown to us.

3 The Bermuda Triangle

The mystery of the thirty-fifth parallel is echoed by strange disappearances that occur farther west, near the thirtieth parallel.

The area of the sea bounded approximately by Florida, Bermuda, Puerto Rico, and Jamaica is called the Bermuda Triangle in America and the Magic Rhombus or the Triangle of Death in Europe. In this area, not only do crews disappear, but also their vessels, which makes the problem even more baffling.

In all of the world's oceans, ships have been lost without a trace because they sank in isolated places, but the Bermuda Triangle lies in one of the most frequently travelled parts of the Atlantic and, besides ships and boats, aeroplanes also disappear there without leaving the slightest bit of wreckage.

The Soviet periodical *Technology and Youth* and the writer George Langelaan, in a book entitled *Les Faits Maudits*, have described the strange disappearances that have occurred since 1954. Here they are, as they were reported in the press.

Five Vanished Torpedo Bombers

At 2.08 on the afternoon of December 5, 1945, five Avenger torpedo bombers took off from the naval air base at Fort Lauderdale, Florida, for a routine flight. Weather conditions were good: the sea was calm, the sky was clear. At 3.45, when the planes were on their way back, it was noted on the base's radar that they were not approaching in the usual way. Then the control tower received a disconcerting radio message from the pilots: they could not see land and did not know where they were. Subsequent messages from them were incoherent.

The men in the control tower were bewildered. It seemed that the pilots must have gone mad. They were apparently not worried by their situation; they began talking among themselves, asking absurd questions which left no doubt that their minds were deranged. They did not know their position and seemed not to understand when they were asked to try to determine it.

The Sea Is Strange

It was known, however, that they were off the coast of Florida between the Bahamas and Bermuda – that is, they were in the Bermuda Triangle, though it had not yet been given a name.

At 4.45 a fairly comprehensible message was received. It stated that the pilots did not know their exact position but thought they were about two hundred miles northeast of the base, and that the sea was 'strange.' (It is worth recalling here the 'strange thing' mentioned by the captain of the *Mary Celeste*.)

Subsequently, a big Martin seaplane was sent out to search for them. It flew northeast, carrying thirteen men who were specialists in sea searches. Ten minutes later, radio contact with the seaplane was lost: it too had disappeared!

A general alert was broadcast to all naval forces in the vicinity. An aircraft carrier sent its planes to search for the Avengers and the seaplane. Soon there were dozens of planes combing the Bermuda Triangle, along with more than two hundred fishing boats, yachts, and warships.

Every square foot of the sea was scrutinized, but not one of the six missing planes was found. The sky was still clear and the wind was normal; what could possibly have happened? How could experienced pilots have disappeared on the kind of routine flight they had made a dozen times before? Why did they not send an SOS? Why did they seem so confused and irrational? Why did they not take any of the measures that were standard procedure in case of accident?

These questions have never been answered.

The report of the US Navy was laconic and honest:

it simply stated that no one knew what had happened on
December 5, 1945.

A Hole in the Sea

Beginning in 1948, there was a cascade of disappearances
in the Bermuda Triangle:

- January 29: an airliner that had left London with forty
  people aboard.
- December 20: an airliner flying from San Juan, Puerto
  Rico, to Miami. Its last message gave a position not
  far from Florida. It did not send an SOS.
- January 17, 1949: a four-engined transport plane flying
  from Bermuda to Jamaica with seventeen men aboard.
- February, 1963: the American tanker *Marine Sulfur
  Queen*.
- July, 1963: the trawler *Snow Boy*.
- August 28, 1969: two tanker planes.

The planes and the two ships were lost with everyone
aboard. Wreckage was found only from the two tanker planes.
They had crashed into the sea outside their normal flight
path. Why had they strayed so far? No one knows.

Between 1929 and 1954 (not counting the years of World
War II), the statistics of Lloyd's of London show that
two hundred and twenty-two vessels disappeared without a
trace in all the oceans of the world, but particularly in the
Pacific.

In the North Atlantic, disappearances are not numerous;
yet the Bermuda Triangle is not only in the North Atlantic
but also in one of its most heavily frequented parts. Dozens
of aeroplanes and hundreds of ships and boats are in this
area every day. Under these conditions, how can two ships
simply vanish?

One fact may be significant: on the thirty-fifth parallel,
near the Azores, vessels are found without their crews,
while in the Bermuda Triangle ships and planes also disappear, along with their passengers and crews. In both areas,
no witness remains to give an explanation.

With regard to the Azores, we may deduce that material

objects can subsist but not people, as though all witnesses were systematically eliminated. There seems to be a determination to prevent any first-hand account of what takes place. It is therefore permissible to think that on certain occasions, sometimes in the Bermuda Triangle and sometimes in the vicinity of the Azores, there are unusual events that must be kept hidden from the human race.

Are we to believe that beings alien to our civilization live at those places in secret underwater bases?

It is a fantastic hypothesis, but the facts it is meant to explain are equally fantastic.

Passage into the Fourth Dimension

Other incredible explanations have been proposed, such as modern pirates or, still better – and why not? – a passage into the fourth dimension, as in the Philadelphia Experiment or on a Moebius band. (See my book *Le Livre du Mystérieux Inconnu,* Chapter II.)

Is there a gap in time? Have pilots and sailors, by an unknown phenomenon, been shifted from their own time and transported into either the future or the past?

Have they disappeared through a 'hole' in the sky or the sea; that is, do ships and planes slip into a parallel universe at certain times?

The Land where Time Stops Flowing

Professor Todericiu has stated some hypotheses on the subject of the Bermuda Triangle. Its mystery has a very ancient origin. The second-century writer Aelian spoke of it in his *Variae Historiae,* a work which is full of ridiculous tales but also contains some curious details and undoubtedly reveals certain genuine facts.

Aelian reports the following in Book III, Chapter XVIII. In a well-known conversation with Silenus, the Phrygian Midas referred to America (a land beyond the great ocean). He said that near the city of Anoston there were two rivers, the River Gaiety and the River Sadness, and that between them, in a certain part of the sea, men forgot everything they had done and entered a new dimension of time.

It is extremely curious that Aelian speaks of America and mentions a place where men forget their whole past! He also states that they forget all their knowledge and become very young. They thus disappear by living in a time whose direction is the reverse of ours.

This is one of the first allusions to a fourth dimension, and the place involved is approximately situated in the Bermuda Triangle.

The stories of the Holy Grail state that in the kingdom of King Bran, at the western limit of the lands of the Celts, lived Queen Rianon, who created such a magical atmosphere when she spoke that time ceased to flow at her court.

Thus at the times of Aelian (second century A.D.) and the legend of the Holy Grail (Middle Ages), there was belief in pre-Columbian America and the 'Land of Knolls,' that is, a vast continent beyond the sea. And there was belief in the existence of a land and a kingdom where men unknowingly entered a parallel universe.

These traditions deserve to be taken into consideration.

The fantastic truth can be hidden only in an explanation of the same nature.

A Magic Zone

Off the coast of the Azores runs the immense fracture in the ocean floor which extends from Iceland to the Antarctic. Matter from inside the earth constantly spews from this fracture and moves in two directions: eastward and westward.

Off the coast of the Bahamas lies the Sargasso Sea, a veritable cemetery where the hulks of wrecked ships and all sorts of floating debris are gathered.

It is a strange coincidence that tradition locates Atlantis between the Azores and the Bahamas.

There are also unusual features in the air: hurricanes arise in the Bermuda Triangle and the high pressures of the Azores condition the climate of all of Europe.

It is likely that the earth's magnetic field is exceptionally intense at these places. There must be electrical interactions between the sea and the sky that are still unknown because they are very rare. These interactions are perhaps capable of creating fantastic phenomena which would explain the mystery that intrigues us.

Scientists of the Max Planck Institute in Mainz, Germany, have detected an abnormally high concentration of nitrous oxide (laughing gas) in the vicinity of Iceland and the Faroe Islands. They believe that the oceans have a kind of metabolism, one phase of which, catabolism, may give rise to chemical reactions related to organic decomposition. This chemical process may be particularly intense in areas of eddies where floating debris is concentrated, such as the Sargasso Sea, through which the thirty-fifth parallel passes.

There must be periodic production of unknown chemical compounds that have effects on human beings similar to those of certain gases developed for chemical warfare: annihilation of the will and the sense of direction, or hallucination capable of deceiving sailors and aeroplane pilots. This would explain part of the mystery: sailors and pilots who seem to lose their reason and plunge into the sea, perhaps impelled by mysterious occult forces . . . .

It would be a satisfactory solution to the whole problem if it also explained what becomes of the ships that vanish in the Bermuda Triangle, but it does not.

The enigma remains, defying the science of rationalists and the sagacity of those who believe in the Mysterious Unknown.

Part 2

SUPERIOR ANCESTORS

4 I. Our Ancestors were not Apes

One of the most extraordinary phenomena in the history of science is the French school of prehistory, with its inventions of cave men, the ages of bronze, iron, and polished stone, and other nonsense in the same vein.

It is not my intention to forge a wondrous prehistory, but to adapt my theories to the laws of reason, the scientific rules of discovery, existing evidence and documents, plausibility, and the data of the traditional heritage.

This reasonable line of approach leads not to the conclusion that our ancestors were apes, but that they were superior men.

Nothing New under the Sun

The human race is still at a rudimentary stage of knowledge. We know only a tenth of what our children will know in the year 2000.

Does this mean that our species started from nothing? Not at all: our ancestors, who had amazingly advanced ideas in astronomy (the Egyptians), who knew the atomic theory (Leucippus), cosmogony (Moses), the smelting of metals, etc., had inherited their knowledge from someone who knew more than they.

The English chemist Frederick Soddy, who won a Nobel Prize in 1921, stated the view that traditions provide justification for believing that there were once human races, now vanished, that not only reached our level of knowledge but also had powers which we do not yet have.

This is also the opinion of the Soviet professor J. B. Fedorov, who maintains that all the civilizations on earth had their origin in a mother civilization that is unknown to us because it disappeared, either beneath the ocean or into space.

But long before modern times, the ancient world had the certainty that Superior Ancestors had preceded us on our planet.

'The Chinese speak of a world anterior to ours and reckon its duration as several *lekes* of one hundred thousand years each,' wrote Monsieur de Longueville Harcouet in *Histoire des personnes qui ont vécu plusieurs siècles et qui ont rajeuni* (1735).

Their traditions and those of the Hindus refer to an empire that was engulfed by the sea – the continent of Mu – and in the West, proof of the existence of ·Atlantis has been found.

The spermatozoon has the shape of a spiral and advances like a helix to bring life; our solar system moves in a spiral path which is taking it from the original nebula toward the Hercules star cluster, in which it will some day be amalgamated.

In Ecclesiastes 1:9-11 we read: 'What has happened will happen again, and what has been done will be done again, and there is nothing new under the sun. Is there anything of which one can say, "Look, this is new"? No, it has already existed, long before our time. The men of old are not remembered, and those who will follow will not be remembered by those who follow them.'[1]

Is Man Regressing?

It would be illogical to follow the conventional views of outmoded prehistorians and certain archaeologists, for two reasons:

1) The history of the world and of civilizations is fundamentally conditioned by cataclysms which periodically disrupt the globe. (See *L'Empire de l'Arc-en-ciel*, by Father Pierre Perroud, a missionary in Peru, and Jacques Helle, Editions Rhodaniques, Saint-Moritz, Switzerland, 1963. This book is of prime importance

[1] All Biblical quotations are from *The New English Bible*, Oxford University Press, 1970. (Translator's note.)

for knowledge of Incan civilization.)

2) It is not at all obvious that civilizations are progressing; the opposite, in fact, seems to be true. If we consider the cranial capacity of Neanderthal man (1600 cubic centimetres), the known history of dolphins and apes, and even the history of our ancestors according to traditions, it appears likely that our human race is regressing. If we are to believe translations of clay tablets, the science of the Babylonian priests was transmitted to them by giant Initiators who came to earth after the Deluge.

Furthermore, any study in archaeology or prehistory must take account of two extremely important phenomena:

1) Isolated cultures: even now, when space travel has begun, there are still Stone Age cultures in remote areas. On July 20, 1969, almost simultaneously with the first arrival of earthlings on the moon, a previously unknown tribe was discovered in Colombia, still living at the level of the early Stone Age.

2) Incongruous discoveries: objects that have been displaced for one reason or another, and then found in places where they normally should not be, may give rise to false datings and conclusions. For example, the Chinese ivory tokens found in excavations in Ireland, or the Sumerian statuette found in the Moroccan desert. (This statuette must have belonged to the feudal lord Glaoui. Other Sumerian and Egyptian objects from his private collection are probably still hidden in Morocco today.)

With these simple but essential facts in mind, we can give the coup de grâce to the concoctions of official prehistorians.

We Do Not Descend from the Ape

If some of our contemporaries claim to be descended from the ape I have no objection, and in a sense I can believe them! But not Einstein, Pierre Curie, Rodin, Pasteur, Descartes, Rabelais, Plato, Pythagoras, Leucippus, Buddha, the

Celts, the Hyperboreans, and the authors of the Vedas and the Avesta, who knew that the earth was round, that the universe was composed of atoms, and that certain planets were inhabited; who had interplanetary spacecraft, knew the rotational cycle of Venus, may have made atomic bombs, and certainly knew how to cut and melt stone and transport squared blocks weighing thousands of tons! Not our remote ancestors, who no doubt used a universal language and left us a heritage of engraved signs, symbols, and monuments that bear witness to their advanced knowledge.

Were the Atlantans Stone Age men? And what of the people who built Thule, Cuicuilco (in Mexico), and Abydos, at a time when Sumerian shepherds did not even know how to make a clay plate – did they live in trees or caves?

No man of good faith and common sense will give the slightest credence to such absurdities.

'Prehistorians' officiate, reign, and pontificate in universities, museums, and academies, and at secret meetings where they hatch their plots, but the doors of the future are irremediably closed to them.

Free minds rebel against closed minds.

The sacred old world is collapsing under its own weight of crimes, exactions, stupidity, and oppression. The Christian Church is crumbling everywhere; Irish Protestants massacre Catholics and burn their houses as in the heyday of religious warfare, Buddhist priests fan the flames of the war in Vietnam, atheistic Communists subjugate the countries of eastern Europe, racism is rampant in the United States and South Africa . . .

Descendants of apes would never have invented and established such a sectarian civilization, with a God who bears such a close resemblance to a devil!

Man is an Extraterrestrial

The genesis of man is, to be sure, a mystery; but logically, rationally, it must go back to billions and billions of years ago.

Since the universe has existed either for all eternity or for a nearly infinite number of years, it would be ludicrous to believe that the process of evolution let vast periods go by

without making man appear, reserving that privilege for our
paltry last million years, only a brief instant on the overall
scale of time. It would be arbitrary, and would give our
species an importance that our reason rejects. We know very
well that we are only minute cogs in the great universal
mechanism and not its main element, much less its ultimate
product!

Yet conventional prehistorians maintain this unacceptable
view and go even farther by doing everything in their
power to present man as an essentially earthly creature. As
though, since the Great Beginning, millions of other planets
could not also have engendered the human race.

Logically, then, we must acknowledge that our creation
goes back an incalculable time and that the first man was
certainly an extraterrestrial, that is, born somewhere other
than on our earth, which did not yet exist.

It is quite conceivable that our planet, in its five to ten
billion years of existence, may also have engendered a native
human race. But this hypothesis by no means excludes a
first extraterrestrial genesis, or crossbreeding between native
earthlings and peoples from beyond the earth: the angels of
whom the Bible speaks, the Initiators who appear in all
mythologies.

The Wondrous Hypothesis

It is an unforgivable crime – committed by prehistorians
– to teach that man descends *exclusively* from the ape. Such
a genesis is within the realm of possibility, although the links
between us and the ape have not been found; but even if
they were found our knowledge would be little more advanced and we would be no more satisfied!

Man descends from the ape? Let us grant it for the
moment: our history now goes back to a rather disagreeable
point of departure and we have accomplished nothing except
to make the Darwinian theory of evolution credible. A
fine result!

But there is a second hypothesis, more plausible and much
richer in teachings, which leads us to believe that earthly
man had Superior Ancestors. In this case, man's adventure
becomes prodigious, fecund, and exalting!

If other men, antediluvian – 'pre-historic,' taking the word 'prehistoric' in its conventional meaning – existed, fascinating pages of history still remain to be discovered.

How did they live? Where were their cities? Did they commit the same sin of scientific pride that we are now committing? I am inclined to think so!

Atlantis and Mu are not dreams of spiritualists, but realities of a mysterious era. We preserve a nostalgia for them in our memory chromosomes, and we also find convincing traces of their existence.

In this sense, the Atlantans and the Hyperboreans were our direct ancestors, the magicians of a civilization of electrical forces, controlled waves and nuclear energy. If they made disastrous discoveries, we have an explanation for the punishment of the Deluge, the loss of the 'earthly paradise' and the chain of deteriorated but long-lived traditions that have come down to us. We also have an explanation of initiation, the vestiges of unknown civilizations that have so far left us perplexed, and the scientific inventions and ideas of the ancient Egyptians, Greeks, Hindus, Incas, and Mexicans.

We have no right to exclude this thesis from the search for our genesis, because it alone leads to the fantastic past and no doubt to the truth.

II. Eight Heart Transplants a Hundred Thousand Years Ago

That past was indeed fantastic and of course it was the present of our Superior Ancestors. A hundred thousand years ago they performed heart transplants, like Christian Barnard in our time – or rather, better than Barnard, since theirs were successful!

'Impossible!' prehistorians will say. 'A hundred thousand years ago was the time of Pithecanthropus (one to five hundred thousand years ago), or Mauer man, or the beginning of Neanderthal man.[1] Can you imagine a semi-ape, barely capable of making a flint tool, performing the most difficult surgical operation on a human body?'

It goes without saying that the opinion of the conspiracy does not impress me. I will simply present the facts, as they have come to me from the Soviet Union via Bucharest, giving references that can easily be checked.

Skeletons a Hundred Thousand Years Old

In 1969, during an exploration in central Asia, the Soviet professor Leonidov Marmajaijan, heading a group of researchers from the Universities of Leningrad and Ashkhabad, discovered a cemetery in a cave. In one large grave they

[1] Prehistorians always deal in vague approximations; depending on the school to which they belong, they assign an age of fifty, eighty, or a hundred thousand years to Neanderthal man. Similarly, they give him a cranial capacity that varies between 1350 and 1600 cubic centimetres (which represents a difference of age on the order of one to two hundred million years!) In reality, Neanderthal man, exemplified by the man of La Chapelle-aux-Saints, France, had a cranial capacity of 1600 cubic centimetres.

found thirty skeletons in a perfect state of preservation.

On their return to the University of Ashkhabad they subjected these skeletons to carbon 14 dating, which indicated an age of more than twenty thousand years. (As I have repeatedly pointed out in my other books, carbon 14 datings are illusory when they refer to ages greater than ten thousand years.) More thorough scientific investigations led to the conclusion that the skeletons were about a hundred thousand years old. Moreover, some of them showed curious traces of operations in the chest cavity. In view of the importance and antiquity of the discovery, Soviet scientists decided to perform a minute osteological examination.

The results were published under the title *Report of the Marmajaijan Scientific Expedition in Soviet Central Asia in 1969, on behalf of the Turkmenistan Anthropological Society.* With the approval of the Society, the report was presented to the Soviet Academy of Science in late November, 1969.

It states that eight of the skeletons show signs of serious bone injuries, made while the subjects were alive. These injuries seem to have come from fights against animals (bears, leopards, tigers?) because some bones have claw marks on them and others have deep marks made by the bite of powerful jaws with large teeth.

Operation Christian Barnard

In one skeleton, the investigators noted 'the removal of the centre of an area penetrated by a trephination.' (No other translation can be given without distorting the text.) But the most astonishing thing is that they found *traces of a surgical operation on the bones bordering the chest cavity.* The ribs on the left side of the skeletons had been cut, either with a sharp flint blade or in some other way. Careful study of the zone of operation showed that after part of the ribs had been cut away, an opening had been made and widened by retraction to permit the operation.

Since the bones around this opening were covered with periosteum (a fibrous membrane that covers bones and enables callus to form), the scientists of Leningrad and Ashkhabad drew the following conclusion: 'After the success of this major operation, the patient recovered and lived at least three to five years, as is shown by the thickness of the periosteum.'

And the ribs that were cut are precisely those which correspond to the 'cardiac window' used in our time by Dr Barnard and his emulators!

Before this discovery, there had already been observations of operations on the bones of the chest cavity in skeletons found in the Middle East (Palestine, Assyria, Iran), dating from more than fifty thousand years ago. The same was true of a young woman who lived during the Upper Paleolithic near Les Eyzies, France, but in this case the observations were made only on bone fragments, which meant that the conclusion was only hypothetical. It is also interesting to note that a carved fourteenth-century altarpiece in the cathedral of Palencia, Spain, shows a leg transplant. The donor is a black man, the recipient is a white nobleman. The surgeon is still holding the leg he has just amputated.

After the Soviet scientists' discovery, there can be no doubt that the Neanderthals who performed *successful* heart transplants a hundred thousand years ago had extremely advanced scientific knowledge.

It is possible that the operations were performed by someone other than they – Initiators or surgeons of a superior class – but the fact remains that our ancestors had scientists.

A Heart Transplant in the Time of the Pharaohs

In the library of Alexandria, Egypt, a papyrus written in Coptic, based on an older text, tells how a soldier was able to recover from a spear wound *in the heart*. He was serving in the royal guards when he received the wound, which normally would have been fatal. He was a protégé of the Pharaoh, who ordered his physicians to do everything in their power to save him. A surgeon had the idea of replacing the soldier's heart with that of a young bull. The papyrus describes the operation and ends by stating that it was successful.

This information comes from Professor Doru Todericiu. In spite of my inquiries and investigations, however, I have not been able to make a precise identification of the document in question. It may be the Ebers Papyrus, which is a treatise on the heart.

Ancient Egyptian medicine was highly developed in treating disorders of the respiratory tract, the alimentary canal, the urinary passages, and the head. Physicians used suppositories, enemas, and laxatives. Dentists filled cavities in teeth. Oculists successfully treated trachoma, cataract, and night blindness. The Edwin Smith Papyrus proves that the ancient Egyptians practised scientific bone surgery. Hippocrates and Galen did not conceal the fact that part of their knowledge came from the works they had consulted in the temple of Imhotep at Memphis.

With the ancient Egyptians and the Neanderthals of central Asia, heart transplants may have been an exceptional operation performed by scientists who were alien to our planet. If they were performed during the reign of King Zoser (Third Dynasty), when the wise and divine Imhotep was alive, it is worth noting that at this time, about five thousand years ago, the 'Venusian Initiators' were also working miracles among the Assyrians, Babylonians, Phoenicians, Mayas, and Aztecs. Thus the Superior Ancestors responsible for heart transplants may not have been native earthlings.

Extraterrestrial Initiators

Whatever may be the truth whose surface has barely been scratched by a few men of superior awareness, historical and protohistorical facts prove that highly developed people came to the earth in the past to teach our ancestors. The sacred writings of all countries describe the coming of these aliens, whether angels or astronauts, and tradition maintains that they were Venusians.

About five thousand years ago, Initiators engendered the Mayan civilization in Mexico. The same thing happened in the case of the Incas, the Assyro-Babylonians, the Phoenicians, and the Persians. (See my books Le Livre des Secrets Trahis, Chapters VIII and IX, and Le Livre des Maîtres du Monde, Chapters I, II and III, both published by Robert Laffront, Paris.)

Without this intervention, it is impossible to explain the

sudden blossoming of these people's civilizations, which were all placed under the sign of Venus and had 'gods', that is, superior beings, who were called Venusians: Quetzalcoatl, Orejona, Viracocha, Ishtar, Astarte, Anaita.

Ten thousand years ago, an identical miracle made Egyptian civilization blossom, with 'divine kings who came from the sky.' Everything moves in recurring cycles.

Earthlings are now on their way toward becoming the Initiators and 'gods' of another planet. And it would be in keeping with the universal order if, in the near future, other extraterrestrials came to our own planet, bringing a fantastic and no doubt reassuring confirmation of this thesis.

Conventional (that is, outdated) prehistorians reject these prophetic views and call them whimsical. But for those of us who dare to be men of tomorrow, conventional prehistory is only adulterated and foolish fiction, incredible because it is untruthful.

5 The Puerta del Sol and the Mystery of the West

Ancient Peru fascinates everyone interested in archaeology and the Mysterious Unknown of civilizations. Yet the reign of the Incas lasted little more than a thousand years and it is probable that the extent of their power and the development of their culture have been exaggerated.

They were not the first inhabitants of the *altiplano*, the high plateau that extends from Peru to Bolivia and from Ecuador to Chile. Before their advanced civilization, others had appeared all over South America. The extensive, enigmatic remains found in Brazil, at Ylo, in the Nazca pampa, and at Tiahuanaco bear witness to the fact that ten thousand years ago in the Andes there were civilized people who may have been the last Atlantans.

K'emko in Peru

The Capital of the Incas was Cuzco, in the Andes, but near the fortress of Sacsahuaman which defended the city, on the rocky spur of K'emko, there are caves, a menhir, and hewn stones that do not belong to Incan civilization.

They have sometimes been attributed to the Aymaras, ancestors of the Incans, but the K'emko ruins are actually much older, probably by several thousand years, and seem to be related to the pre-Celtic civilization of Carnac in France and Stonehenge in England. K'emko, moreover, strangely resembles a tumulus.

The Incas had their political and cultural centre on the high plateaux around Cuzco. The most important remains of their cities and fortresses, still very well preserved, are found not far from this capital.

To go from Cuzco to Ollantaytambo, we travelled along

a rough but scenic mountain road at an altitude of between ten and twelve thousand feet. It winds through gorges where our expert guide, Madame de Carthagène, showed us the few Incan graves that have been discovered.

They are holes in the sides of rocks, just long enough to hold a body. When their openings had been sealed, they soon blended in with the surrounding rock, which explains why archaeologists have been able to find so few of them. The shepherds of the *altiplano*, however, in both Peru and Bolivia, are more skilled in locating these graves – perhaps because they have spent more time looking for them – and rob them of the gold that was placed in them for the use of the deceased in his future life.

Madame de Carthagène gave us some amusing details on this subject. In Cuzco and La Paz the Indians, genuine Incas but less civilized than their ancestors, are fond of gold teeth. Their natural teeth may be perfectly sound, but gold teeth are fashionable on the *altiplano*. They go to a dentist and ask him to pull five or six teeth and replace them with a gold bridge.

'But that's expensive,' says the dentist. 'Do you have any money?'

'No.'

'Do you have any gold?'

'Gold? Oh, yes.'

No bargain is concluded, but the next day the Inca comes back, takes a handful of gold or ancient jewels from his pocket and says simply, 'For my teeth.' And that is how a dentist on the *altiplano* can make a fortune in a few years.

Ollantaytambo

The little village of Ollantaytambo is traversed by a clear stream. The houses along its only street all date from the time of the Incas. They are made of stone, and there are earthen structures for animals.

Life seems to have stood still here for a thousand years. Although the wheel is known (we came to the village in a car), it is strictly forbidden. The people carry everything on their backs, including their harvested crops.

Above the village, the fortress rises in narrow terraces

on which llamas and white alpacas graze. Enormous rocks, carved in the shape of benches, stairs, or pulpits, are scattered everywhere. They are called 'the weary stones.' Perhaps they did not have the energy to climb to the top of the fortress alone!

Machu Picchu: the Mystery of the Stones

From Cuzco, one goes to Machu Picchu on a little mountain train that leaves early in the morning. The trip, by way of the valleys of the Salty River and the Urubamba, is extremely scenic. The tropical forest on both sides of the railway track is rich in different species of trees, but the overhanging mountaintops are bare of plant life because they are at an altitude of about sixteen thousand feet.

Machu Picchu, the secret city of the Incas, was rediscovered only in 1911 by Hiram Bingham, at the cost of terrible efforts. Reaching it is now easy, but in the time of the conquistadores it was all but impossible.

It is thought that Machu Picchu may have been the retreat of the Virgins of the Sun, but this is only conjecture because the Incas never even revealed its existence.

It is a vast site, dominated by the mountain of Machu Picchu, on which one can still see terraces cultivated by the Indians in the fourteenth century. It is a massively constructed city. Everything in it seems to have been built for religious practices.

The terraces that lead to the habitations are laid out exactly as at Ollantaytambo. Peaceful alpacas graze freely on them. The walls are made of great stone blocks arranged as at Sacsahuaman. Some of them are astonishingly similar to the walls of Winapu, on Easter Island. There are squared blocks sixteen feet long; how they were transported remains a mystery.

We saw one rock, about five feet high and three feet thick, that had a shallow and absolutely straight saw-cut on one side. At intervals of about eight inches along this cut there were notches into which wedges, probably wooden, had been driven to split the rock. It was split into two equal parts, although the fracture on the side opposite the saw-cut was less straight. We were amazed by the precision of the work

and by the workmen's knowledge of the grain of stone in a
shapeless mass that seemed to have none. In any case, it
is now established that the Incas worked stone by breaking
it along the line of the grain with wedges, without magic or
any supernatural means.

The Incan Mirage

Most of the other Incan archaeological sites, except for
K'emko, do not seem to be very ancient. Pachacamac is
relatively recent and of no great interest. The ruins of the
Temple of the Sun on Titicaca Island are nearly nonexistent
and what remains of them is disappointing. The ruins on the
Island of the Moon reveal no greatness. The same is true of
what remains in Cuzco, whose second Temple of the Sun,
now transformed into a Christian church, bears no resemblance to the lyrical descriptions of Garcilaso de la Vega.
What was once the Curicancha (Enclosure of Gold) is now
nothing but a plot of empty ground that slopes down to a
narrow, muddy brook: the fabulous Guatanay!

I was greatly disappointed by what I saw. It was not
easy to give up a legend that had pleased my imagination
and my fondest feelings.

The Incan king, like the 'powerful' Egyptian pharaoh,
was unquestionably a minor ruler without military power,
the leader of a small people spread over vast spaces; and
Incan civilization, however brilliant it may have been, was
incapable of extending all over the empire.

It was not by chance, or because they were regarded as
gods, that Pizarro's hundred and two foot-soldiers and sixty-
two horsemen so easily conquered a territory six times as
large as France.

Tiahuanaco

Tiahuanaco, in Bolivia, fifty miles from La Paz, is a vast
plateau at an altitude of thirteen thousand feet, surrounded
by undulating mountaintops.

Before reaching the village by way of a rocky path, one
walks alongside the site where the Puerta del Sol stands,

small but rich in legends and prestige. The monument is, regrettably, hideously protected by a metal fence that takes away part of its charm.

Is it a Venusian calendar? Perhaps. In any case, the figures of the frieze are as they have been described: remarkably intact and sharply carved, representing four-fingered personages.

What is less well known is that a little more than half a mile away there are ten other gates, some of them larger than the Puerta del Sol, lying in an enclosure. They seem to have been abandoned by people who built a city or a sanctuary about which we have no information.

An important centre must once have existed at this place, however, because all over the plateau, around an immense earthen tumulus surmounted by a menhir, there are magnificent, purely Incan statues, menhirs, remains of structures, and broken stone phalluses. The whole site is puzzling but deeply moving.

A long wall beside the road is flanked every hundred feet or so by menhirs similar to those in Brittany. The real Tiahuanaco, in fact, is a city of menhirs. They are everywhere, by the hundreds, most of them embedded in more recent structures.

A half-buried temple, the *templete*, bears witness to what I will call the Celtic antiquity of *the original Tiahuanaco*.

A little museum of pottery and carved stones has been built between the Puerta del Sol and the *templete*. In it we saw a strange block of black stone, a disc similar to the millstones of Mexico and the museum at Carnac, France, and a series of human skulls ranging in size from that of Cro-Magnon man to that of giants who must have been at least ten feet tall. The largest of these skulls has a height and a width of about fourteen inches.

To what race did those men belong? What was the origin of the civilization that produced the tumulus, the menhirs, and the phalluses?

The Bretons of San Agustin

In Mexico, Peru and Bolivia, no ancient statue has slanted eyes. The eyes are round or, more often, square or rec-

THE PUERTA DEL SOL

tangular, as at San Agustin, Colombia, where one finds the pure Breton type of France and Great Britain.

A rigorously logical idea immediately comes to mind. The pre-Celts entered America from the north; from Canada they passed into the United States and then into Mexico.

What became of the Mayas of the Yucatan? According to standard textbooks, they vanished without a trace. But to an honest archaeologist who sees the menhirs and the megalithic enclosures of La Venta at the site of San Agustin, the connection is obvious. Those Mayas were the builders of San Agustin; centuries later, they continued their migration to Peru, and then to Bolivia, where their style and their megaliths are found at Tiahuanaco.

Medzamor: a Steel Mill Five Thousand Years Old

More and more, discoveries in Europe tend to establish that part of the world as the home of the first civilized men of whom we have any knowledge.

If we dare to trust accounts describing finds of unknown or mysterious objects and materials, metal-working civilizations existed in the European Occident thousands of years before Sumer and the pseudo-Bronze Age which outdated educators drum into their students.

At this point I would like to repeat something I have already said before. In the enthusiasm of discovering new, exciting, and revolutionary ideas, my young readers sometimes broaden their scope unjustifiably. I want to stress that with regard to most of the sciences I formulate working hypotheses, often in the form of intellectual games. I urge my young readers and friends to trust their teachers and follow them in their presentations of accepted theories. I make an exception only for prehistory: conventional prehistory is false and nonsensical.

At Medzamor, in Soviet Armenia, Dr Koriun Meguerchian has discovered the oldest metallurgical factory in the world. Experts have established that it was built five thousand years ago.

At Medzamor, vases and objects made of all the common metals have been found: knives, spearheads, arrowheads, clasps, rings, bracelets, etc.

The foundry had a series of vats, hollowed out of rock, in which ore was crushed, pounded, washed, refined, and enriched until pure metal was obtained. Twenty-five furnaces have been uncovered, but more than two hundred are thought to be still buried.

Medzamor was an industrial centre of the period derisively called the Neolithic. Imported ore was treated there, and the finished products were distributed among the peoples of the Near East. Craftsmen worked with copper, bronze, lead, zinc, iron, gold, tin, arsenic, antimony, manganese.

And also steel!

Steel tweezers, slender and still shiny, have been found. They are a little more recent – they date from only three thousand years ago!

Fourteen varieties of bronze were smelted in the plant and used for different purposes.

These discoveries have been verified by scientific organizations in the Soviet Union, the United States, France, Britain, and Germany, yet they have not altered the viewpoint of prehistorians.

And for a long time there will continue to be talk about the Age of Polished Stone, as though anyone on earth had ever seen a field of polished stone axes!

The metal-working people of Medzamor had a three-story astronomical observatory in the shape of a triangle whose apex was pointed towards the south, where stars are most numerous.

And yet, despite these scientific complexes worthy of a better fate, the civilization of Medzamor is virtually unknown.

Unusual Metals and Science

Medzamor provides a good approach to the subject of unusual discoveries. I must point out that my knowledge of some of these discoveries comes from reports without solid references or from traditions which, of course, cannot be verified.

A solid, pointed metal cylinder about seven inches long was found in a Spanish silver mine that was worked in the sixteenth century. Examination of the immediate environment of the object placed its age at several tens of thousands of years.

According to B. Laufer in *Prehistory of Aviation*, the Chinese Emperor Tsin Shi (c. 250 B.C.) had a 'magic mirror' which, like modern X-ray devices, made it possible to see the bones of the body through the flesh.

Skulls of Indians who lived more than three thousand years ago were discovered at an archaeological site near St Louis, Missouri. The investigators were astonished to see that cavities in the teeth of some of these skulls had been filled with a kind of cement.

In a study of dental caries in ancient Egyptian remains, Dr Lucille Homy and the dentist Richard Koritzer, of the Smithsonian Institution in Washington, observed that caries occurred at the rate of ninety per cent from the Eighteenth Dynasty onward, while the rate was only three per cent from the Sixth to Twelfth Dynasties. This would seem to show that the earliest Egyptians had medical knowledge that we do not possess in the twentieth century.

Menhirs on the Moon

According to the magazine *Interavia*, photographs taken by Lunar Orbiter 2, from a distance of twenty-three miles, indicate that intelligent beings erected menhirs on the moon at an undetermined time in the past. The photographs show the shadows of eight of these megaliths, which are between forty and seventy-five feet high, with a diameter of about fifty feet.

Photographs taken by the Soviet Luna 9 show similar megaliths a hundred and fifty feet high.

All over the globe, archaeological discoveries are proving that long before the Paleolithic of prehistorians, even before the civilization of Atlantis, our ancestors had technical knowledge which annihilates the allegations of conventional doctrines.

In South Africa, an official report by experts states that human beings exploited hematite mines at Ngwenya, in western Swaziland, twenty-five thousand years ago.

In Malta – it is said – vestiges of an ancient railroad have been found, with cross ties and rails.

In the early Middle Ages, according to the writer Maurice Guignard, the priestesses and grand master of Odin 'had for thousands of years been miniaturizing their means of production. They collected cosmic energy in an emerald cylinder and transported it in a small accumulator called *Völuvölt.*'

The American clairvoyant Edgar Cayce said essentially the same thing in 1940, with regard to the Atlantans.

The Oldest Shoe in the World

In the Gobi Desert in 1959, the Russo-Chinese expedition headed by Dr Chou-Myn Chen made a strange discovery: the perfect, almost incontestable imprint of a shoe sole, about size nine, in a rock two million years old. It is thought that the imprint was made in soft sand and that sediment was later deposited on it.

The English naturalist Charles Brewster is said to have found the remains of eleven steel nails in limestone from the Cretaceous period, seventy-five to ninety million years ago!

It is known that the ancient Incas alloyed silver and platinum several centuries before it was done in Europe. The melting point of platinum is 1773.5 degrees Centigrade!

At Chan-Chan, Peru, objects plated with gold and silver have been found, which indicates knowledge of electrolysis. Similarly, Egyptian vases several thousand years old seem to have been covered with a thin layer of gold by an electrolytic process.

Where could these peoples, living so far away from each other, have obtained the secret of such knowledge, if not from Superior Ancestors?

Levitating Stones

Andrew Tomas gives a perfectly authentic report on something which, he says, reproduces an achievement of vanished ancient science. In the village of Shivapur, near Poona, India, is a little mosque built in memory of Qamar Ali Dervish, a holy man of the Sufis, a Mohammedan sect which teaches that if man is purified by meditation, ecstasy, and strict observance of certain rules he can rise to the level of divinity. On the ground near the mosque are two round stones weighing ninety and a hundred and twenty pounds respectively. Every day pilgrims stand beside these stones and invoke Qamar Ali for a long time; then eleven of them put their hands on the stone weighing a hundred and twenty pounds and suddenly lift it to a height of about five feet, using only the tips of their forefingers.

The same phenomenon, produced with the ninety-pound stone by nine people is nearly identical to the one I described in the second chapter of *Le Livre du Mystérieux Inconnu*, with four people.

In *Magie chaldéenne*, Charles Lenormant writes, 'It is certain that in very ancient times the priests of On . . . by means of magic words, caused storm to arise and lifted into the air, to build their temples, stones that a thousand men could not have moved.'

I will not carry credulity to the point of asserting that this miracle unquestionably took place, but it may be that Lenormant is referring to an adulterated tradition based on a science unknown in our time.

In *La Généalogie humaine*, Annie Besant attempts an explanation: 'These stones were not lifted by an accumulation of muscular strength or by ingenious devices more powerful than anything we can produce today; they were lifted by people who understood and controlled the earth's magnetism. They lost all their weight and floated in the air, so that the pressure of a finger was enough to move them and place them in the exact location assigned to them.'

We must, of course, make a distinction between the probable and the imaginary, but so many discoveries have been made all over the world, and so many incredible traditions have persisted through the centuries, that a parcel of truth seems to be trying to draw our curiosity toward the fantastic frontiers of a past that refuses to die out.

And it is a filial duty for us, the men of the twentieth century, to refrain from thoughtlessly breaking the umbilical cord that still binds us to those who were our great ancestors.

6 Celtic Mythology and the Great Pyramid of Plouézoch

The Three Invasions

The history of the Celts is approximately known through ancient Irish and Welsh manuscripts. The *Book of Invasions* says that at the time of the great Deluge the magician queen of the Green Island perished with all her race. On a First of May, Prince Partholon and twenty-four couples came from Greece. On a First of May exactly three hundred years later, an epidemic wiped out the descendants of the Greeks. Then came the invasions of the Sons of Nemred, originally from Scythia, and the Firbolgs, a small Gothic people.

On still another First of May, 'from beyond the ocean river,' the Mag Meld ('Plain of Joy'), came the Tuatha De Danann tribe, who were undoubtedly Quiche Mayas from South America.

The Tuatha De Danann

As soon as they landed in Ireland, the Tuatha De Danann attacked the Formors and defeated them at Moytura (in Gaelic: Mag Tuireadh, 'Plain of Pillars,' that is, raised stones, or menhirs), near Cong, in what is now County Mayo. (*Mythologie générale,* by Félix Guiraud and G. Roth, Larousse, Paris.)

These events, write Guiraud and Roth, took place at about the same time as the Trojan War, which would explain the arrival of a Greek prince and place the time at about 1300 B.C. But in my opinion the events were much earlier.

In any case, more than three thousand years ago there were already menhirs on the plains of Ireland, and the Celts apparently did not clearly understand their significance, since they called them 'pillars.'

The Tuatha De Danann brought magic objects: the Nuada Sword, the Lug Spear, the Dagde Cauldron, and the Fal Stone, or Stone of Destiny, which cried out when the legitimate king sat on it.

The invasion of these magic-wielding foreigners was relatively peaceful, for although it gave rise to fighting that was described with great exaggeration by chroniclers, it seems that the Tuatha De Danann were accepted by the majority of the natives. Their conflicts with them strongly resembled tribal rivalries and were often happily concluded by marriages.

These foreigners from South America apparently behaved like genuine Celts returning to their homeland. They had no language problem with the Irish, came to terms with them as one does with close relatives, and educated them.

The Mayas of Mexico Return to Europe

It would seem, then, that the descendants of the Hyperboreans from the mysterious Thule in the mountains of Greenland, or of the Aryans from the plateau of Iran, had made several round trips between the two continents that once bordered the land of the Atlantans. Many Amerindian stories support this hypothesis, which conventional historians ignore.

How are we to explain the following two facts?

1) The Initiators of the Incas and the Mayas, who were white, bearded gods, one day *went back* to their country, across the eastern sea.
2) The Tuatha De Danann came on a First of May from across the western sea; they returned to their country, again on the sacred date of May 1.

The Tuatha De Danann, who were 'of a divine race,' left after having lost a long war, but before leaving *they demanded the observance of a kind of memorial worship, which is very edifying in view of the fact that they had been defeated!*

Everything becomes clear if we grant that the Tuatha

De Danann, or Mayas from South America, were Celts who had previously left Europe. (Let me specify that by 'Celts' I mean Aryans from the plateau of Iran; we do not know their name, but their main migration formed the Celtic branch.)

This return to the ancestral homeland is described in the Popul Vuh, the sacred book of the Quiche Mayas, in which we read, 'They were at Ha'kavitz when the four leaders of their migration disappeared in a mysterious way. Although very old and having travelled a great distance for a long time, they were not ill when they took leave of their children, saying that their mission was accomplished and they were returning to their homeland.

'They urged their successors to go back to see the land from which they had come, leaving them as a keepsake a wrapped package corresponding to the *quimilli* of the Nahuatl-speaking peoples.

'Long afterward, three of their sons set off eastward, across the ocean . . .

'When the Quiches left Tulan, their fathers said, "Your home is not here; you will find your mountains and plains beyond the seas. You will be upheld by Belih [Bel] and Toh [Thoth, Thor]." '

They returned and tried to settle in Ireland, the kingdom that had once belonged to them; they also wandered in their former lands of Wales, Gaul, Iberia and Russia, where, I believe, they founded initiatic centres that gave rise to the flowering of Druidism.

The Great Pyramid of the Celts at Plouézoch

This view will raise the hackles of our good historians; they will be sure to call it ludicrous because it convincingly illuminates a past which, for conventional minds, is nothing but darkness and satanic shadows!

Perhaps they will demand traces of the Mayas' presence in Europe. If so, there is no shortage of them!

Besides the Popul Vuh, I believe that several documents of the Mexican Codices must contain accounts of that journey back to the ancestral lands. But the major proof

of it is given by the large Mayan monuments that one can
see in France.

'Here's something new,' you may think. Yes, everything
is new to those who cannot or will not see, but if you
are curious enough to see for yourself, go to Brittany and
drive six miles north of Morlaix, a little beyond the village
of Plouézoch. When you come to the sea, turn left, drive
past a few fishermen's houses, and there, at the top of a
hill, you will see . . .

I went there with Yvette Charroux in the spring of 1969;
we both exclaimed together, 'A Mayan "pyramid"!'

It is a monument in the shape of a long, truncated pyramid,
exactly like those at Monte Alban and all over ancient
Mexico, made of the same material, with the same lines and
arrangement of masses. It is a colossal monument that has
been colossally ignored.

As you can see from a comparison of the two photographs,
it is quite similar to the stepped structures of the Mayas
and the Incas.

It is Two Hundred and Fifty Feet Long

The Plouézoch pyramid is about two hundred and fifty
feet long, fifty-five feet wide (at present) and thirty feet
high. Its long sides lie in an almost east-west direction, but
slightly northeast-southwest. It thus faces Stonehenge and
Iceland, which can be regarded as 'the island of the first
fathers, lost in the tumultuous sea.'

The pyramid has four levels and covers four or five large
rooms whose entrance is partially obstructed. In the past, it
sheltered a dozen dolmenic chambers, two of which, decapit-
ated by stone-pillagers, are now visible on one of its sides.

This impressive monument overlooks the sea from the
top of a hill. Its great size is no doubt unique in the whole
Celtic region. For this reason, I believe it was the Great
Pyramid of the Celts, serving as a tomb and perhaps as a
chamber of immortality for the great leaders of the Tuatha De
Danann or the kings of Armorica, which was not yet
Brittany. (The Bretons are descended from peoples that
came from Great Britain no earlier than the fourth century

A.D. The real natives of what is now Brittany are the Armoricans. The name Armorica is Celtic and means 'at the edge of the sea.' In the time of the ancient Celts, as in the time of the Romans, Armorica must have been composed of the territory between the Rhône and the ocean.)

The pyramid was originally higher and considerably wider at the places where dolmens appear. Through the centuries, the inhabitants of the region have removed many stones and used them for building houses.

The Pyramid of Carnac

A similar pyramid stands at Carnac, France, where it is called the Saint-Michel mound.

Sacrilegious Christians have tried to efface this Celtic monument. They have partially covered it with earth to make it into a mound and on top of it they have built an ugly little church dedicated to Saint Michael, the leader of the celestial militia who slew the wicked dragon. The dragon, of course, was paganism, Celtism, Druidism, initiation — everything that symbolized the religion, culture, and spirit of the ancient Occident.

When you push aside the gorse that grows on the slopes, you distinctly see the stone steps of the original pyramid. The interior is of fine masonry and includes a long circular hall connecting dolmenic crypts made to be used as tombs.

There are four known pyramids in France, at Plouézoch, at Carnac, at Falicon, near Nice, and at Couhame near Autun. But there are certainly others which escaped the great destruction ordered by Charlemagne.

The situation is too new, archaeologically speaking, for us to be able to say whether the Mayas took the pyramid style from Celtia to Mexico, or whether they brought it from Mexico to Gaul and perhaps to Egypt, before transplanting it all over the world.

The pyramids in Brittany appear to be definitely older than those in Mexico and perhaps those in Egypt.

Is this a typically Atlantan architecture?

It is interesting to note that drawings intended to represent the monuments of the Atlantans are always based on the pyramid, as though our memory chromosomes suggested that style to us through an obscure but genuine recollection of a past that goes back to before the Deluge.

They Came in Flying Machines on a First of May

In the Celtic tradition, the magician-king Bran is a traveller from the 'mysterious regions' who goes westward to the land of the Beyond, in a chariot that never touches the water.

His brother, Manannan, worshipped in our time by the Witch Queen on the Isle of Man, is a powerful magician whose horse flies through the air. He also travels across the sea in a boat without oars or a sail.

The Celtic goddess named Belisama ('flamelike') can no doubt be identified with the planet Venus and the wife of Bel-Baal, that is, Astarte, queen of the skies of Baal. She was the female equivalent of the Gallic god Balan or Belin or Belinus.

It should be noted that, among the Phoenicians, Baal was the 'north lord,' the same as Bel among the Assyro-Babylonians.

Here, then, is a genealogy which combines the Celtic gods and the Phoenician gods, the planet Venus, mysterious flying machines, America and the Venusian gods of the Incas, and Mayas, Viracocha, and Quetzalcoatl, who 'set off eastward, across the ocean,' that is, in the direction of Europe and Africa.

These similarities among the South American, Celtic, Phoenician, and Assyro-Babylonian myths clearly indicate their common origin and the identity of their heroes.

In Hindu and Persian mythology, the ancestor of the white man is Aryaman, the Gwyon of the Celts; he came from the Milky Way, which means that he travelled in a spacecraft.

In Phoenician and Assyrian mythology, Baal-Bel and Astarte-Ishtar came from the planet Venus. Their counterparts among the Persians are Ahura Mazda, the flying god, and Anahyta, the Venusian goddess.

The Egyptians believed that the first divine men came from the sky of Horus in flying machines. As for the Incas and Mayas, there are clear representations of spacecraft at Tiahuanaco, Palenque, and Monte Alban, and in dozens of Mayan manuscripts.

And among the Celts, Bran's chariot, which did not touch the water, and Manannan's flying machine, which took him from Ireland to England in one night, give us clues that can be added to evidence from other sources.

The supreme God of the Gauls is nameless, because he is the only God. But, as with the God of the Christians, a Trinity emanates from him. We find it, for example, in the three-headed statues in Autun, the Hôtel-Dieu in Paris, the Beaune museum, etc. This Trinity is Teutates-Taran-Esus.

The myth of the Initiator-serpent (the ram-headed serpent) is associated with the Celtic gods, who generally hold two ram-headed serpents in their hands

On the famous Gunderstrup Celtic vase in the Copenhagen museum, the god Curnunos holds a ram-headed serpent and there are many flying griffins. It is known that the serpent is the symbol of space travel and that it gave rise to the myths of the flying dragon and the flying serpent.

How did the Tuatha De Danann come from America?

They 'knew how to hide themselves behind the cloak of invisibility.' They were able to appear and disappear – like, one is tempted to say, the mysterious UFOs (unidentified flying objects) that haunt our skies!

The whole history of the ancient world now becomes perceptible and can be formulated as follows. Five thousand years ago, when the comet Venus entered the solar system and was stabilized in it, there was a great Deluge (the second Deluge) and Initiators spread over nearly all of the globe. They had flying machines and taught writing, the arts, and techniques of metalworking.

In Phoenicia, they were called Baal and Astarte; in Assyro-Babylonia, Bel and Ishtar; in Peru, Viracocha and Orejona (see the third chapter of my *One Hundred Thousand Years of Man's Unknown History*); in Mexico, Quetzalcoatl and Kukulkan; in Celtia, Belin, Belisama, Gwydion, Bran, and Manannan.

It even seems possible to determine, not the exact year in which these events took place, but the day of the month: the First of May, for it was on the First of May that the Tuatha De Danann landed in Ireland, on a First of May three hundred years later that they set off again, 'beyond the ocean river,' and on a First of May that Prince Partholon and the Sons of Nemred came to the Green Island.

And since then, the First of May has been regarded as the sacred date of the pagan Celtic religion: May Day, or Beltane. And Beltane is strongly reminiscent of the festival of Bel-Baal the Venusian!

May Day

Etymologists are not in agreement on the origin of the name 'May;' for some of them it is the month of Jupiter (*Deus Maius*, 'Great God'), for others it is the month of Maia, the Queen of the Earth.

Since the most ancient times, the First of May has always been the prime sacral date, perhaps because it was on a First of May that the extraterrestrial Initiators landed, or the comet Venus entered into orbit around the sun.

In Celtic witchcraft, May Day is religiously consecrated to the Great Goddess, with a secret ceremony which the Witch Queen of the Isle of Man refuses to divulge. For the same unknown reasons, the pagan festival known as Walpurgis Night takes place on the eve of May Day. To escape the fanaticism and murderous fury of the Church, it was camouflaged as a tribute to the Christian Saint Walpurgis, whose vestments are preserved in the Eichstaedt convent in Bavaria, and the instructions given by the initiated Celts were observed in Germany, France, Great Britain, and the Netherlands.

In our time, groups of initiates are still working towards the goal of making the Celtic May Day the festival of all the peoples of the earth.

Two thousand years ago, great crowds gathered in the forests and mountains on May Day to pay homage to the great Goddess and celebrate the coming of spring, first with religious solemnity, then with healthy merrymaking.

It was on the 'Fields of May' that the Franks held their great yearly assemblies and the Romans celebrated the festival of grain and flowers, dedicated to the goddess Maia.

Worried by this fervour which was prejudicial to its God and its saints, the Christian Church began an insidious campaign of derogatory propaganda that eventually bore fruit.

History of the First of May

The good pagan gods were presented as demonic monsters and Walpurgis Night was depicted as an unholy Sabbath, with witches riding broomsticks, human sacrifices to Satan, and other nonsense in the same vein. The Brocken, highest peak of the Harz Mountains in Germany, became an accursed place and was stigmatized by a bad reputation that extended to all celebrations of the eve of May Day.

Yet despite slander and attempted Satanization, the First of May was such an essentially sacred date that it finally imposed itself all over the world.

Alfred the Great, King of the West Saxons, who reigned from 871 to 899, was the first to have the idea of instituting, on a First of May, the forty-hour week, with days divided into eight hours of work, eight hours of leisure, and eight hours of sleep.

On May I, 1886, three hundred and forty thousand striking American workers demonstrated for a forty-hour week. The demonstrations turned into an insurrection and many men were killed. On May 1, 1908, despite a lockout, the workers' demands acquired the force of law.

During the German occupation of France, from 1941 to 1944, the First of May officially became the Festival of Labour. When the war ended, the Liberation government reacted by requiring all civil servants to work on May 1, 1945, and the Communist union, the CGT, supported this decision.

In 1946 the First of May became an international workers' holiday, primarily because of the efforts of General de Gaulle in France, Stalin in the Soviet Union, and Evita Perón in Argentina.

The Celtic festival of May Day has now spread to all parts of the world, by a just recurrence in which white magic, the colour of hawthorn, plays a part that very few people suspect!

Druids who Killed

It was because of their proximity to the vanished continent that the peoples of Mexico and of the Atlantic coast of Europe, particularly the Celts, were those who best kept the reflection of Atlantan civilization.

Julius Caesar wrote in his *Commentaries on the Gallic War* that the Druids made human sacrifices to their gods, on dolmens; and megaliths have indeed been found with hollows in the shape of a man (as in Peru) and channels for the flow of a liquid (in Mexico). Tiberius, who ruled Rome from 14 to 37, forbade the Gauls to practise human sacrifices.

The reality of these sacrifices is well established, but they have nothing to do with real Druidism.

Those 'killing Druids' were actually only sorcerers. Their bloodthirsty rites were as far removed as possible from the teachings of the great initiates. They operated in the backwaters of Europe, where there were few outside contacts and the great currents of civilization did not pass.

Baal Worshipped under the Oaks

The real Druids, or 'Men of the Oak,' were priests who officiated in God's name: in forests and, more precisely, at the foot of the king of European trees, the oak.

Their religion was universal and was taught from Gaul to India. The Pelasgians, the Phoenicians, the Canaanites, the Philistines, and even the Hebrews had their Druids.

It is historically established that priests officiated under oaks (or other trees where there were no oaks) all over the Middle East and particularly in Phoenicia, where the worship of stones was held in high regard.

The widespread occurrence of the so-called pagan rites of the Celts leads us back to this conclusion: these identical priests, common religions, and gods who bear the same names imply an identity of origin. The Pelasgians, Greeks, Phoenicians, and Hebrews were Aryans.

The Real Druidism

The Druids, like the priests of the Incas and Mayas, said that they descended from the God of the Seas, who had given them all their knowledge. Caesar reports that, according to their doctrine, the Gauls descended from Dis Pater (God the Father).

Who was Dis Pater? He was God, unknowable and unnameable. But the unitiated Celts, of course, gave him names or transfigurations: Cernunos, Esus, Taran, Teutates, Belinus, Beli.

Dis Pater had a wife, the Mother Goddess. Esoterically, she was as abstract as her husband, but the uninitiated called her De-meter (Earth-mother), Morrigain, Morgana, Koridwen, Dana, or Ana.

The sorcerers of Brittany and Great Britain taught magic; the Druids of the Gauls taught history, philosophy, science, and astronomy. They believed in another world, *orbis alius,* and a metempsychosis reserved for heroes.

According to Diodorus Siculus, the Druids spoke the language of the gods. Perhaps they knew the power of waves and applied it in speech.

Lug, Ptah, and Apollo

The main god of the Celts, always unnamed and unnameable – the Dis Pater of the Gauls – is a trinity represented with a triple head.

The Kymris Druids (Belgium, northern France) believed in metempsychosis and the eternity of matter and spirit. Their concept of the Other World seems to be a recollection of knowledge that they could no longer understand.

According to the Barddas, the Druids symbolically conceived three circles of life: the *abred,* the inner circle, which contained the germs of all things; the *gwenved,* the middle circle, representing bliss; and the *keugant,* the outer circle, containing only God.

They believed in five elements: *kalas* (earth, solid bodies), *gwyar* (wetness,) *fun* (breath, air), *uvel* (heat, fire, light), and *nwyvre* (emanation, spirit of God). All life was born of the

combination of *nwyvre* with the other elements. God was
nwyvre.

The Druids of Ireland, Wales, and Brittany believed in
little more than magic.

The wife of Dis Pater was the Great Goddess, Demeter,
the Cybele of the Greeks, but in the tribe of the Tuatha De
Danann two tuterary divinities were honoured: Bile, or Bel,
and Dana, his wife. From them were descended Ogmios and
Gwydion, civilizing heroes whose castle was in the Milky
Way (Caer Gwydion). Their descendants also included Lug,
skilled in all the arts, Llyr, or the ocean, Bran, Manannan, and
Queen Morgana.

This genealogy will shed light on the situation and place
it much farther back in time, long before the Trojan War.

The greatest of all the Celtic heroes, Lug, 'the prodigious child, master of all the arts,' was a Tuatha De Danann.
He was the hero not only of Ireland, but of all Celtia, particularly Gaul.

Cities all over Europe were named for Lug: Lugdunum
(modern Lyon), Lugdunum Clavatum (modern Laon), Lusig-
nan, Loudon, and Montluçon in France; Lugano, Locarno, and
Lugarus in Switzerland; Luga and Lugansk in Russia: Leiden
in Holland; Luggude in Sweden: Lugoj in Rumania; Lugo
in Italy and Spain, and many others. Thousands of localities
still bear the name of this hero and perpetuate it from the
Urals to the Pillars of Hercules.

Lug, the Celt *par excellence*, who is also identified with
Ogmius and Gwyon the Initiate, is to western Europe what
Ptah, Prometheus, and Apollo are to Egypt and Greece. He is
very likely the same person.

The West Has Been Sabotaged

Control of the world has always belonged to the great
navigators, whether they sailed the Atlantic, the Pacific; or
the great universal ocean that is outer space. In recent times,
Portugal, Spain, France, and England shared control of the
world known to them and the world is now dominated by
the two great space-travelling nations: the USA and the
USSR.

In more ancient times, the same position was occupied by

the Genoese, the Venetians, the Phoenicians, and the Cretans. In still more ancient times, mastery of the sea and land belonged to the Pelasgians, Shardana, and Vikings, who came from the northern seas and erected megaliths.

The ancient chronicles of Gaul, Germany, Spain, and Russia certainly related the exploits of those great peoples, but, except for the Irish and Welsh manuscripts that have miraculously been preserved, nothing of early European history has come down to us; everything was destroyed by the Christians.

In official textbooks there is no trace of the real history of our ancestors, and anyone who speaks of it is likely to be regarded as a godless, unscrupulous heretic.

The Celts Colonized the Globe

Yet that history is prodigious, since those peoples, the Celts, Scandians, Vikings, Pelasgians, descendants of the Atlantans and intrepid navigators, who conquered the world, spread from the Iranian plateau to Ireland, Iberia, the Mediterranean basin, and India, crossed the Atlantic in their masted ships, initiated the native Americans, formed the Mayan and Incan peoples, and finally sailed all over the South Pacific, peopling the thousands of islands of Micronesia and Polynesia in the area of what was once the vast empire of Mu.

This version of human history is, of course, contrary to what is taught by the apostles of 'classical and obligatory truth.' But the real truth, suppressed so long, will soon illuminate our knowledge of the past.

One fact will become inescapably obvious to archaeologists: the menhirs, phalluses, and megaliths of France, Great Britain, Germany, and Russia were the work of the same people that carved the giants of Tula in Mexico, Tiahuanaco in Bolivia, and Easter Island; the same people that erected megaliths in the Mariana Islands, the Guanche islands of the Canaries, Senegal, Gambia . . .

Part 3

LOST CIVILIZATIONS

7 Mysterious Civilizations

It is sometimes difficult to know whether rocky masses reproducing human and animal forms belong to an unknown civilization or whether they are, to use the consecrated expression, 'whims of nature.'

On the Marcahuassi plateau in Peru, my friend the explorer Daniel Ruzco discovered a profusion of rocks resembling bears, sea lions, snakes, lions, etc. He concluded, logically enough, that the stone had been carved by men, and attributed the representations to what he calls the 'Masma Culture.'

In the Fontainebleau Forest, Danier Ruzco, aided by a talented photographer, Edith Gérin, identified some remarkable rocks with human shapes, one of which, the now famous Mater, is reproduced in my book *Le Livre du Mystérieux Inconnu.*

Professor Doru Todericiu has returned to the problem, with the extraordinary sea lion.

The Fontainebleau Sea Lion

It is hard to imagine, says Professor Todericiu, that nature should have amused herself by carving this sea lion in such minute and realistic detail, including the eye and the front flipper.

The image is nearly perfect, but the 'scales' on the back and the flipper (and on all the other rocks in the forest with human or animal shapes) should apparently not be attributed to human work. They are the result of blistering on the surface of the stone when it was molten, and the same phenomenon can be seen on stone in all parts of the world.

This would seem to indicate that the sea lion is a whim

of nature. It would be an acceptable hypothesis if elephants, cattle, lizards, and the Mater were not found in the immediate vicinity!

Using a base of four or five features for each animal shape and four or five animals grouped in a single place, the theory of probability justifies an unequivocal conclusion: *the shapes cannot be accounted for by chance; there was a conscious will to create them.*

In other words, at Fontainebleau and on the Marcahuassi plateau there are too many stone figures to have been produced by chance, and therefore the sea lion was carved by human hands.

Candles Without Fire?

If you have not already been to Montignac-Lascaux in the Dordogne, France, you have missed your chance to contemplate the greatest wonder of the past, the present, and no doubt the future, because the caves are now closed to the public. (And for a good reason: to protect the paintings from further damage by the algae that have attacked them. Only a few qualified visitors are admitted from time to time.)

The site is composed of a series of connected rooms whose walls are covered with paintings from the Magdalenian period, fifteen to twenty thousand years ago.

Cultivated men from all over the world have come to admire those matchless yellow, red, and black paintings, and Lascaux has been called the 'Louvre of Prehistory.' But what is less well known is that there are also extraordinary engraved drawings on the cave walls.

The Magdalenians did not live in these caves, but it seems that they made them a kind of temple, or better, a museum of painting, to leave proof of their genius for future generations.

The comments of the guide who accompanied us expressed the views of conventional prehistorians.

'The people who made these paintings must have had dwellings,' I said to him. 'Did they know how to build walls and houses?'

'No,' he answered, 'they didn't know how to build walls.'

'But how did they go about painting those pictures ten

or twelve feet above the floor?'

'They used scaffolds. Look, you can still see the holes in the rock where they put in crossbeams that must have held up planks.'

I asked the opinion of Doru Todericiu, professor of science and technology at the University of Bucharest, who was with us.

'It's absolutely contrary to logic,' he said. 'The history of technology shows that scaffolding cannot precede knowledge of masonry, because it follows from the development of masonry. Therefore, if the people of Lascaux made scaffolds, they already knew how to build a wall. To deny it would be like saying that the candle was invented before anyone knew how to kindle a fire.'

'Then you maintain that the Magdalenians knew how to make dwellings with masonry walls?'

'Yes, it's unquestionable.'

They Made Sticks of Ferric Oxide

The idea that the people of Lascaux were primitive savages is absolutely groundless.

What did they paint with? Prehistorians answer (and it is true): with yellow ochre, sticks of manganese, and sticks of ferric oxide. These sticks had the consistency of a modern lipstick, but were much larger.

In the twentieth century we can go to the moon, but ask four hundred people, chosen at random in the streets of Paris or Berlin, to make sticks of ferric oxide or manganese – not one of them will be able to do it!

The men of Lascaux had to use sophisticated techniques: they had to extract the ferric oxide or manganese (the latter is very rare) from earth or rock, pound it, purify it, separate it from the matter around it, reduce it to a powder, and mix it with a greasy substance to give it the desired consistency.

Are we to believe that such advanced technicians did not know how to place stones on top of each other to make a wall? How can anyone dare to state such an absurdity?

Furthermore, two distinct techniques are used in each painted animal: the bodies are drawn with lines, and pulverized paint is used for manes and muzzles. This indicates an advanced stage of development. And in animals that are shown from the side, the two legs in the foreground, that is, those nearest the observer, are drawn normally, while the two others are drawn with a gap between them and the body, to show that they are in the background. The result is an effect of perspective. But in historical times, perspective was not used until the fifteenth century!

The pictures show shadows and highlights, there is a plan of construction, an idea of composition that makes use of hollows and protuberances in the rock. In short, each picture proves that the painters of Lascaux were men who possessed a culture much more advanced than that of the average inhabitant of the European countryside today.

To maintain that these people had not gone beyond the stage of living in caves and using clubs and crude flint tools, and that they looked like the 'apeman' depicted by the statue at Les Eyzies, is to contradict all the rational teachings of the history of science and technology.

The Marvellous Horse

The painters of Lascaux were artists with impeccable taste, capable of making perceptive decisions, yet their genius is now ignored or unjustly underestimated. The fault lies with prehistorians, who are often skilled in clearing a site, identifying its architecture, removing pottery, and finding small objects, but are absolutely incompetent when it comes to making qualitative, intellectual and psychological judgments. If they found a jet aircraft that had crashed in a field containing flint tools, they would conclude that it was an artifact from the Solutrean or the Upper Paleolithic!

In prehistory, the main error consists in relying on archaeologists to interpret finds. This ought to be done by art historians and professors of science and technology.

Furthermore, it is scandalous that archaeological discoveries in France, and only in France, are concealed from the public until the pundits have agreed on which of them will receive the glory of publishing a report.

That is what has happened at Lascaux. The engraved drawings have at least the same value as the paintings, but it is forbidden to photograph them, and almost forbidden to see them. On the left wall of the 'nave' there is a small horse head, about eight inches long, which reminds one of Cranach and the best of the so-called primitive engravers of the artistic period that preceded the Renaissance.

There are hundreds of drawings at Lascaux, but nothing is published about them and they are not shown; they are kept sequestered in their 'galleries,' some of which have always been forbidden to the informed public.

Similarly, the engraved stones of Lussac-les Châteaux were kept sequestered from 1937 to 1969: the Conspiracy has complete power over most of our historical heritage. As for those few parts of it that escape its jurisdiction, it simply declares them to be false!

Other examples: Glozel, whose engraved bones are the finest in the world, and a number of caves containing paintings and drawings as beautiful as those of Rouffignac and Lascaux.

The Ancient Egyptian Plasma Generator

An Egyptian wall painting shows an invocation to Ra, the sun god, in a curious stylization: the worshipper is represented by a force-accumulating pillar and the head is in the shape of the Greek letter tau, the symbol of rebirth. Above the head, two human arms are gracefully raised toward the disc of the sun. Undulations on either side of this central subject resemble materializations of electrical fluid. Two smaller worshippers kneel at the bottom of the picture, and above them are monkeys – baboon Thoths – holding out their arms toward Ra.

Rightly or wrongly, a scientific technician was struck by the rare stylization of this picture and decided that its central subject might well be a plasma generator. Its functioning would be explained as follows: a jet of plasma is obtained by thermal means (fire) and conducted into a tube; inside this tube are two electrodes connected to an inner circuit, and the apparatus is placed between the poles of a powerful electromagnet.

It would no doubt be hazardous to assert that the ancient

Egyptian artist had intended to depict the process of plasma manufacture, but the schematic similarity forces us to seek an explanation.

The Soul of the Universe

It is not impossible that an essential, premonitory correspondence exists between the imaginative creations of yesterday (in this case, the Egyptian painting) and the concrete achievements of today or tomorrow (the plasma generator). Superior works in the graphic arts, and even in poetry, could thus prefigure future scientific developments. They would be visions of the future, or remembrances of the past future; in this latter sense there would be a reconstruction, through the workings of memory chromosomes and in an elusive artistic form, of the very ancient scientific secrets of our Superior Ancestors. And such magic phenomena as the projection of words over great distances, magic mirrors, and flying carpets would be prefigurations of radio, cinema, television, and aviation.

This hypothesis inclines us to think that everything in the universe is directed and that our destiny is inscribed for all eternity. Some will see in this the will of God, others the organizing field conceived by Professor Todericiu: waves that precede and accompany all structurings (atoms, molecules, crystals), determine the modifications of organisms, and dominate their chemical and physical properties.

G. Stromberg calls these waves 'the soul of the universe.' If they exist, they belong to the original plan, the unknown reason of universal life.

The Stones of Guatemala

In one of my other books I reported some information concerning the mysterious round stones in the jungle of Guatemala, arranged according to size to represent a map of the sky.

It turns out, upon investigation, that those stones are only a whim of nature.

The National Geographic Society and the Smithsonian

Institution examined similar stones, much larger and more numerous, in the mountains of northwestern Mexico, near Guadalajara, in the triangle formed by Ahualulco de Mercado, Ameca, and La Vega.

The appearance of the lower part of each stone shows that for a time it was in a kind of matrix; its surface is yellower and less smooth than that of the upper part.

According to geologists, these spheres were formed during the Tertiary by crystallization at one thousand to fourteen hundred degrees Fahrenheit. Those found in Guatemala and Mexico unquestionably have this natural origin. They lie in disorder, they did not fall from the sky as has been claimed, and they are not vestiges of any civilization.

The legend was attractive but false.

Strange Petra

On Mount Hor, between the Dead Sea and the Red Sea in the Middle East, a narrow, winding gorge known as El Sik leads to a kind of natural amphitheatre surrounded by high walls of rocks. This is the site of the ancient city of Petra, also called Wadi Musa (Valley of Moses), which was the capital of Palestine III under the Roman Empire.

According to Moses, the first inhabitants of Petra were the Horites, who lived in caves.

In the high cliffs, the observer can admire a temple, a theatre, and palaces built into the sides of the rock. According to archaeologists, they were constructed by the Romans during their occupation of the region. Several tombs, much older, have been found in the city.

In this case, reality is stranger than anything one could imagine, because those façades of palaces, a temple, and a theatre are false: there is nothing behind them but a small room hollowed out of the cliffside, with a few benches carved from the same rock. The porticoes, porches, and windows lead nowhere, as in a theatrical set. Everything is simulated, deceptive; only the outside is real.

The pink sandstone palace, with its columns, pediments, foliated scrolls, and bas-reliefs, is an integral part of the mountain and has never been inhabited.

It is hard to believe that these strange, useless monuments were made by the Romans, who were certainly great builders but never worked gratuitously, especially on such a scale. And there is nothing in any ancient text to support this hypothesis.

The Nabataeans founded Petra in about the seventh century B.C., but their city has been found in the hollow of the valley.

Who, then, built the palaces and the temple? When and why?

It is thought that their construction began in the eighth century B.C. and was continued during the Nabataean domination.

For some archaeologists, Petra bears witness to a lost civilization which may have taken refuge in this desert region after a great cataclysm. For others, the palaces, the temple, and the false theatre either sheltered tombs or constituted a *secret sanctuary* where initiation into high magic was practised.

It is possible that those structures with no apparent purpose were conceived as a kind of parallel universe, or consecrated to gods whose names and worship the builders did not want to reveal.

They may have been dedicated to the Master of the Universe, the One God, unknowable and unnameable, who was perhaps the God of the Atlantans.

A Temple in the Brazilian Wilderness

In 1939 the archaeologist Harold T. Wilkins obtained, through W. G. Burdette, the American consul general at Rio de Janeiro, a copy of a Portuguese document entitled *Historical Account of a Well-Hidden and Ancient Habitation and its Inhabitants, Discovered in 1753.*

When bandits explored – and pillaged – the almost impenetrable wilderness in the province of Bahia, they discovered a ruined temple, ancient walls, and caves that had once been inhabited. On these ruins, overgrown with tropical vegetation, they saw inscriptions in an unknown language. One of the bandits had the intelligence to copy them.

We can only guess at the identity of those mysterious

inhabitants of the Brazilian wilderness, but they unquestionably developed an original and advanced civilization, as is
shown by the invention of their writing and the ruins they left
us.

An Electric Lamp

There is abundant evidence showing that elsewhere in Brazil,
and all over South America, including Peru, the civilization
of the Incas and Aymaras was preceded by an unknown
civilization, equally powerful and probably more advanced.

In 1601 the Spanish writer and traveller Barco Centenera
visited the ruins called El Gran Moxo near the sources of the
Rio Paraguay, that is, in the vicinity of the Sette Sgunas
(Seven Lakes) in the middle of the Matto Grosso, latitude
14°35′ south, longitude 57°30′ west, near the modern town
of Diamantino. He found a kind of large electric lamp in good
working order. It was certainly not powered by batteries, but
it gave light uninterruptedly and there is reason to believe
that the source of the light was chemical and electrical.
This is what appears from its description: 'A column surmounted by a moon or large sphere, which brightly illuminated
the surrounding area.'

The secret of this lamp was apparently universal, since
similar lamps were found on the other side of the earth,
near Mount Wilhelmina in Netherlands New Guinea. They
were composed of spheres about ten feet in diameter, mounted
on columns. They are thought to have been made of a
fluorescent mineral substance, and they gave a white light like
that of a neon or mercury vapour lamp.

The Radiant Rock of Ylo

The archaeologist Harold T. Wilkins (Introduction to the
Mysteries of South America, London, 1950) discovered an
extraordinary monument that seems to be related to the
ancient spherical lamps. At Ylo, on the Pacific coast south of
Arequipa, Peru, stands the Tombo del Ynca (Tomb of the
Inca). It bears an ancient inscription that is said to reveal

the location of the entrance to a tunnel leading to the 'Ancient Lost World [of] mysteries and gold, whose hidden door lies fouled with gases behind one of *Los Tres Picos* (The Three Peaks).' Wilkins believes that the tunnel is at the southern end of the Atacama desert in southern Chile.

The indecipherable inscription is phosphorescent and the top of the rock itself gives off a light like that of the lamp in El Gran Moxo.

The Treasure of Los Tres Picos

The legend of the treasure of Los Tres Picos is not well known among treasure-hunters. Perhaps it must be identified with the treasures of Pez Grande and Pez Chico, which I unsuccessfully tried to find during an expedition to Peru. (I have related the history of these treasures in my book *Trésors du Monde*.)

Here is what my friend the explorer Florent Ramaugé says on the subject.

'An old Inca of noble lineage, heir to the traditions and secrets of his ancestors, did not want to die without confiding to someone what he knew about the treasures hidden by the Priests of the Sun in the Andes.

'He chose a Spaniard whom he considered trustworthy and said to him, "The treasure of Pez Chico is in the Carahaya Andes. You will find a cave that is illuminated by the first rays of the rising sun. Its interior is closed off by large blocks of stone, but you will find a space between them large enough for a man to pass through. It leads to a passage under the mountain.

' "You will have to open three doors to reach the secret sanctuary. The first door is of copper and is opened with a gold key, the second is of silver and is opened with a copper key, the third is of gold and is opened with a silver key. You will find great wealth, including a disc of pure gold which you will bring to me, for I want to contemplate it before I die. But you must take none of the other treasures amassed in the sanctuary, because they belong to the Sun God."

'The Spaniard was driven mad by what he found. He returned to the Inca and tried to force him to reveal the secret of the Pez Grande.

' "It is under the statue of the Sun God," said the Inca, "but you will not find it!"

'And the Spaniard was buried in the cave, just when he had succeeded in pulling down the statue.'

And so the secrets of both the Pez Chico and the Pez Grande were lost, but the rock of Ylo may hold the key to them.

8 Atlantis Rises

Mu, the mysterious continent that lay in the middle of the Pacific, arouses less interest in Europeans than Atlantis, probably because it was farther away. Its authenticity is even more controversial, and yet I think the two problems are inseparable: if Atlantis is not a myth, then Mu necessarily existed also.

A sensational discovery in the Bahamas has brought the subject of Atlantis into greater prominence and seems to have added one more important piece of evidence to all the others that official science refuses to accept.

The Initiates Knew

In initiatic circles it was known as early as 1968 that 'something was going to happen' with regard to Atlantis.

In 1940 the great clairvoyant Edgar Cayce, always ahead of his time, predicted the discovery of the submerged walls of Bimini in the Bahamas and gave information about Atlantis that came to him directly from the Beyond. In that same year he also predicted that Poseidonis would be the first island of Atlantis to reappear above the surface and that it would happen in about 1968, or by 1976 at the latest.

Then the Master of Villeneuve, head of the French Rosicrucians, published the same prophecy in an important brochure. (*L'Empire Invisible*, by Raymond Bernard, Editions Rosicruciennes AMORC, Villeneuve-Saint-Georges, France.)

Finally, on the thirty-fifth parallel and in the Bermuda Triangle, in the Atlantic, amazing and incomprehensible phenomena began occurring.

These prophecies and events were in the purest esoteric tradition. In 1968 no rationalist would have been willing to accept them; but, in a realm outside the exact sciences, certain individuals have perceptions that are nearly always confirmed by verified facts.

The 'Atlantis affair' had such a foretaste of authenticity that in May, 1970, I had an imperious desire to do a little exploring in the Canaries, Madeira, and the Azores. I found that the situation was normal. The inner fire was smouldering in the infernal fissures of Lanzarote Island; the waters of Furnas, at San Miguel, were boiling and rumbling in mud craters, the sand and lava of the newborn island beside Fayal were slowly cooling. Off Flores and Corvo the sea was calm and the gulls were soaring placidly.

In the Bermuda Triangle, nothing was happening that was not commonplace and reassuring.

The Walls of Bimini

The French diver Dimitri Rebikoff seems to have been the first to notice the impressive underwater geometric masses near the west coast of Bimini. In collaboration with an American professor, he took some convincing aerial photographs: those geometrical masses were ancient walls!

For more than thirty years, thousands of underwater fishermen had been frequenting Bimini, a little island in the Bahamas about fifty miles from Miami, and diving in the same area where Rebikoff found the walls, but none of them had even noticed those strange lines of rocks about two hundred and fifty feet long and twenty feet below the surface. Only when they had been photographed from the air were they seen to be composed of huge blocks sixteen feet square. They rise less than two feet above the sea bottom. The size of the sunken part is not yet known.

There are other walls near Andros Island, and probably elsewhere.

A timid estimate has been advanced by archaeologists: the Bimini walls are said to date from six or seven thousand years ago, for the sole reason that the Atlantic was then twenty feet below its present level!

If this were true, Bimini would not be an Atlantan ruin; but it is obvious that the estimate has no serious basis. It is hard to imagine buildings being constructed with their foundations at sea level in a region periodically ravaged by hurricanes. We must logically assume that the walls of Bimini were built at least fifteen to twenty feet above sea level, which places the time of their construction at twelve thousand years ago, or longer. This date will surely be pushed back even farther when the height of the walls buried under the sand is discovered.

With the minimum of twelve thousand years, we reach the date of the Deluge, which means that the Bimini ruins must have belonged to an antediluvian Atlantic continent whose name has been familiar since Plato: Atlantis.

Buried Secrets at Bimini

Edgar Cayce had an almost classical vision of what Atlantis had been. It underwent three cataclysms, he said: the first two, in about 15,600 BC, divided the continent into islands, and in the third, twelve thousand years ago, the remaining land was submerged. The original continent extended from the Sargasso Sea to the Azores, with an area equal to that of Europe and Asia Minor combined.

Before the last cataclysm, the Atlantans emigrated to Peru, Egypt, Mexico, New Mexico, and Colorado. Their civilization was at first brilliant, but then they sank into abject sensuality, which led to their annihilation, as in the case of Sodom and Gomorrha. According to Cayce, they built up destructive forces which, in combination with the natural forces of electricity and expanding gases, set off a volcanic eruption in the region of what is now the Sargasso Sea.

Cayce predicted that it would be possible to find traces of Atlantis in three places: Egypt, Bimini, and the Azores. But although I do not make a blanket denial of his prophetic gifts, I can guarantee that no traces of Atlantis will ever be found in the Azores, even if the sea bottom should rise above the surface.

He is said to have made this prediction in 1940, during talks that were not published. He added that a record of the systems by which the Atlantans manufactured energy would be found near Bimini, along with part of a temple.

In 1970, discovery of the Bimini walls brought dramatic confirmation of these astonishing prophecies, although the

Atlantan 'records' still remain to be found.

The epicentre of the earthquake that divided Atlantis into five islands was, said Cayce, in the Bahamas. The three largest islands were named Poseidia, Aryan, and Og. When the poles shifted and Lemuria (Mu) sank beneath the Pacific, Atlantis was at the zenith of technological civilization. After the second eruption there was a migration into the Pyrenees. In other migrations, the Atlantans mingled with native peoples of Africa and South America, producing the Egyptians and the Incas.

Atomic Stones

The Atlantans, said Cayce, had discovered the secret of concentrating solar energy in a stone with 'magnetic properties' that enabled it to emit more energy than it received. This energy (which we could now call a product of atomic disintegration) was distributed for use in industry, transportation, and even housekeeping.

The great atomic stone was placed inside a dome with sliding panels, like that of an astronomical observatory. Its invisible radiation acted on receiving stones which supplied motive power for air, land, and sea vehicles. The great stone was a cylindrical crystal with many facets; its top was shaped in such a way that it captured solar energy and concentrated it in the middle of the cylinder.

Cayce mentioned some stones found in the Yucatan in 1933 and said that they would prove the truth of all this if their meaning were understood. I have been unable to learn anything about these stones.

It is possible that reckless use of atomic energy by the Atlantans caused an unexpected deterioration of the environment. Atomic-energy plants, overproducing and perhaps improperly regulated, may have been the direct cause of the second destruction of Atlantis.

The truth is that Cayce's visions now seem childish and outdated, even if his 'crystal' prefigures the laser. Science-fiction writers have long since found better and more scientific devices than the 'solar-energy stone,' which had illustrious predecessors in such things as magic rubies, diamond settings in rings that worked wonders when they were turned, the star at the end of a fairy's magic wand, and Aladdin's lamp!

But Cayce demonstrated the reality of his clairvoyance by speaking of Bimini. If Bimini is true, why should the rest not be true also?

The Invisible Empire of the Rosicrucians

According to secret documents in the library of the Rosicrucians, Plato was a depository of the Atlantan tradition and his account is genuine.

Part of the teachings of the Rosicrucians has presumably been revealed to members of the association by the French Grand Master Raymond Bernard in a book entitled *L'Empire Invisible*. He writes as follows:

Atlantis was a highly civilized continent with means of transmission and transportation compared with which ours are as nothing. In its time, it was the *heart of the world*.

'Colonized' peoples received knowledge in keeping with their capacities. In particularly 'open' countries, a direct relationship was established by the College of Sages, that is, the highest initiates of the time, guardians of the secret wisdom, and this relationship was marked by a *pyramidal temple* in the image of the supreme pyramid where the College had its seat in Atlantis, and where its knowledge was preserved.

Only one pyramid, however, has reproduced the supreme pyramid, and even then in a different 'measure': what is known as the Pyramid of Cheops. It perpetuates in the face of the world the *totality* of Atlantan wisdom, whereas others reveal only *part* of it.

In the rather near future, 'discoveries' beneficial to mankind will put an end to many arguments.[1]

The Atlantans knew the nature and power of certain cosmic forces, particularly telluric currents, and carefully applied them to agriculture and the harmonious maintenance of the overall balance of these currents, to avoid all geo-

[1] Raymond Bernard prophesied, a year and a half in advance, the discovery of the Atlantan ruins at Bimini.

logical catastrophes that it was within man's power to avert.

The pyramids also fulfilled this function because of the duly studied locations in which they were built. Elsewhere, points of protection were sufficient. This was the case, for example, with dolmens and menhirs. They precisely marked places of conjoined forces and focalized universal energy, where efficacious ceremonies could be held.

It was the same with megaliths, many of which can still be seen all over the world in estates, fields, and even cities; but their sole function was to amplify cosmic energy and improve harvests.

It can be considered, moreover, that all these secondary elements were attached, from the standpoint of energy, to the supreme pyramid. The entire earth thus constituted a kind of efficient receptacle for the whole of cosmic forces . . .

When the supreme pyramid had been unfavourably altered as the result of ignorant and ambitious intrigues, the planetary catastrophe that engulfed Atlantis transformed the surface of the earth and became engraved in the folk imagination under the inaccurate name of the Deluge.

In the basis of the teaching of *authentic* African secret societies, *a particle of the Atlantan wisdom has been preserved.*

At the time of the catastrophe, the supreme sages took refuge in Egypt. *They had safeguarded the scientific and technical knowledge that made Atlantis a continent whose civilization has never been equalled, not even in our time . . .*

The sages did not reconstitute the Empire, because of what had happened and because this was in accordance with the universal plan.

It is the whole world that is called upon to become the *New Atlantis* . . . The human will is always free. Once again, and for the last time, mankind will face an ultimate choice from which will result either an era of extraordinary civilization or the end, not of a continent this time, but *of the world.*

The time of choice is approaching. It will be marked

by the reappearance of Atlantis, the resurgence of the
vanished continent before the astonished human race.

The Sages have guided our development. They have
given men the discoveries that were suggested to him, as
soon as he was able to understand, receive, and use each
of them without danger; they have delivered, in the strictest
sense of the word, the scientific and technical knowledge
acquired by the Atlantans and preserved by them and their
successors . . .

The knowledge of the Atlantans came from *another*
galaxy and was brought by those who became the first
rulers of Atlantis. Some of those Extraterrestrials returned
to their home; others remained on earth, to carry out a
mission. All the world's civilizations come from this second
group.

Raymond Bernard is convinced that the present Atlantans,
who will replace the former College of Sages, are acting
in concert with the High Council of the A . . . . (The secret
name is not divulged by the Rosicrucians.) The Atlantans
will reappear openly when Atlantis rises. They are now
scattered over all the continents.

The human race will return to Atlantis, then later, perhaps,
set off for new conquests which in future centuries will bring
about the union of planets and galaxies, so that the plan
will finally be carried out; at that time, the awakening of consciousness will be universal.

The Last of the Atlantans

The Canary Islands, or the Elysian Fields, or the Garden
of the Hesperides, or the Happy Islands, were known all
through antiquity. After the Arabs, the Carthaginians, and
Juba II, king of the Two Mauretanias, Pliny spoke of them
in his *Historia Naturalis*.

After the Spanish conquered them in 1478, all their inhabitants, the Guanches, died out; they committed suicide
rather than submit to foreign domination.

The Canaries are isolated in the Atlantic a little above
the Tropic of Cancer. Along with Madeira and the Azores,
according to tradition, they constitute the only existing

vestiges of Atlantis.

'The Guanches,' said Dom Inigo, a native of the country, 'descend from King Uranus, first sovereign of the Atlantans.'

The Mexican monarch Montezuma II reportedly said to the Spanish conquistador Hernando Cortez, 'Our forefathers were not born here. They came from a faraway land named Aztlan, where a high mountain stood, with a garden inhabited by the gods.'

This high mountain may have been the Pico de Teyde on Tenerife Island in the Canaries. It is now twelve thousand feet high, which allows us to assume that before the submersion of Atlantis, taking into account the ocean bottom in this area, it must have had a height of more than twenty thousand feet.

Before they died out in the fifteenth century, the Guanches had a tradition according to which they were the last people in the world, all the others have perished when they were swallowed up by the sea. (Marcel N. Schveitzer: *Guide Bleu d'Espagne*, Hachette, 1963.)

In view of this, one might think that their writing was directly derived from that of the Atlantans, but, by an inexplicable phenomenon, it is practically unknown in Europe, and even in the Canaries.

It took us two full days of research, on Gran Canaria, first to persuade our guides that Guanche writing existed, and then to find examples of it. After we had searched the mountains and valleys of the island over a distance of more than sixty miles, it was Yvette Charroux who finally discovered some engraved rocks, not in the *Lobo de los letreros* as we had expected, but on a kind of basaltic outcropping in an isolated valley at the centre of Gran Canaria.

We recognized and photographed designs similar to those of the Celts in Brittany: spirals, circles, serpents, stylized persons, and a remarkable 'sorcerer' that is an exact replica of the one in the Villar cave in the Dordogne, France. Still more important, we took pictures of genuine writing and submitted them to Abbé Hirigoyen and the magazine *Découvertes* for expert examination. The writing is unquestionably composed of letters, some of them resembling our letters V, N, S, T, and I.

On the flat surface of rocks, shepherds or vandal discoverers have written their names and sometimes dates, so that it has become difficult to distinguish what is from the time of the Guanches and what is from later.

To the best of my knowledge, this writing, known to a few German archaeologists, is unknown to the French and Spanish, and I am probably reproducing it for the first time in France.

It may be extremely important because if identical writing is found on the walls of the submerged structures at Bimini, there will be no doubt that we are in possession of the writing of the Atlantans.

The Caldeiras of the Azores

Northwest of the Canaries, in the middle of the Atlantic, the Azores vie with them for the privilege of being the last dry land of Atlantis.

It can scarcely be supposed, however, that Atlantans walked on a soil which, twelve thousand years ago, was at least twelve thousand feet above its present level, with peaks twenty thousand feet higher.

The Canaries are volcanic islands, most of which came from craters that are now worn down and reduced to basalt and limestone. The Azores are greener, moister, less volcanic than Lanzarote or Fuerteventura, and their land is rich. They resemble the Jura and Savoy regions of France. The transmutation of lava is more advanced, either because of the almost daily rainfall or because the islands are older. There are no active volcanoes in the Azores, but the soil is sometimes terribly hot, and in the Furnas region on Sao Miguel Island water boils and explodes in the *caldeiras* ('cauldrons') that are heated by the inner fire of the earth.

As in the Canaries, one has a feeling of uneasiness, almost of danger. The fire of Gaea is just below the surface and it is easy to believe that these islands are either land that erupted out of the ocean or vestiges of Atlantis, which was ravaged by volcanoes.

In 1954 an island abruptly rose from the Atlantic beside Fayal island. Part of Atlantis had reappeared, but in the form of a bare, hot, sandy soil that had been repeatedly churned by geological convulsions, so that there was no chance that any Atlantan remains might have survived.

It is in the Azores, however, and particularly on Sao Miguel, that traditionalists locate Poseidonis, the capital of Atlantis.

This is also the opinion of our friend José da Silva Fraga, who told us, in excellent French, the legends of the double lake of the Sete Cidades.

The Lake of the Seven Cities

'The Azores,' said José da Silva Fraga, 'were once called the Enchanted Isles. They appeared and disappeared like mirages, and they have given rise to the legend of Sao Brandan Island.

'Traditions – which necessarily came from Europe, since the islands were uninhabited when Cabral discovered them in 1432 – say that a submerged continent surrounds the nine islands. It can only be Atlantis, of course . . .

'From the promontory named the Vista de Rey (King's Vista) on Sao Miguel, there is one of the most beautiful views in the world. You look out over a vast, green basin studded with hydrangeas and azaleas. At the bottom of it are two lakes whose harmonious curves are intertwined to form the symbol of infinity. One lake has blue water, the other had emerald-green water, and seven legends explain the difference.

'One of them tells the story of the kingdom of Atlantis and its sovereigns, King White-Grey and Queen White-Pink. For a long time they were in despair at not having any children. Finally they had a beautiful little daughter, but a powerful and rather disagreeable fairy forbade them to see her until she was twenty years old.

'On Sao Miguel, below the Vista de Rey, the king built seven cities of happiness for the little princess to live in. No one, not even the sovereigns, was allowed to enter them. Then, as in all legends, the king broke the prohibition; but just as he was about to enter a city and see his beloved daughter at last, the ground trembled, volcanoes spat infernal fire, and water rose to engulf the seven cities.

'At the bottom of the green lake are the princess's little green slippers; at the bottom of the blue one is her blue hat.'

This is only a legend, of course, but it is the only one that explicitly gives the location of the capital of Atlantis.

Since 1898 there has been no doubt that land once rose above the ocean in the vicinity of the Azores. It was in the summer of 1898 that a cable ship had to drag the ocean bottom for the Brest-Cape Cod cable, which had broken at latitude 47° north and longitude 29°40′ west, five hundred miles north of Punta Delgada. From a depth of ten thousand feet, the dragline brought up a kind of volcanic rock known as tachylite.

Petrologists who examined it noted that it had the appearance of a colloidal substance; if it had solidified at a depth of ten thousand feet, under a pressure of several atmospheres, it would have crystallized in a tangled pattern. Conclusion: the rock had solidified in the open air, that is, on dry land.

A continent at that place could only have been Atlantis.

Homo Atlanticus

In September, 1928, an amazing discovery was made by Dr Marcel Baudoin, a French archaeologist who has remained in undeserved obscurity, but whose name should be associated with that of Boucher de Perthes, the father of prehistory.

At the Havre-de-Vie estuary, Dr Baudoin noticed a large block of quartzite, weighing more than three thousand pounds, which was covered by the ocean at high tide. First with surprise, then with great excitement, he saw that on the surface of the stone there were carvings of a man's head surrounded by cups, the imprints of bare human feet and horses' hooves, and large grooves. From the environment in which they were found, he was able to date the carvings at about 5000 B.C.

He published an article on his find in the October 8 issue of *Le Phare*.

'I have just discovered,' he wrote, 'the man who made the supposedly celtic carvings of cups in our rocks, who erected dolmens and menhirs, made statues and flint axes, and knew how to use the first metals.

'The rock of the Havre-de-Vie estuary is located in the village of Plessis-le-Fenouiller, near Saint-Gilles (Vendée). It is called the "Great Stone." The carving, in the shape of a medallion, is the size of a human head and the depth of its relief is between ten and fifteen millimeters.

'It depicts a man with a strongly aquiline nose, round eyes, and a heavy mass of hair shaped into a chignon at the top. Our ancestors the Gauls also wore their hair in this style.

'The portrait, in my opinion, is that of the man who came from across the Atlantic to bring civilization to the Celts. He bears an astonishing resemblance to the men drawn in the Mayan codices or carved on the steles of Mexico. He is *Homo Atlanticus,* the man of Atlantis, of whom no representation was previously known.

'I have made a cement casting of the carving which can now be seen in the Open-Air Museum of Prehistory that I created at Croix-la-Vie.'

The large stone of Plessis-le-Fenouiller was removed in about 1930 and transported to a museum at either Noirmontier or La Roche-sur-Yon, but I have been unable to find any trace of it.

The Open-Air Museum of Prehistory still exists beside a street in Saint-Gilles-Croix-de-Vie near Dr Baudoin's house. It consists of castings of extraordinary carvings. Some of the originals are in French caves, others are in provincial museums, and still others are at sites whose location has become unknown since Dr Baudoin's death.

The museum forms a wall fifty feet long and seven feet high, on a little side street that bears Dr Baudoin's name. It is a curious place, analogous to the Palais du Facteur Cheval at Hauterives (Drôme), but the municipality does nothing to preserve the wall and in a few years it will no longer exist.

Dr Baudoin's conclusions (which, it must be acknowledged, are often adventurous) have been ignored by prehistorians. The citizens of his home town have done little to preserve his memory; his records have disappeared and it took me a whole day of research to assemble the information I have set down here. I owe it to the kindness of Dr Julien Rous-seau, of Beauvoir-sur-Mer, an excellent historian of the Vendée.

If the man of Plessis-le-Fenouiller was a contemporary of the dolmen-makers, he was certainly not an Atlantan, but it seems more logical to assume that the image on the medallion represents a god or a venerated ancestor for whom the Celts of Poitou showed their respect by surrounding the portrait with cups of sacred water and hoofprints of the horse, an animal that is traditionally one of the major symbols of Atlantis. If this is true, Dr Baudoin may indeed have discovered a portrait of *Homo Atlanticus*.

1 The Long Man of Wilmington, Sussex. This outline of a man, 250 feet long, is formed by an immense ditch, like the Candlestick of the Andes and the Nazca lines. The ditch was dug by an ancient, perhaps pre-Celtic, civilisation which has not been identified, but there is reason to believe that the architects of Wilmington were the ancestors of those of Peru.

2 The Candlestick of the Andes.

3 The Nazca Pampa. From the air it looks like a giant runway. The slanting black line is the Panamerican highway.

4 The Condor. A mysterious drawing 1,250 feet in length.

5　The round stones of Guatemala and Mexico – volcanic 'bombs'.

6 The enormous blocks of stone which form the first wall of the Inca fortress of Sacsahuaman, near Cuzco.

7 A panoramic view of Machu Picchu in the Andes; the secret city of the Incas which was not 'rediscovered' till 1911.

8 The plateau of Tiahuanaco – barren stone and a long stone wall which has menhirs built into it. In the distance is the Puerta del Sol.

9 Details of the Puerta del Sol. Said to represent a Venusian calendar, the construction of the monument goes back into the unknown depths of time. The central figure, the god Inti, has only four fingers on each hand. In the heads of the smaller figures are enigmatic designs resembling space suits and rocket motors.

10 The Throne of the Incas – or sundial – is hewn out of the mountain-side and overlooks Machu Picchu.

11 A detail of the Celtic pyramid at Plouézoch. It has been disem-bowelled by stone-pillagers, and one of the dolmenic crypts it once covered is now exposed.

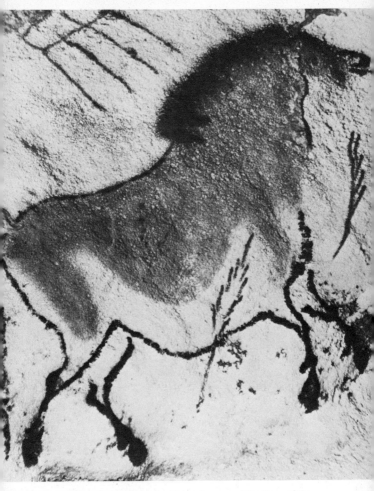

12 Cave painting of a horse at Montignac-Lascaux. The lines of the legs farthest away stop short of the body in order to suggest perspective – a technique not used in historical times until the fifteenth century in Europe.

13 The 'Breton' of San Augustin, Peru. His non-slanted eyes bear
witness to his occidental origin.

9 Mu

Belief in the existence of vanished continents rests on tradi-tions and sometimes debatable documents, but also on valid scientific evidence.

The theory of the German geophysicist Alfred Wegener states that long ago there was a single continent which was split into separate pieces because of geological upheavals or because the land mass slid over the sima, the lower layer of the earth's outer crust. This is known as the theory of continental drift.

Recent studies in marine geology cast new light on the phenomenon: the ocean floor seems to have spread in the course of the millennia, separating the emerged land mass into distinct continents.

The Original Motherland: Pangea

The process continues: there is still undersea volcanic activity and lava still pours from fissures and craters below the surface. A 'carpet' of matter from inside the earth continu-ally spreads out from the great submerged mountain ranges of the Atlantic and the Pacific. Because of this, North and South America, one side, and Africa and Europe, on the other, are moving away from each other.

Daniel Behrman writes that the original continental mass, Pangea (from 'pan,' all, and 'Gea,' goddess of the earth), began breaking up more than a hundred million years ago.

It is thought that there were three continents at that time: South America-Africa, Asia-Europe, and what is now India, which was then off the coast of Kenya and Tanzania.

On this theory, the configuration of the globe developed as follows:

L.W.   D

- A hundred and twenty million years ago, the mountain range in the middle of the Atlantic was formed with the separation of Pangea: the Americas drifted westward, Africa drifted eastward.
- Sixty million years ago, the Atlantic existed, but Brazil was still very close to Guinea. India was approaching Asia.
- Thirty million years ago, South America was moving farther away from Africa, Africa was approaching Europe, India was moving still closer to Asia.
- Fifteen million years ago, South America was joined to North America (which may have been separated from eastern Asia), Africa was joined to Asia Minor, and India was joined to Asia. The pressure of the drifting continents formed the mountain masses of Lebanon, the Caucasus, and the Himalayas.

Gondwana

Study of the residual magnetism of rocks seems to indicate that at the end of the Tertiary the magnetic pole was at about latitude 65°, between Hudson Bay and Greenland.

This location corresponds to that of Hyperborea, the land described in Aryan mythologies.

If at that time the earth was vertical in relation to the plane of the ecliptic, instead of being tilted at an angle of about twenty-three degrees as it is now, the seasons were the same everywhere and Hyperborea, amid its mountains of ice, must have had nearly ideal diurnal temperatures, as ancient writings maintain. This would explain the fossil remains of giant ferns and tropical plants that are found in Scandinavia and even farther north.

This is the view of Robert Dietz, a geologist of the Environmental Science Service of Washington. With the debris of Africa, South America, Australia, and India, he has theoretically reconstructed a continent that has been given the name of Gondwana.

For other advanced geologists, Gondwana was a southern continent which, in the Secondary Era, was matched by a northern continent, the Scandinavian Shield.

Lemuria

The Puranas, an ancient Sanskrit work, speaks of continents rising one after another, each being the home of a race. Seven of them are named, on which seven great races have lived or will live.

According to the German naturalist Haecken, the human race was born in Lemuria, now submerged into the Pacific, and he named that continent Shalmali. Its destruction by fire and water accompanied the appearance of Kusha (Atlantis), where the powerful civilization of the fourth race was developed.

The British Association for the Advancement of Science has announced that a new continent is being formed in the 'circle of fire' of the Pacific, where the Bagoslov Islands, off the coast of Alaska, have already reached an altitude of a thousand feet. This may be the Shaka of the Puranas. It is predicted that the new land will be a thousand miles long and will extend toward Japan, the Philippines, Malacca, and Borneo.

In the traditional writings of the peoples of Ceylon and Madras, we read that the homeland of the Tamils (a Dravidian people still living in southern India) was south of Java, which was one of the first lands to emerge near the equator, and that this land was Lemuria, birthplace of all civilizations.

The writer Wishar S. Cervé believes, on the basis of information received from Rosicrucian sources, that man first appeared in the United States. As for Lemuria, it was a continent that stretched eastward from Africa to the Pacific at a time when, according to Wegener's theory, the Americas, Europe, and western Africa formed a single land mass. Then, after geological upheavals, Lemuria occupied only the area of Micronesia and Polynesia. The Americas moved toward it while Atlantis emerged from the ocean.

Cervé also believes that the mysterious people who are said to live on Mount Shasta, in northern California, are the last descendants of the Lemurians.

Prehistorians, geologists, and traditionalists are more or less in agreement on the location and identity of Atlantis, but with regard to the submerged continent of the Pacific there is nothing but confusion. The fact is that Gondwana,

Lemuria, and Mu seem to be one and the same continent called by three different names.

Assertions without Evidence

I have already reported Colonel James Churchward's extraordinary story in my book *One Hundred Thousand Years of Man's Unknown History;* I will here give only the main points of it.

Churchward served with the British Army in India for thirty years. At an unspecified date during that time, in a temple that he does not identify, he discovered some Naacal tablets. (The Naacals, according to ancient Indian authors, were a mysterious people who came to Burma from their native land to the east. They had been sent to teach their writing and language to the West, that is, India.) The tablets revealed that fifty thousand years ago, in the Pacific, there was a continent named Mu which was the birthplace of the white race. Mu and its sixty-four million inhabitants were destroyed by a cataclysm and a Deluge twelve thousand years ago.

In support of his assertions, Churchward speaks of twenty-six hundred tablets found in Mexico, near Mexico City, by a geologist named Niven. These documents are not taken seriously by scientists, but that, of course, does not necessarily mean that they are false. The fact remains, however, that Churchward's statements are generally unsubstantiated, except by references to 'evidence' whose authenticity is far from obvious.

Churchward's Inventions

Nevertheless, I am almost tempted to take Churchward at his word, because his writings give the impression that he was an honest man, an admirable investigator, and a well-informed and often erudite archaeologist. For example, he fixed the time of the Deluge at twelve thousand years ago long before Scandinavian glaciologists had given proof of it.

In my opinion, it is likely that he either had access to

secret documents or was an exceptionally gifted clairvoyant. But unfortunately his stories are too often marred by enormous errors, whimsical interpretations, and even pious falsehoods.

He speaks of Mexico and the Mayas, Egypt, Assyro-Babylonia, the Incas, etc., with irritating offhandedness. For him, as for most overzealous partisans of Mu, every archaeological discovery, every unknown writing, every mysterious sign, and every unusual fact that has not yet been classified by science belongs to Mu and proves the existence of Mu.

Observing this principle, he gives a translation of the stele of Uxmal, in Mexico, 'dedicated to Mu!' I am well acquainted with Uxmal and its magnificent 'Sorcerer's Castle,' of Advino, and I can certify that Churchward's 'translation' is a pure fantasy.

He gives a false reproduction of the frieze on the Puerta del Sol and represents the central god with five fingers, whereas the most striking thing about him is that he has only four.

And yet that visionary sometimes has flashes of genius and shows amazing knowledge. He unquestionably lies now and then, but he does it to accredit a view which he believes to be true – and actually is true. For the continent of Mu certainly existed, and, without knowing it, he brushes against the truth when he writes that Mexico is more ancient than Egypt. He shows brilliant insight when he establishes an intelligent connection between the Quechuan language of the Incas and the Quiche of the Mayas.

And finally he has the immense merit, which makes up for his failings, of calling attention to the unknown civilizations of the Pacific: the Cook Islands, the Marianas, the Marquesas, etc., for, on the whole, it is in the Pacific Islands that we find the most significant clues to the existence of a very ancient civilization.

Vestiges that Speak

On most of the islands of Polynesia and Micronesia there are remains of cities, temples, harbours, and statues whose size and elaborate architecture indicate a civilization incom-

parably more advanced than that which exists on those
same islands today. Beside huts with roofs of palm leaves
or corrugated iron stand columns, porticoes, and piers whose
colossal stones were hewn and put in place by ancestors with a
much more highly developed technology.

Churchward and Louis-Claude Vincent have drawn up
detailed lists of these vestiges which, let us hope, will eventually be given careful consideration by informed archaeologists.

It is not easy to go to those remote islands, far from
commercial shipping lanes, lacking airports and sometimes
inhabited by people so hostile or poor that only an organized
expedition has any chance of doing fruitful research. What
I am about to write on the Pacific remains is therefore only
a compilation of reports from explorers who went there
in the past or authors who do not speak from first-hand
knowledge.

In 1789 nine mutineers and eighteen Tahitians, men and
women, reached Pitcairn Island, twelve hundred miles west
of Easter Island, aboard the famous ship HMS *Bounty*. They
founded a colony which later prospered. On their arrival, they
saw ruins of houses, a temple, kilns, and twelve-foot statues
on platforms.

In the Gambier Islands there are perfectly preserved
mummies and walls made of coral.

The Caroline Islands are strewn with ruins. The most
impressive ones are on the island of Ponape, where, it is said,
there is a large temple and a megalithic harbour with canals.

Churchward says that the temple is built over a network
of cellars and crypts connected to a canal, and that at its
centre is a room in the shape of a pyramid.

There are similar ruins on Kusaie, one of the Caroline
Islands, especially near the village of Lele. A cyclopean enclosure and a cone-shaped hill surrounded by high walls
testify that civilized people lived there thousands of years
ago. The natives say that these people were very powerful
and travelled far to the east and west in great vessels.

On other islands there are pyramids similar to those found
in the Society Islands.

The Arch of Tongatabu

Reference has often been made to a huge megalithic arch on the island of Tongatabu in the Tonga Islands, south of Samoa, but to the best of my knowledge no photograph of it has been published.

The site is named Haamunga. The arch consists of two enormous blocks of stone surmounted by a third which is morticed into them. It is about twelve feet high and its total weight is estimated at about ninety-five tons.

Churchward points out, with admirable sagacity, that the island is composed entirely of arable land and that the nearest quarry is two hundred and fifty miles away. The ancestors of the Polynesians therefore had to have large ships and an advanced technology to transport, square, and erect the stones of the monumental arch. There is reason to believe that it served as the gateway to a complex of buildings.

The Columns of the Marianas

The Mariana Islands are in Micronesia, between latitude 13° and 21° north and longitude 142° and 144° east, north of the Carolines.

They are volcanic islands, exposed to terrible typhoons and earthquakes, yet there are still large ruins on them, including, on Rota Island, vast areas surrounded by round columns that must once have supported a roof.

Churchward writes that the columns on Tinian Island are pyramidal. They were discovered in 1835 by Dumont d'Urville, who believed that they were cairns. Some of them were surmounted by semispherical stones.

There are pyramids on Swallow and Kingsmill Islands, and it is possible, if we are to believe certain reports, that a fortress of vitrified stones similar to those in Scotland and France was built on one of the Samoa Islands.

In Hawaii, the Marquesas Islands, Australia, and all around Tahiti, there are imposing ruins, most of them earthen pyramids like those discovered at Rapa Iti by Thor Heyerdahl.

Are some of these ruins vestiges of Mu? Yes, say Church-

ward and Louis-Claude Vincent, and it may well be tha
they are right.

It is undeniable, however, that the ruins of monuments
that remain in Polynesia do not give evidence of a civiliza
tion as advanced as our own, far from it. If Ponape, Tonga
tabu, and Kusaie belonged to the Muians, we must assume
that their civilization was not even as highly developed a:
that of the ancient Assyrians, Mayas, and Incas.

It is from this viewpoint that I give Atlantis primacy over
Mu. The vanguard of civilization before the Deluge wa:
certainly not at Ponape or Easter Island, for what remain
at Tiahuanaco (Bolivia), Venta (Yucatan), and in Egypt i
incomparably superior on every level of culture, thought, and
architecture.

10 Mysterious Easter Island

The title of this chapter was inspired by the book of my friend Francis Mazière, *Fantastique Ile de Pâques* (Robert Laffont, Paris), which has spurred still greater interest in that lonely island of the Pacific, twenty-five hundred miles west of Chile.

Near the edge of the sea and on the plateau, hundreds of statues, upright or lying on the ground, scrutinize the earth, the sky, or the sea in a mysterious wait that intrigues and disconcerts archaeologists.

'They are so many witnesses to a fabulous civilization,' says Francis Mazière, 'witnesses weighing twenty tons. How were those statues brought to the seaside from the volcano where they were carved? Were they lifted, rolled, pulled?'

Mazière gives us to understand that 'the first inhabitants of Easter Island were able to tap parapsychological forces to which we are no longer sensitive.'

Statue Ways

The mystery of enormous stones transported miles from their place of extraction arises in the same way at Baalbek (Lebanon), in Egypt, Mexico, Peru and Bolivia, and at Carnac and Loudon, France. At Loudon stands the gigantic Bournand dolmen, fifty-six feet long whose largest slab weighs three hundred and fifty thousand pounds.

Most of the Easter Island statues are from twenty to thirty feet long, and the largest is about seventy feet long. According to Thor Heyerdahl (see *Aku Aku,* Rand McNally, 1958) and modern archaeologists, they were detached from the sides of the volcano Rano Raraku and pulled on descending ramps called 'statue ways' to the places where they were erected. In 1956 Heyerdahl organized a successful repetition of the procedure, in which the natives used only ropes and stone axes.

The mystery does not reside in the way in which the statues were transported, but in the people who performed the feat. There are those who believe that they were related to the civilization of Mu.

The largest statue, the one seventy feet long, called 'the Giant,' is not separated from the side of the volcano, but the American archaeologist William Mulloy, who has studied the problem, believes that it would have been transported like the rest.

Abandoned hard basalt axes and picks are found at the site. The statues are of softer volcanic rock. Their backs were carefully polished so that they would slide on the 'ways.' The eye sockets were carved before the statue was transported, but the eyes themselves were carved later, during an 'eye-opening' ceremony, when the statue was in place. It then took on life and power, and its gaze, turned inland, watched over the village and its inhabitants.

Four Fingers, as at Tiahuanaco

As usual, official archaeologists have chosen the most ludicrous hypotheses to explain the origin of the Easter Island civilization. The ancient islanders, they say, came from Asia, which is not surprising because, according to them, everyone came from Mongolia: the Mayas, the Incas, the Africans, the Chinese. It is implausible but 'classical.'

Thor Heyerdahl and, more recently, other sailors, have proved that communication by sea was possible between South America and Polynesia, and this view is supported by all the ruins that remain.

At Vinapu, on the south end of the island, there are enormous stone slabs that have been carved exactly like those at Machu Picchu, in Peru. The Incan word for 'sweet potato' was *kumara*; the Easter Islanders used the same word for the same plant. The statues on the island all have big ears, like the *orejones* ('big ears') of Peru. The platforms (*ahus*) on which the statues rest are reminiscent of Incan structures and the platforms at the pre-Incan site of K'emko.

And finally, the explorer Croce-Spinelli reports having seen a statue with four-fingered hands. If this is confirmed, it will establish a connection between the civilization of Easter Island and that of Tiahuanaco, the only other place in the world where representations of human beings have that feature.

The Bird-Man

In 1971 the island had about fourteen hundred inhabitants. Most of its plant life is grass, with a few coconut trees, but it is believed to have been forested in the past, and much more heavily populated.

The great annual rite was that of the 'bird-man.' In August or September the people climbed a mountain and lived in dark dwellings – forty-seven underground houses – which can still be seen at Orongo. The tribes waited for the arrival of the first migratory bird, a tern, and the laying of the first egg, to which magical properties were attributed. Each chief appointed a man to try to obtain it; if he succeeded, he would bring great honour and profit to his tribe.

The man who found the first egg, usually on the little island of Motunui, swam back with it and for a year he was venerated as a demigod charged with terrible *mana*. His *mana* was so powerful that no one dared to touch him, for fear of receiving a lethal discharge.

There are many carvings of the bird-man on the rocks of Orongo.

This is nearly all that is known, or thought to be known, about the history of the Easter Islanders. It is not much, but it may be enough to establish a theory which so far does not seem to have occurred to archaeologists.

Non-Asian Statues

This theory is unconventional, of course, and so rational that it will stir up great resistance.

First of all it must be said that the Easter Islanders did not descend from peoples who had migrated from Asia. There is no evidence that they did, and some evidence that they did not.

On Easter Island, besides the large statues, there are
small idols to which little attention is paid. They are identical to those of Tiahuanaco (Bolivia), San Agustin (Colum-
bia), Tula (Mexico), and prehistoric sites in France, Germany,
and Scandinavia. They are statues or simply round heads,
crudely carved and no doubt very old, whose eyes are only
holes in the stone.

As for the large statues, they are boldly carved, with
long faces and noses and deep-set eyes. In short, they have all
the characteristics needed to establish a non-Asian origin.
All the more reason' for conventional prehistorians to persist in their blind stubbornness!

According to Churchward and Vincent, the original Easter
Islanders were survivors of the cataclysm that destroyed Mu
twelve thousand years ago. This is not impossible, but since
the island has no high mountains we must assume that it
was submerged at the time of the Deluge, and therefore
emptied of its inhabitants.

In my opinion the Easter Islanders came by sea, probably
from far away, like the sailors of the *Kon-Tiki* . . .

White Sailors with Oval Eyes

All through the Popal Vuh, the Mayas proclaim that their
ancestors were white, bearded, blue-eyed, and originally from
the *east,* across the tumultuous sea.

'Very well,' said prehistorians, 'that shows that the ancestors of the Mayas were beardless Mongols who came
from the *west.*'

As at Tula, Venta, San Agustin, and Tiahuanaco in
South America, the carved heads of Easter Island have oval
eyes (some of those in South America also have round,
rectangular, or square eyes). With a few exceptions, the giant
statues on the island do not have clearly carved eyes. The
effect of eyes is given by the play of light and shadow,
or by two holes in the sockets. But there are many smaller
statues that have large oval eyes, such as the 'Mater of
Orongo' discovered by the American archaeologist Edwin
Ferdon in the ancient solar observatory of Orongo. The little
statues found in family caves depict beardless men with big

ears and almost round eyes. Not one of the island's statues
has slanted eyes.

Yet prehistorians say, 'It was Mongols with slanted eyes
who were the ancestors of the Easter Islanders.'

That is how history is manufactured!

There is an unquestionable connection among the arts
of Mexico, Colombia, Bolivia, and Easter Island.

There is a perfect identity of style between the walls of
Vinapu, on Easter Island, and those of Machu Picchu and
Sacsahuaman, in Peru.

From Mexico to Easter Island, the statues gradually
become almost caricatures and all have one thing in common:
big ears, like Orejona, the Venusian mother of the human
race who landed at the edge of Lake Titicaca.

Francis Mazière writes that the Easter Islanders were buried
in chambers within the *ahus* (platforms) and that their bodies
were wrapped in mats of *totora,* a reed that grows in the
region of Lake Titicaca, as were the bodies of the Celtic
Guanches of the Canary Islands and the Incas of Lake
Titicaca.

The Statues with Pukaos

There are two types of statues on Easter Island, says
Francis Mazière: those whose lower part was carved to be
buried in the ground, and those which, truncated, once stood
on the great *ahus,* or platforms. The first seem to guard the
volcano, the second are erected not far from the coast and
generally look toward the southeast, west, or northwest.

Pierre Loti, who came to Easter Island in 1870, gave
an interesting description of the site:

'The statues? There are two kinds: first, the ones on
the beach, which are all lying down and broken, and then the
others, the frightening ones, from a different period and with
different faces. They are still upright on the other side of the
island, in a lonely place where no one goes any more.'

The statues once had red stone *pukaos,* or topknots, on
their heads. These *pukaos* were knocked off when the statues
were overturned during the 'war of the idols' in the seventeenth century, but since then some of the statues have been

lifted upright and the *pukaos* have been put back on their heads.

'What race did they represent,' wrote Loti, 'with their turned-up noses and their thin lips thrust forward in an expression of disdain or mockery? They have no eyes, only deep cavities under their large, noble foreheads, yet they seem to be looking and thinking . . . Some of them wear necklaces of inlaid flint, or tattoos carved into the stone. They are probably not the work of the Maoris.'

'There are two hundred and seventy-six giants here, upright or lying,' says Francis Mazière, 'and we now know that there are probably as many underground.'

These statues, say the archaeologists William Mulloy, Jacques Ertaud, and Croce-Spinelli, are turned away from the sea so that their eyes, charged with *mana* (magic power), look towards the villages whose safety is in their keeping. This seems to be the function of the statues: to radiate *mana* for the benefit of the Easter Islanders, direct descendants of the great stone ancestors.

The Myth of the Bird-Man

One might be inclined to think that, as in the traditions of the rest of the world, the bird-man of Easter Island is a kind of resurgence of the Jewish and Christian angels, the Egyptian bird-kings, or the flying men of other mythologies. But not on Easter Island, and only there, one might say, no story of men coming from the sky has been perpetuated in the memory of the natives, which is quite strange. This anomaly suggests a theory.

When the man who had found the first egg of a migratory bird returned from the little island of Motunui, more than half a mile from Easter Island, he carried his precious booty in a basket or a piece of cloth attached to his head. The egg, it has been said, represented fecundation and was a sign that the island had not been abandoned by the rest of the world. The bird that had laid it thus became a living symbol of a motherland that existed elsewhere. It was a symbol of migration, according to Ertaud and Croce-Spinelli.

The man who had found the first egg, the bird-man, became a religious leader until the following year, a kind of sorcerer who was 'charged' with *mana*. He had immense powers that resided primarily in his head, which had touched the egg, for it was the egg that gave him his *mana*.

The Topknots of the Statues

The statues were buried with as much as two-thirds of their length underground, sometimes at the very edge of the sea, so they could place as much land as possible under the power of their gaze. But they acquired this power only when their topknots had been put in place and their eyes had been 'opened.' They came down from the mountain 'blind,' that is, without their eyes having been carved. When they were erected, holes were carved in the eye sockets: the statue's eyes were thus opened, and it was *given life*. And only after it had been erected was the red stone topknot put on its head and fixed in place with a mortice. The statue then took on all its magic significance: it became an accumulator, a *charged* idol radiating *mana* from its open eyes.

The meaning of the statues seems clear: they represented ancestors, but not chiefs. Each one represented a bird-man charged with *mana* and the topknot was the basket he had carried on his head when he swam back with the egg he had found.

A Story of Astronauts

There is one important rule that must be taken into account in the study of mythologies: all traditions, stories, philosophies, and transmissions of every kind become adulterated and deformed after a few centuries or millennia.

The angels of the Bible were not angels. The divine kings or hawk-kings of the early Egyptian dynasties were not hawks. Quetzalcoatl, in Mexico, was not a feathered serpent. The gods in the mythologies of the Middle East who had horns or wings, or rode snakes, were not divine beings.

There was nothing magic about the power of those so-called gods, angels, or divine beings. They were actually men and their power was their intelligence, their knowledge of *a science that was supranormal at the time when they appeared*.

Everything becomes rational, logical, and convincing if

we identify those flying men as aviators or, still better, astronauts! But many people are so made that they would be ashamed to advance such a hypothesis even at a time when earthlings have already set foot on the moon. Backward and outdated, they are waiting for the colonization of Mars and Venus. Then they will say, 'We always knew that those flying men, hawk gods, angels, serpents, and dragons were really astronauts, interplanetary travellers no different from us. The earth was visited by Initiators.'

That is what ordinary people will be saying in a few years!

So we may as well say now that *mana* is only a legend, that the statues of Easter Island have no terrible power, and that the myth of the bird-man is an adulterated tradition.

I believe that this tradition, like those in all other parts of the world, is based on something that actually happened long ago: the arrival of Initiators with great scientific knowledge who came from the sky, that is, who came in 'flying machines,' whether aeroplanes or spacecraft. And they probably came from the same planet as the flying men of South America, Asia, and Europe.

It seems well established that the cult of the bird-man who finds the first tern's egg dates from relatively recent times. The fashion or rite of the *pukao* probably goes back to about the same time: there may not have been topknots on all the statues; only fifty-three have been found.

Even while we accept the hypothesis of extraterrestrial intervention, which connects the history of Easter Island with the other mythologies of the world, we may still assume that the island was colonized by pre-Incan navigators from Peru, as Thor Heyerdahl has written. But, with equally good reasons, certain advanced archaeologists believe that Easter Island was a dependency of Mu before the Deluge.

Part 4

INITIATION

11 The Green Lion of the Initiate

The word 'initiate' come from the Latin *initiare,* from *initium,* 'beginning.' Does this mean that an initiate is someone who knows the beginning, in the sense of the genesis of all things, the creation of the universe?

I do not think so! The divine intelligence, or God, if he has consciousness, knows whether or not the universe was created and, if so, by what process; but men, even the most learned, are completely in the dark on this subject – except, of course, for those who are ignorant enough to feel that they *know.*

It would be sacrilegious to qualify God, to define him, even with the best of adjectives. Even initiates do not know who God is. For the initiated rabbis, he was the Mysterious of the Mysterious and was designated by the name of Ain Soph.

If men are to know a beginning, it must be a beginning in time, and it is far from probable that there ever was one. And it is obviously impossible to know the beginning of eternity. In this sense, 'initiation' would be a meaningless word, since only God could be an initiate.

As for men, they are, and can only be, lifelong seekers.

Initiation

'Friends of truth are those who seek it, not those who boast of having found it,' said Concorcet, and this is also the motto of the Freemasons in France.

We must take the word 'initiate' to mean 'someone who is *beginning to understand something.*' And his knowledge does not go very far.

'Life,' wrote Ballanche,[1] 'is a kind of initiation which serves to manifest the intellectual being and the moral being in man.'

That is exactly what I believe, but it is rejected by those for whom initiation is based entirely on mysteries and whispered magic words with, of course, transmission through the centuries of grandiose secrets that could not be appreciated by the common run of mankind – as though the secrets (always intellectual in nature) known in the time of Pythagoras were beyond the grasp of twentieth-century minds! As though Leucippus, Democritus, and Epicurus, great initiates if ever there were any, had not *revealed the secret of the atom*! But twenty-five hundred years had to go by before clear-headed men understood the meaning of that revelation.

The initiate seldom needs to make a mystery of transcendent knowledge: the best way to conceal it is often to announce it to the general public. Those who are worthy of understanding take the opportunity to enrich themselves; as for the others, the vast majority, they wait without impatience or curiosity until the time comes for them to understand and believe.

Divulgence and Secrets

There are sometimes evil forces that forbid all initiatic revelation.

Father J. Ventura, an eminent preacher and theologian of the early nineteenth century, would not have hesitated to inflict torture on initiates guilty of speaking of atoms and atomism. Atomism was regarded as nothing but crass materialism. 'It is atheism,' said Father Ventura, which meant

[1] Pierre-Simon Ballanche (1776-1847) was a mystical philosopher who believed in palingenesis (return to life after real or apparent death) on all levels. One of his maxims was: 'Progress is not made by evolution, but by revolutions. Social and physical cataclysms are inevitable.' He was one of the first to announce (with regard to Chateaubriand) that 'the reign of the *sentence* has passed in favour of the *idea*.' This prophecy, which was ridiculed by the obscure Sainte-Beuve, proved the profundity and integrity of the great philosopher's thought.

that those who held the theory deserved to be burned at the stake.

But truth, even purely scientific truth, is never a negation of God – quite the contrary. To say that the universe is fundamentally composed of atoms is to lead the mind toward a perception of the real universal intelligence. The idea that God created the universe with words is a sacrilege which leads the imagination toward the false God of the catechism.

The statements of men such as Father Ventura show that revealing knowledge sometimes involves a danger of death. That is what I meant to convey in the twentieth chapter of *Le Livre des Secrets Trahis*, where I wrote that when the rose opens to its heart, it is about to reveal its innermost truth at the cost of its death. To speak certain truths always means placing oneself in mortal danger, today as in the Middle Ages.

That is why the initiate remains silent on some occasions, but when his life is not threatened and when revelation is not socially dangerous (as it might be, for example, in the case of an atomic physicist who spoke outside his own narrow circle of colleagues), he has a duty to speak with discernment, that is, to those worthy of receiving what he has to say. In most cases, however, the initiate does not take this precaution, because *he does not know that he is an initiate,* or at least it gives him no concern, no problem.

Awareness of initiation is so rare that, with a few exceptions, only heads of esoteric schools and groups, and a handful of unknown masters, know that they possess superior knowledge. They teach and transmit it to 'the few.'

Have they received it from a master? It is probable; but it is certain that the initiate is never a mere means of transmission: *he must acquire most of his knowledge by his own work, experience, and meditation.* This is the price he must pay to be worthy of transmission.

Stimulating the Mysterious Regions

Since initiation is not knowledge of the truth, it can only be a search for truth and a conquest of permissible knowledge by a marvellous return to the beginning of heredity (heritage) and tradition.

To become initiated is to stimulate the mysterious regions of the self, to cause the intimate divulgence (called revelation by some) which enables us to regain part of what is within is.

Revelation is not always a representation of truth: more often it is an expression of phantasms, illusions, and even madness. The paranoiac or the megalomaniac is subject to such disturbance when he believes that he has been given a mission by superior entities. Only the sane, well-balanced man can trust his revelations to some extent. The madman believes in them by a physiological process that makes him lose his *self*. He says, 'I am Napoleon,' and this is purely and simply an integration of an external self. The madman is no longer *himself* as a personality: he is *the other*. But unfortunately he retains what is worst in him: his madness. He is alienated (from the Latin *alius*, 'other') and thereby loses his social and civil rights.

What does the anchorite do in his cave? He thinks, reflects, meditates. How? By making his temperature rise, thus sharpening his apperception, and by causing mysterious inner chemical combinations, one of which is known: the flow of glucose into the brain, resulting in an interaction with the neurons that are stimulated. The forbidden doors are then partially opened and the memory chromosomes bring answers and images by a biological process which relates the anchorite to the Ancient of Days (God) through long lines of ancestors.

Initiation in this sense is the possibility of regaining the total knowledge contained in the archives of our personal universe, which is identical to the external universe. Everything is within us. Avicenna, the illustrious eleventh-century Arab philosopher and physician, wrote these sublime words: 'You believe that you are nothing and you contain the universe.'

It is the biological way, or Sacred Vehicle, that communicates to us, by our genes, chromosomes, and nervous system, the memory of the total knowledge possessed by our successive creators: God, Adam the first hermaphrodite, then Adam, Eve . . . and finally our parents.

Pandora's Box

Man's chromosomal 'library' contains almost all of his unknown history, from the 'first' creation of the universe to the fantastic advent of the science of future times. Everything is enclosed, imprisoned in the billions of little boxes constituted by his neurons and the cells of his grey matter.

Billions of these boxes have already been opened and we know their contents, but more billions remain closed. Woe to anyone who might open them all! The human neurological complex may well be a kind of Pandora's box!

Yet the initiate, by his perhaps sacrilegious curiosity, questions his stimulated but inactive neurons. Behind the forbidden doors is knowledge. Initiation consists in making the eliciting mechanism function: opening the doors.

This is also the goal of magic, but whereas the initiate works and tries to make himself worthy of revelation, the magician or sorcerer breaks open the door like a burglar by using hallucinogenic drugs, spells, or incantations.

There are said to be three ways of acquiring knowledge by oneself: work and merit, prayer (asking), and magic (commanding). Prayer would thus be halfway between work and sorcery, or between what is moral and what is not. But the most important part of our initiation is, of course, transmitted and taught to us by our parents, teachers, friends, and acquaintances.

Practically speaking, the initiate and the sorcerer both have knowledge. The difference between them lies almost entirely in their ways of acquiring and using their knowledge. The sorcerer's initiation, besides becoming more and more empirical, more and more rare and ineffective, is limited in time and is often illusory because it lacks a valid base and sufficient general knowledge.

The physicist, the biologist, and the mathematician are initiates in the true sense of the word: they seek and can explain, at least to some extent, the beginning (*initium*) of all things. They use the external way: study, oral transmission, experiences external to the physical body.

The Rosicrucians and the known or unknown Masters are initiates who make greater use of the internal way: study and, above all, investigations into their unknown self and solicitations of their mysterious forces.

It should be noted that the sorcerer's initiation deals only with inferior knowledge without ever approaching the great enigmas of universal order and creation.

In the noblest sense, initiation, on the view being presented here, consists in improving the human biological complex. That is what Pierre-Simon Ballanche meant when he wrote that life, in its most fecund evolutionary system, is an initiation from which man can draw his most valuable intellectual and moral resources.

False Saints and False Initiates

There is a parallel to be drawn between a number of dubious 'saints' and an equal number of sham 'initiates.'

Saint Theresa of Avila, selfish and insensitive to pity and human suffering, sought only, as she herself wrote, to 'enlighten her soul.'

Theresa had her first visions during the fever of an illness that nearly killed her. Later, her life was made up of visions, fasting, vigils, mortifications of the flesh, prayer – in short, everything that moves one away from God and initiation. Her rule was perpetual prayer, which necessarily leads to cerebral derangement. She was entirely absorbed in her beautiful 'mirror soul,' so that she never gave any thought to helping the poor, the humble, and the persecuted. On the contrary, that diabolical creature called the Inquisitors 'angels' and the Grand Inquisitor the 'Great Angel.' Could anything be more nightmarish?

The false initiate damns himself for ever by seeking enlightenment in selfish spiritual elevation.

Real Initiates: Saint Martin and Saint Vincent

The good Saint Martin and the admirable Saint Vincent never had equivocal ecstasies or dubious levitations; they were too busy helping their unfortunate brothers. Buddha, Pherecydes, and Pythagoras did not mobilize their life-forces to serve a monstrous narcissism. They did not take, they gave. They did not remain silent, they spoke.

The false saint, like the false initiate, is a proud and useless Narcissus.

If Theresa of Avila and Thérèse de Lisieux had taken care of the sick, they would not have had time to have visions. They would have done better to take a calming potion that would have enabled them to regain their common sense, rather than communing with the God who inhabited them during their ecstasies.

The human brain, it is said, contains ten billion neurons, or nerve cells, only a third of which are used by our conscious faculties. Man's unknown powers are therefore greatly superior to his known ones, and consequently the miraculous belongs to the former, while the commonplace belongs to the latter.

Inheriting One's Father

The Australian Bushmen live almost entirely in the Stone Age, but they have traditions and a pagan (therefore authentic) philosophy which bind them closely to the truths of nature.

Although they give positive value to their earthly life, they regard it as only a reflection of a superior life lived by their ancestors in the 'time of the dream.' They draw psychic strength from this anterior life by means of a kind of talisman called a *churanga*, a magic tablet of wood or stone with designs carved into it, which they must never lose, under penalty of death in the next world. When he goes off on an expedition, a Bushman hides his precious *churanga* in a place known only to himself, for if an enemy should gain possession of it he would also possess its owner's soul.

When the Bushman passes from the present conscious stage to the 'dream' stage, he sees the time of God and undergoes a return to matter, a reincarnation in reverse.

The conscious state is the state of ignorance, so he must always be attentive to advice and warnings given by the ancestors, as well as indications given by nature.

The initiate, according to this belief, is the man who knows that he is not doomed to annihilation, but that he is meant to enter into communion with the universe and universal life itself. If he fails, everything will disintegrate, for like all men, he contains a summary of the universe within himself.

The Bushman also believes, not that he must inherit *from* his father such things as his soul, mind, and physical features, but that he must *inherit his father,* that is, continue his father's existence in the earthly world.

This Bushman philosophy is very close not only to my views on initiation and memory chromosomes, but also to the philosophy that follows from the highest teachings of science.

The Third Eye

In initiation, the third eye, theoretically located in the middle of the forehead, is a mysterious organ capable of perceiving what is too subtle for our coarse senses. It is also the eye of imagination and dreaming. Turned inward, it seems to govern our inner universe.

For the biologist it is the pineal gland (also called the pineal body, the pineal organ or the pineal eye), a glandular body about the size of a hazelnut in the middle of the brain. It apparently is not very useful, since it becomes calcified in adulthood. In animals such as lampreys and certain reptiles, the pineal gland is just under the skin of the forehead and actually has the structure of a third eye, with the retina facing inward. It probably governs an unknown sense which must be closely connected with instinct.

The farther a vertebrate rises on the scale of evolution, the more this eye becomes a gland, losing the nerve fibres that connect it to the brain. But it acquires an exceptional innervation coming from the sympathetic nervous system, particularly the superior cervical ganglion, which receives stimuli from the eye.

The pineal gland acts by releasing a hormonal substance to the genital glands, which seems to inhibit the sexual system. This may be why the initiate endowed with the third eye turns away from the pleasures of the body in favour of spiritual exercises.

Since, with age, the pineal gland shows less resemblance to an eye turned toward the inner universe, it would seem that the child is physiologically better equipped than the adult for perceiving manifestations of the occult and even for becoming a medium or clairvoyant.

The Senses and Intelligence

In the adult the vision of the two external eyes plays a major role, in conjunction with his intelligence, and this combination gives him the ability to create situations, systems, and machines which can replace instinct and the subordinate senses.

Man's instincts, in fact, are being progressively eliminated by the social system he has established. The police protect him from violence and his food is selected, analyzed, and treated to prevent him from running any risk. His sense of smell, so important in prehistoric times, is now used almost solely in the games of love: woman perfumes herself, man smells her odour. The pleasure he derives from smelling flowers is purely æsthetic; moreover, horticulturists are increasingly sacrificing the scent of flowers in favour of their shape, size, and colour. If human beings still have a sense of taste, it is because it gives them physical pleasure.

In the society of the future, the senses may atrophy and be replaced by a system of precautions and prohibitions created by the intellect. Man has a growing tendency to become an essentially intellectual being.

Becoming Pure Intellects

It is an obvious fact that our instincts, no longer having any reason to exist, are becoming dulled and will eventually disappear, like the functions of the third eye and the appendix.

What will become of initiation? Will it no longer have anything in common with sensitivity and apperception? That would be logical, and there is reason to believe that evolution will take place in this order: from the senses to the intellect, and from fleeting apperception to clearer understanding.

Yet it is certain that the totality of knowledge does not

belong to man, including the initiate. Something will always remain for him to guess and perceive, and if he no longer has the sensory and instinctual faculties needed for going farther and deeper, he will have to make use of a super-intelligence.

If this hypothesis is correct, the major concern of the initiate should be to develop his cerebral functions.

This was the opinion of Moses, who obliged the Hebrews to retain everything by memory, and of the great rabbis of the Sanhedrin, who felt that to be ignorant was to insult the Lord.

Bragi's Cup

It is the intellect which, to remedy the inadequacy of the senses and the loss of the third eye, leads human beings to use hallucinogens.

The shamans of Siberia make *braga,* a kind of rye beer in which poisonous mushrooms have been soaked. It is one of the oldest known hallucinogens, since it goes back to Odin's son Bragi, god of poetry, eloquence, and wisdom among the ancient peoples of Scandinavia.

In their mythology, Bragi was the equivalent of Apollo. Runic characters were inscribed on his tongue and evil words could never come from his lips. He was a perfect example of the initiate. He and his brother Hermod received heroes entering Valhalla (paradise) with these words of wel-come: 'Enjoy eternal peace and drink *meth* [nectar] with the gods.'

Bragi's Cup was a recipient filled with *meth,* or hal-lucinogenic beer, which the Norse kings drank when they assumed power. The drinking of *meth* was accompanied by a solemn oath.

Bragi's Cup was also emptied on the occasion of certain ceremonies, during sacrifices and in memory of those who had fallen in battle. The cup was then passed to everyone present and, inspired by the hallucinogen, each man spoke or sang a tribute to the dead warrior.

The Memory of Matter

I have already published (in *Le Livre du Mystérieux Inconnu*, Chapter XIII) an essay on the scientific production of phantoms, involving singular phenomena and parallel universes.

Now, in scientific circles on the other side of the Iron Curtain, another hypothesis has been advanced, one that is more in accord with the Mysterious Unknown.

In a room containing five people, a medium, by his nervous sensitivity, succeeds in materializing a motive idea by subjective projection. It often happens that two of the spectators, being particularly receptive, see the phantom, while the two others see nothing and deny the reality of the phenomenon. Still more often, only one of them receives the projection. The experiment is preferably carried out in what is known as an 'inhabited place.'

Some physicists are now inclined to believe in these phantom apparitions. Soviet scientists are convinced that any manifestation of an electromagnetic nature may find favourable circumstances, be inscribed somewhere and remain there, recorded as though in the ferrite of a magetic tape. The recording object may be any of such things as a magnetic iron nail, a bird's feather or nest, a tree leaf, or a piece of ferruginous stone.

We have only an imperfect knowledge of the structure of what is called inanimate matter; perhaps it can behave like a ferrite and, under certain natural conditions, 'play back' what it has recorded.[1] If so, the medium acts as a transistor.

During an event that causes strong feelings (sorrow, fear, suffering), these feelings may give rise to exceptionally intense electromagnetic waves. Most of them are lost, but

---

[1] It is amusing to recall a legend of King Midas which apparently involves a phenomenon of this kind. Tired of shaving a man who had donkey's ears, the king's barber went to an isolated place, dug a hole, leaned down over it and, to relieve himself of his burdensome secret, said to the earth, 'King Midas has donkey's ears.' He then filled in the hole. By the following year, reeds had grown over the spot. When they swayed in the wind they could be heard murmuring, 'King Midas has donkey's ears. . . . King Midas has donkey's ears. . . .'

some become fixed in receivers which, when acted upon in a certain way, reconstitute them later. Then, if the waves encounter a suitable environment, they are converted into sound or light, by a system analogous to that of a bird's feather, particularly the feather of an owl if the events takes place at night. (In Chapter 16 I will develop this scientific discovery identifying birds' feathers as sources of sound emission.) For the Greeks, the owl was the symbol of Athena, and it has long been the faithful companion of seers and sorcerers.

A more fantastic hypothesis attributes to matter, to each object, a personal magnetic memory analogous to the memory of chromosomes.

As for the 'phantoms of Hiroshima,' it is not a hypothesis that is involved, but a fact that could be verified by a hundred thousand witnesses.

The Phantoms of Hiroshima

My correspondent and friend Denise Larroque has informed me of a fantastic vision that occurred in Hiroshima a few months after the atomic bomb was dropped on the city. The information came from an authentic witness, Monsieur G., a Swiss embassy attaché who was twenty-five miles from the point at which the bomb exploded, and later died of radiation poisoning.

'On certain evenings, at twilight,' said Denise Larroque, 'images of the destroyed bridges appeared above the river, with cars, pedestrians, and the usual animation. It was like a projection of a film that had been made before the atomic explosion, and it was terribly frightening to what was left of the population. The members of the Swiss embassy thought they had gone mad as a result of the radiation they had been exposed to. Monsieur G. told my husband and me that the phenomenon occurred only under certain atmospheric conditions, but no one could predict them.'

Was it a resurgence of time, or desire-images, or a collective hallucination? I cannot say, but it is not impossible that the sword of a Roman legionary, the relics of a saint, or Joan of Arc's banner will some day relate strange memories, when biologists or physicists have found a way to stimulate those memory chromosomes and decipher their language.

Miracles in the Brocéliande Forest

The oaks of the Celtic forest had the privilege of letting the sacred mistletoe grow on their branches. In a great ceremony that took place on the consecrated date, the Druids went to cut the mistletoe with a sickle.

In our time, oaks with mistletoe have inexplicably become extremely rare. Despite an active search, I was losing hope of ever finding one when, almost by chance, my friend Henri Touron told me that he had one in the Jollandrie wood, five miles from the town of Charroux. It may be the only one left in France. It has two trunks. Its tuft of mistletoe is about sixty feet above the ground and has a diameter of at least five feet.

Unfortunately, Druids seldom officiate in our time, under oak trees at least. But according to my friend E. Coarer-Kalondan, of Nantes, they still have powerful secrets, such as the ability to make it rain whenever they choose, by using the magic properties of Merlin's Steps, a large stone near the Baranton fountain in the Brocéliande forest. It was beside this wondrous fountain that Vivien the Enchantress met Merlin the Enchanter.

E. Coarer-Kalondan, who is a Druid, has written to me concerning Merlin's Steps:

'I regret that the bad condition of my legs now makes it impossible for me to walk three-quarters of an hour on a path full of holes, mud puddles, and thick weeds; otherwise I would have invited you to accompany me to that extraordinary fountain. If you had accepted the invitation, I would have advised you to take a good raincoat and, when we reached the place, I would have ritually poured water on Merlin's Steps. In less than half an hour, a torrential rain would have fallen on us.

'My Druid friends and I have already saved the forest from fire four times, during periods of severe drought, by proceeding in the proper manner.

'In the past, the Lords of Pontuz, or Pontus, did the same; then it was the Rectors of Tréorantec. Since the Revolution, it has been the initiates of Celtism who have taken up the torch.

'I can speak categorically on this subject. I have personally performed the rite, though I admit that I do not understand how it works or the physical laws that govern it.'

As a Druid, E. Coarer-Kalondan does not lie, and even if the rains were fortuitous, we would have to acknowledge that the old Celtic gods are strangely favourable to them.

Radiesthesia

It is not exactly radiesthesia I wish to discuss, but the gift that certain women have for making a pendulum turn. The pendulum may consist of either a ring or a necklace hanging by a thread. It is held first over the head, then over the belly of a pregnant woman. She must be at least three months pregnant, because it is essential that the baby's heart be beating. If the pendulum turns in the same direction over both the head and the belly, the baby is a girl; if not, it is a boy.

The explanation lies in the difference between the bio-magnetic currents emanating from the two organisms. If the baby is a girl, its sex is in synchronization with the sex of the mother, and the pendulum turns in only one direction.

Some sorcerers maintain that the polarity of the first three fingers of the hand, beginning with the thumb, is opposed to that of the last two, and that during certain occult operations these two fingers must be kept lowered in order to give the three upraised ones all their strength.

The Etruscans, writes Robert Grand in a book being prepared for publication (Clefs pour les tarots, by Suzanne Agostini, Shorong, and Robert Grand), determined favourable areas for the construction of a house by using a lituus, a bent stick with the shape of a bishop's staff. With it, they were able to detect the direction of telluric currents: the 'veins of the dragon.'

Astrology

Scientists are revising their opinion of astrology now that botanists have noticed the determining action of trace elements in the growth or degeneration of plants. Infinitesimal doses of trace elements can give new life to cereal plants suffering from a shortage of boron, iodine, phosphorus, etc.

Similarly, a person's life may be considerably modified by electromagnetic interactions of the same order. It is therefore thought that the influence of certain stars may have a favourable or unfavourable effect on the psychology and physiology of a newborn baby, when he is in an exceptional state of receptivity.

The problem, of course, is to discriminate between favourable and unfavourable interactions. It becomes complicated if we bring in telluric forces and forces of the environment, which are massive rather than infinitesimal.

My friend the astrologer Philippe Vidal has an interesting view of the question.

'While astral influence, whose power of orientation we know,' he writes, 'is inexorable on the great majority of people, whom we may call "Mortals," it seems to be less inexorable, or not at all, on a small minority who may be called "Immortals," because they have reached the highest stage of evolution.

'This principle explains the errors made in astrology and the differences of opinion among astrologers. The mystery may lie not in their art and the capricious influence of the heavenly bodies, but in receptive ability, which differs with individuals. If so, detailed data should be used to determine exactly the degree of evolution of the person for whom one is casting a horoscope.'

This is also the opinion, in a less specific version, of the physicists of the Florence Institute, who believe that celestial mechanics has an unquestionable influence on all living organisms.

12 Mother Water and the
Elixir of Immortality

Initiation is in the vanguard of scientific discoveries, and nearly every day the research of scientists brings proof that secrets transmitted since time immemorial, or brought to light again in the human Mysterious Unknown, were already known and verified by our Superior Ancestors.

When alchemists worked over their athanors, most rationalists felt that they were ignorant empirics doomed to inevitable failure. The Philosopher's Stone, the panacea, potable gold, the elixir of immortality – nothing but silly illusions, hazy dreams for gullible spiritualists!

Then one day a Soviet scientist, working with equipment much more sophisticated than an alchemist's athanor, uttered a cry of triumph and astonishment: he had just discovered, if not the Philosopher's Stone, something that was very much like it!

And the amazing, incredible thing he had discovered was water, little different in its fundamental nature from the water that flows from the kitchen faucet, but nevertheless capable of favouring miracles, including the greatest miracle of all: life.

Polywater

Water has always haunted the human imagination and strange powers have been attributed to it. Its composition, nature and function were thought to be known, but always with a touch of doubt; its limpid fluidity seemed to hold the intuition of a sacred mystery.

Chemists ordinarily give little thought to occultism, but they felt as if the wings of the Angel of the Fantastic had brushed against them when, in 1962 and 1967, the Soviet scientists N. Fedakin and Boris V. Deryagin (professors at the Moscow Academy of Science) obtained in the laboratory a solidified form of water which, instead of crystallizing, had the appearance of a block of Plexiglas.

This water is similar to ordinary water, but it boils at about six hundred degrees Centigrade and freezes at about forty degrees below zero. It is expected that, by varying its method of preparation, its boiling point can be raised to eight hundred, a thousand, or twelve hundred degrees, and perhaps even higher.

British chemists of the Unilever group, the Americans Ellis Lippincott and Gerald Cessac, of the University of Maryland, and Robert Stromberg and Warren H. Grant, of the National Bureau of Weights and Measures, also produced the water in 1970, and gave it the name of polywater.

It has so far been obtained only in very small quantities. It has a mass density of forty; its liquid appearance is that of a colourless syrup and its steam condenses into normal water. It is ordinary water, except that its molecules are polymerized. It is believed that they form a hexagonal network, rather than forming chains as in normal water.

Polywater is obtained by heating distilled water for eighteen hours in capillary tubes at low pressure, which is singularly reminiscent of the procedures of alchemists.

It occurs in nature in small amounts, notably in certain types of clay, in plants and, it is thought, in our own cells, where it may have a function not yet clearly understood, but extremely important in the manifestations of life.

'The dawn of the obscure world' may be connected with the mystery of polywater, which may prove to be *mother water*.

Polywater allows us to foresee fantastic properties related to the sacred springs of the ancients, the mystery of caves, Isis, Virgin Mothers, Aphrodite, Venus, pure water, initiation, and perhaps the 'Fountain of Youth,' which has often been discussed, but with no serious belief in its real existence.

The Cycle of Water

Water is a combination of hydrogen (H) and oxygen (O) with the formula $H + H + O = H_2O$.

The water of the oceans, in constant evaporation, causes the formation of clouds which condense into rain, moistening the continents and returning the water to the oceans in an endless cycle.

This is the conventional account of the cycle of water, and it is partially correct, but since the work of C. Luis Kervran the fantastic truth has come to light: the fundamental cycle of water does not begin with an aerial combination of hydrogen and oxygen, but proceeds from the transmutation of limestone into water.

In other words, the earth's reserves of water do not come from the sky, but are formed within the earth itself; its immense underground deposits and streams of water originate in masses of limestone which, through the millennia, are transmuted into water. Thus we can say that rocks, notably limestone, contain water, not by inclusion under high capillary pressure, as the conventional theory maintains, but in the elementary form of hydrogen and oxygen, in semimolecules of water.

The transmutation of limestone into water begins with elementary particles.

And it is in water and from water that cellular life is born and all kinds of life are manifested.

The Creation of Life

In July, 1970, the principal biologists of the world met at Pont-à-Mousson, France, to try to determine how and under what conditions cellular life came into being.

Here, in a highly condensed version, is the generally accepted thesis.

At a remote time in the earth's history, estimated at three billion years ago by Christian Léourier in his book *L'Origine de la vie,* only inorganic matter existed: the earth, the seas, and an atmosphere composed essentially of oxygen, hydrogen, nitrogen, and carbon. As the result of very powerful electric discharges (lightning) and such factors as volcanic eruptions, radioactivity, and ultraviolet rays, basic compounds were created *spontaneously*: amino acids, nucleic bases, simple sugars, etc.

The amino acids, or agents of life, could only have been formed in an aqueous medium, that is, *in the water of the oceans, which was probably mother water.*

In other words, it can be said that energy propagated in the available chemical medium, constituted by the material of the planet, brought about the formation of the basic molecules of life.

The creation of rudimentary proteins was then the point of departure for increasingly complex cellular organization, leading to genuine proteins. The twenty known amino acids can form an almost infinite number of structures, just as the twenty-six letters of the alphabet can form an almost infinite number of sentences. A whole world of life can flow from them, *provided they are baptized by the mother water of the original earth.*

Initiates have always possessed this knowledge, which is older than the Deluge.

The thesis does not, of course, answer all objections that might be raised against it, but it seems to come as close as possible to the truth about the appearance of earthly life. It also shows that the 'four elements' (earth, air, fire, water), ridiculed by conventional rationalists, correspond exactly to modern scientific data.

The Philosopher's Stone

This brief summary shows that water is the primordial source in which life is manifested. Esotericists and conventional scientists are in agreement on this point.

Water that comes from argillaceous arkose is especially aggressive and lends itself to multiple 'reincarnations' in a number of rocks that are still evolving, but it is harmful to the nourishment of plant and animal cells. But water that comes from granites and calcareous rocks, and particularly from lavas and basalts, contains the basic vital principle, the principle that modern physicists call the Coulomb force.

This was suspected, if not known, by alchemists in all

ages, seekers of the elixir of long life, Pontic water, liquid Philosopher's Stone, the fountain of gold, alkahest or the universal solvent, potable gold, and the fifth elixir, or alchemical dew.

The Philosopher's Stone, the universal transmuter, *is certainly not a myth.*

It would seem, then, that Boris Deryagin and N. Fedakin have found the principle of the Philosopher's Stone dreamed of by alchemists, and that this Philosopher's Stone is related not to the manufacture of gold, but to the secret of life and consequently to the secret of the universal being, that is, God.

Mother water, the source of all birth, death, and resurrection, therefore appears to be the origin of life. This is in agreement with the double mystery of the Virgin Mother and water oozing from caves, which are both primordial virgin water that gives birth, and with all mythological traditions, notably that of baptism: in Celtic baptism, for example, the priest of Teutates, god of birth and death, officiated in a square basin filled with water (the square is the symbol of the four elements).

He Who Moves on the Waters

Venus was born of the foam of the sea (which may be a prudish metaphor), just as mineral, plant, and animal life was born in the mother water of the beginning of creation.

Everything proceeds from water.

The moon, a small planet with much less mass than the earth, cooled too rapidly and was unable to retain its atmosphere, for lack of sufficient gravity. But its external composition (chiefly obsidian, or acidic lavas) was the same as that of the earth's surface when it emerged from the waters. Heavy rain would have been enough to give the moon life!

Man's existence in the foetal stage is that of a veritable *Homo Aquaticus*: the unborn child lives in an aqueous medium which esoterically recalls the remote time when the primordial egg floated on the waters of creation.

In the Vedic cosmogony, the most enlightened of all,

the neutral Brahma (the Lord existing by himself, inconceivable, beyond the reach of our senses) 'resolved in his mind
to make the first material creation emanate from his substance. He first produced the waters, and then he placed in
them a germ that became an egg which shone like gold, as
bright as a thousand suns. In this egg the supreme being
himself was born, in the form of the masculine Brahma,
ancestor of all beings.'

The waters were called *naras* because they were the product
of Nara (the divine spirit). They were the first place of
movement (*ayana*) of Nara, who was therefore named
Narayana ('he who moves on the waters').

The Judeo-Christian religion of Abraham-Sarah (Brahma-
Sarasvati), which inspired other Occidental and Oriental religions, describes the beginning of the world in a similar
but much less enlightened and initiatic manner. In the New
Testament, Jesus copies Narayana's movement on the waters,
but without the true esoteric meaning of the symbol. In any
case, the New Testament account of creation – 'When all
things began, the Word already was' (John 1:1) – rests on
an incontestable physical datum, but attributes a physical
meaning to the Eternal.

Oannes, Melusina, and the Primordial Egg

According to Sanchoniathon's history of the Phoenicians,
they believed that life came from a mixture of clay and
water: the *mot*, or primordial mud.

For the Chaldeans, creation began with hybrid generations,
and at that time fish-gods came out of the sea. Oannes
was the most important of them, but there are other mysterious hybrid gods: the Cabiri of the Phoenicians, the Ceto
or Dercetys of the Syrians, who has the face of a woman
and the body of a fish, the Melusina of the Celts in the
Poitou region of France, the Odacon of the Babylonians, and
the Dagon of the Philistines. (It is interesting to compare the
names of these last two fish-gods with the *dagop*, the sanctuary of Buddhist temples. The *dagop* is the symbol of the
bubble of water which represented the human body in the
mind of Buddha. It is the *naos*, the Holy of Holies, the

tabernacle, the *stupa*, the cupola of sacred edifices in India, the mystic egg, and the Great Magistery of the alchemists.)

All these fish-gods are products of creative water, states mythology, and they have an obvious relation to alchemy, that is, to the primordial egg, dew, and other wondrous waters which alchemists have used as transmuters of various elements.

Mother water is a transmuter, and life is only a transmuting function, as physicists and biologists have shown.

You Are Dust and Water

Despite the deterioration of initiatic meaning caused by the ignorance of priests, the divine identity of mother water has prevailed through the millennia, in the great religions, over false ideas and false gods. Baptism, or rebirth, for example, which effaces sin according to Christianity, is actually a rite recalling the original creation. Masonic baptism, more initiatic and closer to the truth, has a *creative* and *purifying* meaning.

Bel-Mylitta and Ishtar in Babylonia, Bel-Baalitis, Ashtoreth, and Adonis in Phoenicia, Attis and Cybele in Phrygia, Osiris and Isis in Egypt, and Teutates in ancient Celtia are double divine personifications of the fecundating principle: water.

In the mother religion of the Celts, water is represented by the Great Goddess, who prevails over the initial principle of fire (the Agni of the Hindus), from which she comes and to which she returns.

The ancient Persians believed that the earth, as well as all the realms of nature, were born of primordial water.

But in general the creation of 'life,' that is, organic matter, begins with a mixture of clay and silt, or water and earth, or water and clay.

The fact is that whether original man – Adam, Man, Manu – is said to have been created of water, clay, or dust, the basic component does not change, since the clay of the earth's crust is a compound of water under high capillary pressure.

The Semisecret of the Alchemists

Thus we have established a natural relation among original water, the source of all life, the primordial egg of alchemy, and the mother water or polywater of Soviet and American chemists.

The ordinary alchemists of the Middle Ages were only half initiated. Many of them confused the manufacture of gold with that of vital water; they combined sulphur, mercury, arsenic, silver, lead, copper, phosphorus, etc., and all sorts of preposterous ingredients. Others sought the elixir of long life, but without suspecting its exact nature. They had a vague idea of it, however, even though they did not know its composition, since they called it 'the water of youth' or 'the water of immortality,' and knew that discovery of the Philosopher's Stone had to be approached by very long heating of water in a closed container. This proves that the secret had been transmitted by genuine Knowers.

The attraction of the Philosopher's Stone was so powerful that alchemists worked relentlessly, always in vain, but always sustained by the mirage of a real but elusive truth. This was the case, notably, with the Templar alchemists and those who sought to manufacture commercial gold.

But our present knowledge of part of the wondrous secret proves the existence, in the remote past, of ancestors with a culture and civilization superior to ours.

At first, of course, the gibberish of alchemists, the labyrinths in which they like to enclose their thought, arouse justifiable mistrust; but we cannot help being amazed to realize that they came very close to succeeding. The philosopher Chrestien wrote cryptically with regard to 'divine water' that it was 'the explanation relative to limestone' and that it was 'sometimes native water, sometimes limewater.'

Without the assumption of Superior Ancestors, there can be no explanation of the stubborn persistence of those half-initiated empirics and the fact that they knew the first part of an immensely important alchemical operation without knowing its real purpose.

It is incontestable that someone in the past had succeeded in obtaining the mother water of immortality and that the process had been revealed, bequeathed, then adulterated through the years.

The secret was probably distorted twelve thousand years ago, in the horrors of the Deluge. We may also suppose that initiated alchemists were able to call on their memory chromosomes (this phenomenon is sometimes called clair-voyance) and partially reconstitute the operation or be guided in that direction.

The Toad of Alchemy Books

Spiritualists believe that initiates know everything, which is a mistake, but, by corroborating traditions, the discover-ies of twentieth-century science have shown the solid basis of initiatic knowledge. The mystery of mother water, and others equally important to the enrichment of the adept, are contained in the teachings of the Cabalists and the Rosi-crucians, heirs of the very ancient alchemy whose origin is earlier than the god Thoth.

It is already known that alchemists heated and reheated water in their glass flasks for the purpose of finding the Philosopher's Stone, but it is extremely important to make a connection between this beginning of badly transmitted truth and another, equally revealing fact: in the alchemical tradition, the primordial egg *contained a toad*.

Pseudo-initiates, always ready to give knowing, promising winks, never suspected the relation between vital water (the nourishment, grail, and catalyst of DNA) and the toad of long life drawn in alchemy books or found enclosed in blocks of stone at the bottom of quarries. Only real initiates knew that this grail was mother water that came from the non-radioactive transmutation of limestone. And they knew that the polywater produced in retorts with capillary tubes, associated with the symbol of the frog, gave the scientific explanation of the mysteries of baptism, initiatic caves, and virgin mothers. An explanation as clear as spring water!

The Initiated Toad

On some oozing rocks, long streaks of green can be seen. They are the vital jelly of chlorophyll produced and nourished by the rock, and they are its elixir of immortality. This marvellous secret is known by a gentle, harmless animal, the toad, which sometimes lives as an involuntary prisoner in blocks of limestone.

It often happens that when such a block is broken in a quarry, even if it has been taken from a depth of fifty or a hundred feet, a living toad, of normal size and in perfect health, is found in a cavity that snugly fits its body. The germ of the toad was probably carried into the porous limestone by rainwater, perhaps with the aid of a fissure that was later closed.

This phenomenon has been known since the most ancient times. It was explained by the extreme sobriety of the toad and its ability to stay alive with a very small amount of air. It was called both a fossil and a living animal.

In the nineteenth century an engineer named Seguin poured plaster over ten frogs and left them encased in it for nearly ten years. When he broke open the plaster, one of them was still alive. The same experiment was performed in 1852 by the English geologist Buckland with sealed blocks of limestone and siliceous sandstone. All the toads enclosed in the air-tight sandstone died, but those in porous limestone survived, and some of them had even grown larger.

It is now known that toads survive in such situations by means of the rarefied gases contained in stone and the miraculous properties of the mother water distilled by limestone, and it is believed that they can survive for hundreds or even thousands of years. They might be said to hibernate, in a certain sense, but since the temperature in the underground stone is always well above freezing it is not a question of hibernation, properly speaking, but of lethargy.

The toad, enclosed in its prison as in a chamber of immortality, feeds on the constituent elements of the porous stone, which contained 'quarry water' as well as water produced by the accelerated transmutation of limestone, the acceleration being caused by the toad's acidifying 'warts.' Does the toad swallow this water, or absorb it by osmosis,

or transmute it? It apparently operates like a plant, by a
kind of photosynthesis.

From sunlight and from water absorbed by its roots, a
plant produces the organic matter necessary for its nourishment and growth: this is photosynthesis. From vital water,
the toad in a rock must also be able to create the chemical
and organic substances it needs, particularly the ribonucleic
acid required for the synthesis of enzymes and proteins.

From here to believing that mother water is a water of
immortality or, more precisely, a water capable of sustaining
human life and biological equilibrium, there is only one step;
but it would still be adventurous to take it.

Baptismal Fonts and Mother Water from Rocks

Another piece of evidence in favour of initiatic secrets
transmitted since antediluvian times is the prehistoric worship
of sacred fountains in caves.

I believe that in the mists of their consciousness prehistoric
men had preserved a memory of the miraculous powers
of water issuing directly from the mother rock, since in
many caves, and at the base of the large shelters under
rock at Les Eyzies, France, one can see containers carved into
the limestone itself. They hold water that has oozed out, full
of life, and blossomed in the form of chlorophyll as soon
as it left the limestone that distilled it. The Cro-Magnon
men of the Dordogne therefore knew, confusedly, that it
was necessary for them to drink water from rocks, preferably from those of La Vézère, La Tardoire, and La Charente.

The priests of ancient times knew that baptismal water
was not only a symbol. A gardener knows the power of rainwater on plants. Modern great initiates know how to explain
the mystery of so-called sacred fountains of water oozing
from caves, Celtic cups that could never be emptied, and
baptismal fonts which, as their name clearly indicates, *should
be fountains,* that is, stone basins in which mother water
from limestone is formed naturally and *never dries up.*

With water from such baptismal fonts, baptism takes on
its religious meaning, which is unknown to Christian priests.
When a priest sprinkles holy water from a font, he symbolic-

ally evokes the oldest magic in the world: he gives life, just as the gods of mythology make life arise by pouring mother water on earthly clay. This is the deep and scientific meaning of baptism.

According to the New Testament, Jesus began living as the Christ when he was baptized by John: 'At the moment when he came up out of the water, he saw the heavens torn open and the Spirit, like a dove, descending upon him. And a voice spoke from heaven: "Thou art my Son, my Beloved; on thee my favour rests." (Mark 1:10-11.)

The Sarcophagus of Arles-sur-Tech

In the courtyard of the abbey of Arles-sur-Tech, France, is a sarcophagus known as 'the holy tomb of the holy bodies.' It has a marvellous property: it produces water like a spring. It is in a rather dark and damp corner, but the ground is dry and the sarcophagus is separated from the floor of the courtyard by two stones about eight inches high.

It is seventy-four inches long, twenty inches wide, and twenty-six inches high, with walls four inches thick. It has a capacity of about sixty gallons and every year a hundred to a hundred and fifty gallons of very pure water are taken from it. This water is said to have certain healing properties.

The ridged cover of the sarcophagus is joined to it by cramp irons which hold it firmly enough to eliminate any possibility of deception.

It is made of grey unpolished marble, dates from the ninth century, and was found in the ruins on which Abbot Castellanus, founder of the monastery, built his cell. The relics of Saint Abdon and Saint Sennen, patron saints of the village, are believed to have been placed in it.

Its water is incorruptible and is constantly renewed, even in periods of severe drought. On religious holidays the parish priest takes out some of the water by means of a siphon, one end of which is inserted in a small opening under the cover of the sarcophagus. Between June 1 and December 1, 1951, about a hundred and fifty gallons were taken from it. The cover was reportedly sealed shut in 1795.

According to unverified reports, the water flows more

abundantly in dry weather than in wet; it overflowed only once, and that was during a very dry period.

The same phenomenon occurs in the catacombs of Rome and at Bari, Italy, where water has been oozing for eight centuries.

At Edhen, Lebanon, the tomb of Saint Abdon and Saint Sennen is in a chapel built on a rock. The Maronites celebrate their festival there on the first Sunday in May. Prince Joseph Karan, who witnessed the miracle, says that at the moment of the elevation of the Host a stream of water bursts from under the altar and continues flowing with a thunderous roar until the end of the next day.

Scientists have taken an interest in the miraculous water of Arles-sur-Tech, but without being able to explain it. A valid explanation would no doubt involve a process of accelerated transmutation of the marble into water. In 1911 the parish priest deposited the sum of a thousand francs with a local notary, to be paid to anyone who could solve the mystery. The money is still on deposit in Perpignan.

Saint Martin's Stones

In a meadow at Linards, France, beside the road that runs from Linards to Brand-Bueix, there are four stones of a kind that cannot be found elsewhere. They are called 'Saint Martin's stones' because the good saint is said to have left the imprints of his knees and fists in them. Even in dry weather, these hollows are always full of water.

Another hole in a stone, this one on a little island near the mill at Salas, France, 'is always half full of water, even in the middle of the hottest summers, and even though it is above the level of the river.' ('Pierres à légendes et pierres curieuses du Limousin,' by Albert Goursaud, in *Etudes Limousines,* October, 1969.)

At the foot of a fir in the Châteauneuf forest is a rock with a funnel-shaped hole that is always full of water, winter and summer. In the same Haute-Vienne region, there are three other rocks with holes that always contain water: at Quenouille, Bussières-Boffy, and Saint-Laurent-sur-Gorre.

All these rocks are granitic, with small cavities in their

surface which the prehistorian Albert Goursaud explains by the disintegration of feldspar from the effect of erosion. In a few cases they seem to be manmade.

'These cavities,' writes Albert Goursaud, 'have the extraordinary property of keeping water in all seasons. On the few occasions when they become dry, a powder resembling coal cinders is found at the bottom of them. Both the water and the powder have miraculous health-giving powers for people and animals. The peasants carefully gather and preserve them.'

This water, practically inexhaustible, seems to be related to the mother water of the Fountain of Youth.

Medieval traditions say that the dead should be buried under oozings of water – no doubt in the hope of resurrection.

In certain monasteries the bodies of outstanding people were mysteriously buried in places that were directly under a rainspout. It is easy to guess why.

The Astrological Stone of La Merlière

In 1905, at the farm of La Merlière in the commune of Poiré-sur-Vie, France, the prehistorian Marcel Baudoin discovered a block of granular schist on which Celts had carved strange designs.

'These carvings,' he wrote, 'are prehistoric writing older than Egyptian hieroglyphics. They include more than two hundred round cavities, some of them surrounded by a circle. Bearing in mind that the top of the photograph is south, the centre circle, near the north edge, is composed of three concentric circular grooves, from which two straight, deep grooves extend northward, representing the north-south meridian and the line of the solstices (angle of sixty degrees). Beside it is another figure, a circle with two grooves. These are images of the sun at noon and the rising sun of the summer solstice. The other circles or rings are the principal stars, probably of the Pleiades.

'All the round cavities are stars of the sky. With these figures there are also about twenty crosses with one rather long branch. Several of them are on the equinoctial line.

13 Reincarnation and Parallel Universes

Reincarnation is the phenomenon by which a soul passes from a dead body into the body of a newborn baby. If a person's life has been pure, his soul is transferred to a noble body and will have few reincarnations before reaching God's heaven or the stage of perfect being. Otherwise, his soul will undergo penitences and will have to accomplish a long cycle of purifying peregrinations, in proportion to his past shortcomings and merits, represented by karma, or subjection to the linkage of causes.

Karma is the weight of our sins, but also of the debt contracted by our ancestors, which seems to indicate that they are reincarnated in us (from a certain angle of understanding). The law of karma is that every sin must be expiated in a later life.

In the doctrine of the Rosicrucians, the law of karma 'is, with reincarnation, the only rational and satisfactory explanation of the apparent injustice of the inequalities of life. It is universal and applies to all levels of creation, from the infinitely small to the infinitely great.'

The term 'apparent injustice' gives us to understand that the explanations are equally 'apparent.' Reincarnation and karma probably have another meaning in the secret doctrine of the Rosicrucians.

The theory of reincarnation has several variants: palingenesis, metensomatosis, and, especially, metempsychosis (from the Greek *metempsukhosis*, 'transmigration of the soul') which goes back to the earliest ages of the world.

No Reincarnation among the Egyptians

Spiritualism is based on the existence of spirits of the dead and the manifestations by which they make themselves known to the living. It is an art that makes use, in its own way, of souls not yet reincarnated, whether they are waiting in the Beyond or reside there permanently.

Before taking on its present name, reincarnation was called metempsychosis. According to Herodotus, metempsychosis was born in Egypt: 'The Egyptians are also the first to have mentioned the doctrine according to which the human soul is immortal. At the time of bodily death, the soul passes into another creation that is being born at that same time. When it has successively passed into all creatures on land, in the sea, and in the air, it again enters a human body at the moment of birth. It completes this cycle in three thousand years.'

This theory, in my opinion, has nothing in common with the reincarnation of spiritualists because it involves passing through all the realms of nature. Stated more explicitly, it means that the living principle of all things returns to the totality of the universe for a new cycle and that after an end of the world (fragmentation and restructuring of the universe) it again animates a human body.

Pythagoras Did Not Believe in It Either

During his stay in Egypt, Pythagoras became familiar with this theory (which is properly a cosmogony) and brought it back to Greece, where it was interpreted in various ways.

Pythagoras is unequivocal on this point: in his teaching, souls (and he did not mean 'an immaterial substance') impregnate all of nature, including so-called inert matter (sand, stones, earth) as well as plants, animals, and men. According to Cicero (*De Natura Deorum*, XI, 27), Pythagoras said that God was a soul which extended to all beings of nature, and from which human beings were drawn.

The Master could not have been mistaken.

The metempsychosis of the Pythagoreans was repeated indefinitely, without order, with no apparent goal and no fixed rule. It was a game of universal life, in accordance with the law of chance as expounded by Professor Jacques Monod.

Misunderstood, the theory was attacked by the Epicureans. They objected (not without reason, said the Encyclopedists) that if we had lived an earlier life, we would remember what we had done.

As Professor André Bouguenac has said, what is the good of being reincarnated if we have no memory of our previous lives? If we are reincarnated, it is hidden from us very effectively and is therefore not something we should know. Nature always reveals what it is good for us to know. Why not trust her?

The Epicureans also based their objection on the uniform character of animals. Lions, they said, are always brave, and deer are always timid; this would be inexplicable if the soul of a deer could pass into the body of a lion.

The Souls of the Dead Waiting?

If reincarnation is bound up with procreation and the transmission of hereditary traits (and it obviously depends on procreation, in the sense that without procreation our species would die out and human reincarnation would become impossible), that is, if a dead person's soul passes immediately into the body of a newborn baby, what becomes of the baby's own soul?

If the souls of the dead wait somewhere, it is hard to imagine where that place might be! And why should they wait, since the goal of life, in the concept of reincarnation, is to permit the refinement of our psychic qualities so that we may succeed in identifying ourselves with God?

For the ancient Lithuanians, the lives of men and the lives of trees were often connected. If, after a man's death, the tree he had loved did not wither, it meant that his soul had passed into that tree. The Australian aborigines believe that the souls of their ancestors inhabit them and reside in their personal talismans, or *churangas*.

Reincarnation is not Canonical

Most religions accept reincarnation, but not the Christian, Jewish, and Moslem religions, although their rejection of it can be debated.

There are those who believe that the theory of reincarnation, systematically maintained within the framework of religion, is responsible for the periodic famines, chronic poverty, and technological backwardness of India.

The theory of the transmigration of souls (reincarnation in lower species) is even more unjust: what contempt it shows for animals and plants!

We must still determine how reincarnation is defined.

In the Bhagavadgita it is the way of spiritual purification and final union with God. 'As a man casts off his worn-out garments and takes new ones, the inhabitant of the body casts off the worn-out body and enters a new one . . . For he who is born is certain to die, and he who dies is certain to be born. Therefore one must not lament the inevitable.'

The Koran, more finely shaded, leaves room for multiple interpretations: 'God engenders beings and they return unceasingly until they are identified with him,' which must indicate a constant mixing of life, and of all lives, for the purpose of a general elevation, since Mohammed banishes reincarnation from his teaching.

Biologists Say No

On the theory that reincarnation introduces a more refined soul into the body of a newborn child, what becomes of the original soul of the child? For he has a soul attached to his material body, to the personality that is already programmed in the genetic code bequeathed to him by his parents, the memory chromosomes in which the hereditary message is inscribed.

Within the framework of evolution it is foreseeable that in the near future biologists will be able to alter genes, to correct or eliminate the genes of idiocy, criminality, cruelty, selfishness, fear, etc. Already, by the use of drugs, gases, or electrical stimulations, it is possible to transform a daredevil into a coward and vice versa. It is no secret that certain tranquillizers completely change the personality.

Will we some day see the reincarnation of an evil man's soul in the body of someone whom doctors have artificially made gentle and kind for his whole life?

Already, in Paris, Berlin, London, and New York, thousands of people conditioned by tranquillizers are leading honourable lives, whereas without the intervention of a doctor, an intervention irrelevant to their merit and good will, they would be antisocial, irascible, and dangerous.

Has the scientist substituted himself for God? Has he circumvented God's intentions? Is he more powerful than God? Certainly not, if he is part of God himself. Be that as it may, however, the theory of reincarnation, as it is generally understood, has now been vitiated, since doctors, biologists, and chemists have the power to make it inoperative.

Everything seems to indicate that, at death, all the psychic acquisitions of the individual revert to the universal living mass, for the benefit of all.

An Idealist's Eschatology

For the sage, the prospect of giving himself to the least favoured of his fellow men is an infinitely higher ideal than hope of personal reward. Did not even God sacrifice himself to bring about the birth of the human race?

In the Assyro-Babylonian cosmogony, Marduk and Bel sacrificed themselves and gave their blood so that humanity could be born: clay moistened with that blood served to model the first men. Uranos was sacrificed by Kronos, and from his blood came the Giants and the Furies, but also the beautiful Aphrodite. The Egyptian god Atum drew the first divine couple from himself, without the aid of a woman. In Scandinavian mythology, humanity came from the blood of the giant Ymir. The first human couple was born of the sacrifice of Gayomart, according to Aryan mythology. Similarly, subordinate gods sacrificed themselves for the creation or salvation of men: Orpheus, Adonis, Attis, Osiris, Zoroaster, Jesus.

The concept of giving oneself to one's fellow man ennobles and spiritualizes the individual. Instead of evolving toward

a selfless goal, a 'bourgeois capitalist' eschatology, he works
and 'alchemizes' within the general framework of all worlds,
for the benefit of the least favoured, the 'proletarians' of
nature, the limestone of a hill, the rose in a garden, the
donkey in a meadow. He magnifies himself by his sacrifice,
rises by lowering himself. He then identifies himself with
God, who is also characterized by self-sacrifice and self-
abasement.

God stoops to man; man stoops to his brother the pebble
on the ground. These marvellous images sanctify evolution.

Is this not the secret doctrine of Buddha, the doctrine
that flows not from esoteric Buddhism, but from the thought
of the Bodhisattva who liked to identify himself with his
brother the grain of sand?

In the twentieth century it is hard to accept a theory that
seems to belong to a bygone time when the mysteries of
biology were still almost completely impenetrable. Biologists
and physiologists do not acknowledge the principle of reincarnation, except in the sense that the constituent matter
of human beings, and even their psychic and electric properties, pass into the realm of nature.

This is no doubt what is meant by the return to God and
communion with the universe.

God as an entity, monad, or pure spirit has no need of
our spiritual contribution; he already has the maximum
amount of spirituality. God as the universe, however, in his
hypostases or states, at the levels of minerals, plants, and
lower animals, needs the subtler, more elaborate and more
refined contribution of the higher realm, so that evolution can
take place and the level of thought will constantly rise.

The Great Fear of the Common Man

Belief in purgatory and hell comes from the idealistic concept of a reward for the good and punishment for the
wicked, and perhaps still more from fear of death, aroused
by the instinct of self-preservation.

The system assumes the existence of a kind of celestial
railroad station with waiting-rooms for souls and three
categories of tickets: first class (heaven), second class (pur-

gatory), and third class (hell). Such complexity seems to belong to the human imagination rather than to the universal or divine order.

At the dawn of the world this necessary belief was elaborated by the weak or by initiates in order to curb brute power. Intelligence had already shown its supremacy over force.

To a simple mind it seems incompatible with morality, as it is conceived by men, that the wicked should be able to live their perverse lives without being inevitably punished by divine justice. Otherwise, why should anyone be good and just and obey the rules of society? (This is the voice of selfishness: be good, provided you are rewarded for it!) The view reflects an understandable human feeling, but it fails to take account of universal laws.

It is certain that any infraction of the laws of the universe is a serious and even unforgivable crime which has adverse effects on general evolution, and therefore on human society.

Is God good when he lets a church collapse onto his worshippers or allows a man to die in an attempt to save another's life? Is nature good when she kills a sage, gives a sickly body to a newborn baby, or dries up a well in the desert? No, according to human morality; but universal law takes no account of that morality and obeys a superior intelligence.

Another feeling motivates belief in reincarnation: fear.

The believer is capable of all sorts of compromises to assure *the security of his conscience*. It is often because he regards himself as a 'loser in the game of life' that he takes refuge in beliefs that can give him the self-esteem he needs. Convinced that he is in possession of transcendent knowledge, he cannot accept the idea that his little self, judged to be insignificant on the scale of values of ordinary life, will some day disappear and be absorbed into the great, triumphant matrix of nature.

Pythagoras, Albert Einstein, Salvador Dali, the biologist, the mathematician, the physician, and the upright man whose posterity is assured by a large and healthy family know very well that they will some day return to the bosom of nature, but this thought arouses no fear in them. They have accomplished their task; they know that they will be immortal, either as the result of their work or through the children in whom they recognize themselves.

But a man of rather limited intellect whose life has been a 'failure' can comfort himself by believing in cycles of reincarnation that will enable him to achieve his aspirations in another life.

In general, those who believe in reincarnation are sensitive but have difficulty in adapting to society.

These considerations are contradicted by people who claim to be a reincarnation of someone else. Such people are rare, and rationalists deny the validity of their claims, but they do exist.

The unknown reality of universal phenomena is so fantastic that anything we consider impossible in our three-dimensional universe may be possible in a universe with four or five dimensions.

Changing Orbits and Universes

Parallel universes are not merely a figment of the imagination or a working hypothesis: physicists have demonstrated their existence and certain characteristics of them that are still incomprehensible.

I have already described (in *Le Livre du Mystérieux Inconnu,* Chapter XIII) the 'singular phenomena' that take place at the level of the atom, to the great astonishment of physicists: particles changing their orbit, while at the same time remaining, in a sense, in their initial orbit.

Certain waves, studied by many scientists, including Professor Bernard d'Espagnat of the Collège de France, have the gift of ubiquity: they can pass *totally* through one opening and at the same time pass *totally* through another one beside it. It is as if a thread could pass through the eyes of two needles placed side by side, simultaneously.

It would seem that each particle can be both single and double, which appears to violate the elementary laws of our science.

Such observations are frequent in nuclear physics. They have led the Masters to consider the concept of a parallel universe, or even multiple parallel universes.

And what seems to be true of atoms and molecules,

studied from a mathematical viewpoint, may also be true of all stages of matter, organic or inorganic: men, animals, plants, and objects.

The Soul

These facts, studied only in a laboratory, presuppose on the level of the human individual, among other concepts, a nature that is subtle and capable of being integrated into all possible universes, that is, of binding us to the great Whole. I believe that this third nature is what spiritualists call the soul.

The soul is the only human element that has a permanent or accidental induction with certain phenomena called supranormal or miraculous. By its immaterial nature, it belongs not only to our three-dimensional world but also to others, governed by systems of four, eight or n dimensions. The authenticity of a parallel world which penetrates us, but which we perceive either not at all or only indistinctly, is recognized by everyone, from empirics to mathematicians.

We are advancing farther and farther into this system, thanks to the fantastic development of science, particularly the science of electromagnetic waves in television and radio. Anyone who takes part in a television broadcast knows that countless 'selves,' beyond his perception, people the totality of space. Invisible, intangible, yet real, they instantaneously go to millions of distant places and have an existence apparently identical with what takes place in the broadcasting studio, except that they have only two dimensions.

Four ... Eight ... N Dimensions

Man is born, lives, and dies in a universe of which his consciousness and his sensory faculties give him only an incomplete image; more precisely, an image whose colours and general form are within the reach of his coarse senses.

The essence or 'interior' of the universe constitutes the Mysterious Unknown.

This Mysterious Unknown, probably governed by a system with four, eight, or n dimensions, is made dynamic by forces that would certainly be regarded as miracles in our three-dimensional universe.

In a four-dimensional universe as I imagine it, a man in a hermetically closed prison could leave it and return to it at will. We can form a certain idea of this by means of the intellectual recreation known as the 'bottle with neither an inside nor an outside.'

In a five-dimensional universe it would probably be possible to live consciously in both the Middle Ages and the twentieth century, simultaneously. With six dimensions, a man could simultaneously be dead, be alive, hunt aurochses in prehistoric times on earth, pilot a spacecraft to Sirius and transmute himself by the power of thought. In an eight-dimensional universe, anything would no doubt be possible, from travel in time and space to integration into different realms of nature.

Such universes do not necessarily have the structure of the one we know so imperfectly. It may be that an eight-dimensional universe, for example, is analogous to an algebraic equation or the domain of the dream-idea.

These speculations on the unknown have different names: depending on the personality of the thinking being, they may be called science, magic, spiritualism, knowledge, or madness.

Parallel Universes and the Total Universe

In our universe we derive our concept of space-time from a continuous movement that appears to go from the past to the present and from the present to the future. It seems that in reality this concept is strongly conditioned by the three dimensions that govern us. Scientists and spiritualists alike believe that at a higher level, that of universal intelligence or God, time is eternally present.

This conjecture presupposes the existence of an infinite number of harmonics (waves having multiple frequencies of the initial wave) of the present, and an infinite number of selves simultaneously living all phases of life on chains of waves that are infinite in length. This is analogous to what happens with a non-selective radio receiver, in which a broadcast on the hundred-metre band, for example, can be received at all multiples of a hundred, theoretically to infinity.

These harmonics are doubles, phantoms of real life; although they can be received by a radio, they are not perceptible to our senses and therefore constitute parallel universes. The total universe, with four, eight, or n dimensions, or the Supreme Intelligence, is infinitely more complex than ours. We must assume that it includes forms of life unknown to us.

These other inhabitants could be forces, force-ideas, or formal creatures. Their matter might even be in the form of pure, intangible energy.

On this hypothesis, a universe populated by souls of a subtle nature, participating in all universal dimensions, is not a ridiculous concept, but a perfectly logical one.

And so, without abandoning the scientific viewpoint, we are led to conceive of a self that is a persistent double, living in another world after what is called the death of the physical body.

In our three-dimensional universe, matter upon death loses all chance of living again, but the soul remains intact indefinitely, capable of being 'received' like a radio broadcast, provided the receiver is tuned to the right 'wave length.'

Establishing communication between our world and others means opening the way to 'reincarnation.'

It is possible for the neophyte to attain superior knowledge by his work and merit alone, and acquire the genetic code of a Master by a kind of biological alchemy within the conscious and unconscious realms.

A Scientific Process

To sum up, part of a person's self remains bound up with the earthly cycle of his constituent elements, while at death another part, the soul, seems to change orbit like the singular particles of the atom, to rejoin the double of the self that already resides in another universe, parallel or total.

Soul-transference is a purely scientific and electromagnetic phenomenon. It can be explained in a very approximate manner by the following descriptions and images.

1) The soul or a harmonic of every living creature resides in another universe whose laws, structure, and number of dimensions are unknown to us. For a believer, this universe is the thought, word, or breath of God or Brahma. For a physicist, it might be the sum of all possible universes, or the total universe.

2) When an individual dies, part of his soul remains attached to his constituent elements and the other part passes into a parallel universe where it reinforces its harmonic.

3) Each body and each soul has its own specificity, *analogous* to a wave length, which gives the individual his personality.

4) Each physical body (or support) is a receiver tuned to the individual's personal 'wave length.'

5) When an individual is born with a specificity identical to that of a soul existing in a parallel universe, he 'receives' that soul, which fuses with his own.

6) There may be a few physical differences between his body and that of the other soul, but, having the same genetic code and 'wave length,' he becomes a double of the dead man, with an identical intelligence and soul.

7) Initiates have the power of favouring and accelerating this phenomenon of identity.

8) The coincidence cannot be absolutely perfect. There are interferences which give priority sometimes to the first soul, sometimes to the other. This explains the duality that exists in the individual.

9) Unknown Masters are descendants and reincarnations of the great initiates of antiquity.

Part 5

APOCALYPSE

14 Protest

I am not a man who wants to ask you for money or your daughter's hand, so I will tell you the truth.

— Arab saying.

The riots and violent protest demonstrations of 1968 did not surprise those who had attentively studied the general tendencies of social evolution.

To understand these events, we must turn back to the social upheavals of the past: to the student protests of 1407, for example, or, more recently, to the surrealists' agitation in 1927.

At that time, André Breton and other thinkers of the far left launched radically new concepts in the arts, for the purpose of overthrowing the values of a society that was already disintegrating. The general idea was to plunge the bourgeoisie into an apocalyptic atmosphere, confuse the government, and influence its policies. Surrealism gained a dominant position in the arts, but the expected social revolution did not take place. The time had not yet come.

Three Solar Cycles

It is possible to believe that in 1966 and 1967 a very secret conspiracy decided that the times were about to be right for a renewal of the attempt of 1927.

With or without a conspiracy, however, the evolution of the world had to take a decisive turn at that time, for many reasons, the two main ones being that the abscess had reached the point where it had to burst, and that there were cosmic interactions which would necessarily bring about an acceleration of history.

The fateful year was 1968, when solar conjunctions irrevocably disturbed the electromagnetic field of human beings, animals, plants, and even so-called inert matter. An extremely rare phenomenon occurred in 1968: there were three conjunctions of solar cycles at almost the same time.

The eleven-year cycle (ten to twelve years) is well known by the effects of its winds. Another, of four hundred to four hundred and fifty years, increases in intensity for four hundred years, then diminishes for the next four hundred. A cycle of twenty-five hundred years is in correlation with periods of glacial advance and minimum solar activity.

The primary consequence was that the earth's magnetic field was greatly disturbed. As a secondary effect, its variations acted strongly on human electromagnetic behaviour. It was therefore within the natural order of things that glaciers, the earth, plants, and all animal species should be affected by the phenomenon. This was evidenced in avalanches, earthquakes, and cellular, physiological, and psychic perturbations.

Electric induction between the earth's magnetic field and human electric complexes made people inclined toward irascibility and protest.

Everything that is fluid was seriously perturbed in all realms: blood (myocardial infarct), sap, manufacture of silk fabrics, nylon, and viscose. The silk manufactures of Lyon had to cope with strange and often incomprehensible accidents.

The electric climate was propitious to all sorts of violence (robbery, murder, rape, war), perhaps also to all great undertakings, and in any case to those of which one does not usually think.

There were protest demonstrations all over the world, even in places where they were least expected, such as universities in Senegal, Gabon, and Madagascar. There was capitalistic protest: too much French capital was going abroad; religious protest in the Vatican and among bishops; Soviet communist protest against the Israelis; military protest: for the first time, soldiers were disturbed by problems of conscience.

Even Animals Protested

I have questioned a number of veterinarians who recall that in May, 1968, animals were skittish, agitated, and hard to treat. In circuses, animal tamers had difficulty in preventing lions and tigers from attacking them. In Siberia, wolves came out of the forests in packs, which was unusual at that time of year.

Plants were also perturbed. Young trees died for no apparent reason. Apple trees yielded an extraordinary harvest: the apples were exceptionally numerous, but very small.

Avalanches were particularly murderous, notably in France. Earthquakes in Chile, China, and Peru were national catastrophes.

Three hundred people died in a train wreck in Argentina. The French submarine *Minerve* sank in the Mediterranean on January 27, 1968, and two years later the *Eurydice,* another French submarine of the same type, was lost under the same mysterious circumstances.

As for armed conflicts, they became considerably more violent, whether in occupied Egypt or in Vietnam.

Apocalyptic Times

The influence of the earth's magnetic field did not act only on the behaviour of young people: all vital forces in all nations were placed in a state of revolution.

Sociologists, scientists, and all the other intellectual masters who actually rule the world launched slogans and philosophical doctrines designed to disrupt the somnolence and selfish complacency of the sybaritic West. Professors Jacob, Jacobson, Lhéritier, Lévi-Strauss, Monod, etc., conceived structuralism and new ways of thinking the world, mathematicians envisioned new mathematics, and so, from level to level, from escalation to escalation, all hierarchies and all accepted values were placed in question.

In France, students – disturbed and agitated by the aftermath of World War II and the Resistance, the invasion of drugs, the hippie phenomenon, the collapse of religion and social order, the eroticism that had come from America and

Scandinavia; contaminated by films, television, radio, the
press, and misleading textbooks; assailed night and day by bad
singers, aggressive music, and tendentious news reporting –
felt an irresistible call to reform.

The deterioration of the West naturally coincides with
the unleashing of powerful anger among students.

Our Judea-Christian civilization is unquestionably moribund
in the eyes of those who dare to study the past and conjecture the future. It has been branded by the Hebrews and
the Catholics, marked by bloodshed, destruction, genocide,
and privilege as much as by the prodigious creation of
cathedrals and a form of life which, in many ways, has
been attractive and admirable.

More than other young people, perhaps because they are
more sensitive, students have been acted upon by occult
forces emanating from the cosmos, and no doubt also by
a kind of idealism that has come from messianic China.

Mao Tse-tung

Like Jesus, Mao Tse-tung denounces arbitrary power, racism,
and injustice. He says that 'the first will be the last.' To
his followers he is God, the Messiah of the Jews, the Jesus
of the Christians, the man who chastises evildoers and exposes
them to public opprobrium under the name of Children of
Darkness.

Sacred writings, traditions, the Bible, and the Dead Sea
Scrolls are in agreement on this point: the saviour of the
world will be a *Teacher of Righteousness.*

He will come to assure the sole survival of the Children
of Light, that is, the good, humble, poor, and charitable. The
wicked will be punished and will perish. And, speaking in
terms of justice, who are the wicked? They are the powerful,
the rich, bankers, judges, pimps of politics and business, mag-
nates, popes, spiritual misguiders, hippies . . . and protest
demonstrators. For men will be judged by their true worth,
weighed with unrigged scales. And that is what frightens us
Occidentals so much!

Yet what do we really deserve? We have held most of
the world's wealth, science, and power, and what have we
done with it? Which of us, in the inner depths of his con-

science, does not hear the lamentations of slaves, victims of sacrifice, men sent into the slaughter of battle, martyrized animals? Prisoners of arbitrary power, human beings burned by the Inquisition and the Nazis, dogs callously murdered, guinea pigs put to death in slow agony – their wails rise from the darkness to accuse and curse us.

I do not think that the Teacher of Righteousness is Mao Tse-tung, and still less a Jew or a Christian, but in the minds of the protest demonstrators the Saviour of their desire-images closely resembled the master of China: implacable, inaccessible, incorruptible, a man who had come to chastise with fire and the sword. 'You must not think that I have come to bring peace to the earth; I have not come to bring peace, but a sword.' (Matthew 10:34.) Mao Tse-tung speaks of real love: replacing love with justice.

Love: a Satanic Concept

The greatest revolution, which will come from the Orient, will be the abolition of the notion of love that has been the basic principle of Christian philosophy. Not that love is fundamentally pernicious, on the contrary; but it becomes so when it is erected into a social system, because it includes privilege.

Let us take the case of a rich, powerful man who has an only son. This son is neurotic, cruel, and unscrupulous; we may even say that he is a murderer. Yet it is to him that the father will bequeath his factory and the fate of hundreds or thousands of workers, for the father loves his son. The result will be an avalanche of misfortune, injustice, and ruin. The concept of love will have prevailed in the father.

If he acted on the basis of justice, would he not eliminate the 'rotten apple' for the benefit of the healthy majority? Would he not turn over the management of his factory to the best and most highly qualified man he could find?

The concept of love essentially involves a privilege that is given to someone, nearly always wrongly. A man loves his mother even if she is a thief or a murderess, and he will try to protect her against everyone. It is permissible to love such a mother, but one must also love those she has killed. It is here that the weakness in the concept of love appears.

It is obvious that justice must intervene when love threatens to harm society. Justice contains love, but the converse is not true. The just man must first of all love the universal, the human. All men are our fathers or our brothers, all women are our mothers or our sisters. In its deepest essence, love must extend to all realms and forms of existence, from a grain of sand to the person we cherish most emotionally. The grain of sand must not be sacrificed, and this rule of integrity takes the name of justice.

God does not concern himself with considerations of love when he causes a supernova to explode, winter to follow autumn, an island to emerge, or a continent to sink below the ocean.

The Law is the Law, made for all universes, with no other purpose than order and justice.

The Man on a Donkey and the Man in a Rolls-Royce

Benjamin Mendoza y Amor, the Bolivian painter who tried to assassinate Pope Paul VI during his visit to Manila, said later, 'I wanted to rid the world of Christian superstition and the hypocrisy of the Pope.'

In a similar frame of mind, other protesters booed Paul VI when he accepted the hospitality of the rich, powerful, and ostentatious Bishop of Manila, and when he rode to a slum neighbourhood in a Rolls-Royce before walking to pay a 'comforting' visit to the people who lived there. One of these protesters had the clever idea of following the Holy Father through the city, riding on a donkey, 'to teach a lesson of humility to the man in the Rolls-Royce.'

The Protesters of 1407

Events are being repeated at an accelerated rate. Besides the Children's Crusade, twentieth-century student protest had other precedents in French history.

In the Middle Ages, the University had great religious and political influence. Secular science was neglected and the notion of authority – 'The Master said so' – had the force of law, as in the time of Aristotle.

In 1407, during the reign of Charles VI, Guillaume, Lord of Tignonville and Provost of Paris, ordered the arrest of two students of the University on a charge of robbery and homicide. He offered to let the University try them, but it refused to acknowledge them as belonging to it. He sentenced them to be hanged, which was done.

The Duke de Bourgogne, who had reason to hate the provost personally, stirred up opposition to him among the students of the Nation of Normandy,[1] to which one of the hanged students belonged. The whole University soon rose up in rebellion to protest against the violation of its privileges. The schools were closed. When the king seemed to approve of the provost's conduct, the University declared that since its honour had been insulted by the infringement of its right of sanctuary, it would move to another country. Charles VI immediately ordered the provost to take the corpses down from the gallows in person, kiss them on the mouth, and pay the expenses of the funeral. The provost was then dismissed from his office.

The scandalous privilege that the University enjoyed was based on its 'universal' nature, instituted not by Charlemagne, as is generally believed, but by Philip Augustus, who gave it inalienable rights and named it the University because it embraced the universality of the arts and sciences, as well as the universality of masters and pupils. The University, like the Church, was beyond the jurisdiction of secular justice in criminal cases. Philip Augustus commanded all burghers to denounce and even arrest anyone who struck a scholar, and scholars' homes were declared to be inviolable.

This privilege fell into decay by the end of the sixteenth century, but the student protesters of 1968 tried to revive it.

---

[1] The University was divided into five provinces: the Nation of Picardy, divided into five tribes; the Nation of Normandy; the Nation of Germany, divided into two tribes; the Nation of the Continents, subdivided into two provinces; and the Nation of Islanders, which took in the British Isles.

Beethoven and the Pétomane

Protest is now directed against every principle of authority. The sun lights the earth? That remains to be proved!

Without going so far as to deny such obvious facts, we can take it as a certainty that the hierarchy of human values is a hoax perpetrated by conspirators.

The 'great' painters of the current artistic scene, the 'great' literary prizes awarded by conventional-minded and perfectly odourless juries to even more conventional-minded and odourless writers, and the 'great' pundits of radio, television, and the press are equalled only by the famous unknowns (with a few exceptions) of the French Academy, which is at least the best-dressed institution in France.

On November 27, 1970, a Velázquez painting was sold at auction in London. It was bought by Mr Wildenstein, of New York and Paris, for the tidy sum of $5,544,000.

Salvador Dali, a brilliant protester and at least as good a painter as Velázquez, was the only one who made a sensible remark about 'the most expensive painting in the world': 'the picture is abominably painted, pompous, and banal. It can appeal only to schizophrenic snobs and lovers of art and bouillon cubes. Its price is in direct proportion to its total lack of interest.'

An *agent provocateur,* Salvador Dali only said aloud what millions of people, too cowardly to state their opinion openly, thought to themselves.

Yet the time has now come when anyone can loudly express indignation at seeing such men as Racine, Molière, and Corneille inscribed in the curricula of our schools. Protesters do not hesitate to say that they are plagiarists and windbags, that Rembrandt is a bore, Courbet a bungler, and Ingres a hack. Few 'geniuses' find favour in their eyes. Leonardo da Vinci is congenitally awkward; Michelangelo is a pederast who draws men and then adds breasts and long hair to make them into women (it is true!); as for César Franck, Bach, Beethoven, and other sound-mixers, they are to the bourgeoisie what the *pétomane*[1] of the Exposition of 1900 was to the masses.

---

[1] The *pétomane* (from *pet,* 'fart') was a performer who enter-

Salvador Dali was speaking in essentially the same vein when he said, 'Since earliest childhood I have been addicted to the vice of behaving and regarding myself as the opposite of ordinary mortals. I have always been successful at it.'

In a world where one can succeed by turning everything upside down, protest is not a sign of degeneracy, but of a mobilization of the critical sense. Dali defines it as follows: 'Protest, like eroticism, is the monarchical principle which, cybernetically, flows in the molecular structures of deoxyribonucleic acid.'

The great Chinese philosopher Confucius said more simply, 'A father should have a son who argues.'

tained his audiences with his ability to emit varied and abundant sounds from his anus. (Translator's note.)

15 Eroticism

The word 'lingam' comes from the Sanskrit *linga*, 'penis.'
A lingam is a representation of the penis, worshipped in
India as a symbol of the god Shiva. Hindu theogony (genealogy of the gods) states that 'when the fourteen worlds were
formed, with the axis that traverses them, and Mount
Kailasha above, the triangle yoni [vulva] appeared at the
top of the mountain, and, in the yoni, the lingam.'

This lingam is prudishly called the 'tree of life' in other
religions.

The Tree of Life

The Bible speaks of the 'tree of life' and the 'tree of the
knowledge of good and evil' in the middle of the Garden
of Eden. In Genesis we read:

'The Lord God made trees spring from the ground, all
trees pleasant to look at and good for food; and in the
middle of the garden he set the tree of life and the tree of
the knowledge of good and evil.' (2:9)

'The woman answered the serpent, "We may eat the
fruit of any tree in the garden, except for the tree in the
middle of the garden; God has forbidden us either to eat or
to touch the fruit of that; if we do, we shall die." The serpent said, "Of course you will not die. God knows that as
soon as you eat it, your eyes will be opened and you will
be like gods, knowing both good and evil." When the woman
saw that the fruit of the tree was good to eat, and that it
was pleasing to the eye and tempting to contemplate, she took
some and ate it. She also gave her husband some and he ate
it.' (3:2-6.)

The rest of the story is well known: God becomes angry

and Adam ungallantly puts the blame on Eve: 'The man said,
"The woman you gave me for a companion, she gave me
fruit from the tree and I ate it." ' (3:12.) Then Eve in turn
blames the persuasive serpent: 'The woman said, "The
serpent tricked me, and I ate." ' (3:13.)

The raw truth shows through this bowdlerized and deteriorated account and sheds light on the general history of
all civilizations.

The Bible thus states that in the middle of paradise, which
has the shape of a man with his legs and arms spread, there
is a kind of living phallic menhir, represented by the serpent; that is, in the middle of paradise, which is a place of
pleasure, is the phallic tree of life. Four rivers extend from
paradise: the arms and legs. (Many menhirs, at Tiahuanaco,
for example, are in the shape of a phallus with a serpent
carved on it.)

Foolishly, it must be admitted, God has declared that
this menhir is taboo. Adam, simpleton that he is, is willing to
obey, but Eve already has all the shrewdness and cunning of
a pretty woman, and also (since she is more instinctive and
voluptuous than her husband) an innate need to sin. She
does not think of having children and leaving descendants, not
at all: she finds the fruit of the tree of life attractive, good
to eat, and valuable for the intellect.

Original Sin

The marvellous Eve has much more in her lovely flesh
than servile obedience and Judeo-Christian indoctrination;
she has common sense, genius, and a passionate temperament.
She commits *the real original sin*.

Adam is too thickheaded to understand. He does not
even realize that he is the first deceived husband in history.

All this may seem like nothing but a racy story or an
impertinent tale by Sade or LaFontaine, but from it arise
the dominant idea and the basic mythology of all the world's
civilizations: the emblem and worship of the phallus, which
engenders all animal life, and of the Mater whose fertile vulva
is represented by the cave, the cup, and the 'Mystic Almond'
from which the human race emerged.

Yet, by an incredible aberration, in Christian theology

the Mystic Almond is a symbol of the Holy Virgin's *virginity*, even though it is represented, around her images, as radiant and open wide.

This almond may have been the origin of the Gothic arch.

Christian tradition says that the mystic meaning attached to the Tree of Jesse, which blossomed in one night and bore an almond, must be regarded as the origin of the symbol.

This is indeed very symbolic, but it sheds no light on the first love story of our world. With whom did Eve commit her sin, if not with Adam? With the menhir-serpent? This is the opinion of certain exegetists, who point out that if the serpent *spoke*, it must have meant that he (and no doubt other animals) had an intelligence that was at least as well developed as man's, and much richer in experience, since it was older.

Did Eve sin with an animal, as Orejona did (with a tapir) to create humanity in the kingdom of the pre-Incas? This hypothesis is less preposterous than one might think. It would explain, by a badly transmitted old myth, the enigmatic stories of monsters that were half human and half animal, as well as the reason why the jealous God of the Hebrews preserved them from infamous fornications that would have been harmful to the human race; and finally, it would enable us to give an acceptable meaning to *original sin*.

The Lingam

According to Indian sacred writings, the lingam, or tree of life, had three layers of bark: the outer layer was Brahma, the middle layer was Vishnu, and the innermost layer was Shiva. When the three gods had detached themselves, only the bare trunk, placed under the guard of Shiva, was left in the triangle on Mount Kailasha. On the golden mountain is a square table enriched with nine precious stones, and in the middle of it is the *padma* (lotus) containing the triangle that is the origin and source of all things. From this triangle emerges the lingam, the eternal god who makes it his eternal dwelling.

In India, the most highly venerated temples are those

of Shiva. They are always dedicated to procreation by the lingam, though Vishnu sometimes vies with Shiva for that honour, as Khajuraho and Konarak.

It is only to the uninformed, say Hindu scholars, that temples with erotic representations seem to glorify the sex act as the sublime expression of life. In deep truth, the meaning of the love-dance of man and woman is better presented in this ambiguous passage by Raja Rao than in the carvings of Khajuraho:

'Man also seeks his way toward his intimate being: leaving from the ramparts of the city, he takes the royal road, goes through the gates of the temple, passes under the arch, crosses the antechamber and the second antechamber, and reaches the womb-hearth (*gardbhagriha*). And what he contemplates at the end is not God, but his Self.' (*Les Temples de Khajuraho,* preface by Raja Rao, text by Marcel Flory, photographs by André Martin. Editions Delpire.)

In the West, our coarser senses would not be very responsive to these subtleties. If, in our speculations, matter is sometimes closely mingled with energy-spirit, it is not in the sacred language of poets, but in the profane language of scientists.

Oriental Subtlety

It is wonderful to read, in *Les Temples de Khajuraho,* how the refined Parvati speaks of love with her husband Shiva:

'Living in the world that sees only Self, you do not see human woe. Man suffers in his failures, woman in her aspirations. You made them two, so that duality would not be, yet duality and plurality subsist, and neither man nor woman knows the secret wisdom of satiety. . . . Man has lost the sap of his joy because of passion, and woman's deserted womb moans. . . .'

'Very well, then,' replied Lord Shiva, who knew this, but spoke as if innocence were lodged on his curved tongue, 'we shall have a fifth Veda which will make man virile in his knowledge and woman as supple as a betel tendril. And their wisdom will truly be total.'

Parvati later asks:

'What would happen if man *remembered* his past, his spirit, his future?'

'Oh,' replied the generous-hearted god, 'we shall give him a drink like nectar and ambrosia, which, when it has been purified by rites and hymns, will be comparable to the very essence of immortality.'

'Immortality!' said Parvati. 'You will give them immortality in mortal forms!'

'In truth,' said Shiva, 'man was born with immortality as light was born with the sun. Man will know woman and, through her, he will know Self.'

'Marvellous, my Lord, marvellous! Let there be that knowledge!'

And it was thus that the Tantra Shasta was born.

It was also the creation of the status of love, with the nectar of life dispensed during the sacred rites of struggle, and hymns with words tasting of flesh and honey.

Or, as an uninitiated Western professor would say, nectar intended to flow from the plus to the minus.

Khajuraho

Those struggles carved in stone at Khajuraho and Konarak, those rigid men, those women open to the heart – do they sing the hymn of the coming of the nectar?

Nowhere else in the world do friezes of frescoes portray eroticism with such monstrous male vigour or such lithe, lascivious, and imaginative postures. One cannot help sometimes doubting the spiritual purity of their intention, which is supposedly to symbolize the union of the soul with the divinity!

From an Occidental viewpoint, the friezes of Khajuraho are as licentious as the Song of Songs in the Bible. But is it not the ultimate refinement to sublimate what is crude and coarse? At Khajuraho, the scenes with two, three, or four 'interpenetrated' partners are said to show the sage's detachment from the pleasures of the flesh!

Khajuraho is in northern India, northwest of Agra. In

the tenth and eleventh centuries the site contained eighty-five Jainist and Brahmanist temples.

The Kinarak temple is built among the dunes on the shore of the Bay of Bengal, south of Calcutta. Its friezes depict couplings as licentious as those at Khajuraho, to 'symbolize separate principles,' but also, it is said a bit more credibly, because making love is the usual pastime of the gods.

The Strange Worship of Shiva

At Sisupatyam, on one of the gates of the town there are six naked Brahmans kneeling with their eyes fixed on Sita, the chaste wife of Rama, and offering her their virility.

Between Pondicherry and Madras there was once a famous pagoda where one could see an immense lingam wound like a snake around the bodies of several women.

At Rama Eswurim, near Cape Comorin, stands one of the most highly venerated temples of Shiva. Beggars ask for alms beside the roads, holding their lingams in their hands.

In some parts of India, young girls come to sacrifice their virginity to an idol. Duquesne reports that in Goa, before taking a husband, girls go to the temple of Shiva to give the first fruits of marriage to an iron idol that serves as a sacrificer. In other places a priest who has inherited the privilege serves the same function as this idol. In Calcutta the leading Brahman is allowed to spend a night with the girl whom the rajah is about to marry. In Jaggrenat a girl is brought at night to the priests of the temple.

In Hindu mythology, it is by taking the various postures of yoga that Shiva creates the different kinds of living creatures.

In the religion of Shiva, the lingam is the purest, most abstract representation of the creative principle. Coitus is a method of inner improvement, self-realization, and contact with the supernatural. (See *Erotisme divinisé*, by Alain Daniélou, Editions Buchet-Chastel.) The world is an immense sacrifice: no creature can exist without devouring other creatures. Matter itself exists only by combustion, and the sun is the symbol of cosmic sacrifice.

According to 'sages,' erotic representations in India have a magic and educational value; they give an image of the cosmic world.

If a temple has no erotic sculpture, says tradition, it will be destroyed by lightning. Similarly, erotic representations on houses ward off spells and the evil eye.

Is this subtlety, perversion, or hypocrisy? Or all three at once? The Oriental soul may be hard for our Occidental understanding to grasp, but not to the point of making us believe that the moon is made of green cheese!

The Song of Songs

The Song of Songs is an astonishing portion of the Old Testament. It is said to have been composed twelve centuries ago, on the occasion of one of King Solomon's numerous weddings, and it is regarded by Christians as a symbol of Christ's marriage with the Church. The Vulgate translation of the Bible gives the Song of Songs such subtitles as these: 'Eagerness of the Church to receive Jesus Christ,' 'Beauties and perfections of Jesus Christ,' 'The Church is the sole object of Jesus Christ's love,' 'Love of the Church for Jesus Christ.'

In reality, it is a poem of carnal love between Solomon (the bridegroom) and his beloved (the Bride). Here are some extracts from it:

Bride:
I will sing the song of all songs to Solomon that he may smother me with kisses. . . . I am dark but lovely, daughters of Jerusalem, like the tents of Kedar or the tent-curtains of Shalmah. Do not look down on me; a little dark I may be because I am scorched by the sun. . . . My beloved is for me a bunch of myrrh as he lies on my breast. . . . Night after night on my bed I have sought my true love; I have sought him but not found him.

Bridegroom:
I would compare you, my dearest, to Pharaoh's chariot-horses. . . . How beautiful are your breasts, my sister,

my bride! Your love is more fragrant than wine, and your perfume sweeter than any spices. Your lips drop sweetness like the honeycomb, my bride, syrup and milk are under your tongue, and your dress has the scent of Lebanon. . . . My sister, my bride, is a garden close-locked, a garden close-locked, a fountain sealed. . . The curves of your thighs are like jewels, the work of a skilled craftsman. Your navel is a rounded goblet that shall never want for spiced wine. Your belly is a heap of wheat fenced in by lilies. Your two breasts are like two fawns, twin fawns of a gazelle. . . . You are stately as a palm-tree, and your breasts are the clusters of dates. I said, 'I will climb up into the palm to grasp its fronds.' May I find your breasts like clusters of grapes on the vine, the scent of your breath like apricots.

It is all charming, in a rather childish way, but where the devil can anyone find Jesus Christ and the Holy Church in that erotic idyll?

The Apis Bull

Eroticism, or the search for sexual sensations, is not a perversion unless it involves morality or physiological danger.

The Celts honoured the phallus as a symbol of reproduction and the continuation of life. Their roughly carved menhirs were often penises, either rising from the ground, as is usually thought, or plunging *into* the entrails of the mother-earth. Was worship of them mingled with eroticism? It is rather unlikely, but we do not have enough evidence to decide with certainty.

Eroticism is a refinement beyond the intellectual scope of barbarian peoples, but it appears naturally in every advanced civilization.

The Greek celebrations in honour of Aphrodite had a licentious character that was described by ancient authors, particularly with regard to the orgiastic festivals which took place at Corinth and Paphos.

Aside from being a salutation to life, phallus worship must originally have expressed gratitude for the beneficial hybridization brought by 'angels from heaven' who came to procreate with earthly women.

The first Initiators were undoubtedly beings who possessed great knowledge, but they were also engendering males, famous heroes who became gods. The religion they inspired was later extended to engendering animals: the bull, the stag, the goat, the cock.

The Apis bull of the Egyptians was an earthly representation, a reincarnation, of the horned god Osiris. The apis bull had to be black with two white spots: a triangular one on the forehead and a crescent-shaped one on the right side. He had to have a protuberance under his tongue in the shape of a scarab beetle, two kinds of hair on his tail, etc. In all, there were twenty-nine distinctive signs.

This superstition, similar to that of the 'living Buddha' (the Dalai Lama) in Tibet, was obviously contemporaneous with the worship of Cernunnos, that is, between the Tenth and Eighteenth Dynasties.

When the Apis bull had been recognized, he was taken with great pomp to Memphis, where only women were allowed to approach him – and they asked him to make them fertile. For this purpose they lifted their skirts in front of him and presented their open vulvae to him.

The Sex Fair

The deterioration of morality and the corruption of justice in our civilization have produced reactions in twentieth-century Europe that include a phase of exacerbated eroticism. Hippie protesters have launched a movement that has led to the production of licentious films and plays. The hypocritical bourgeoisie, alarmed but prudent, has offered only flabby resistance to this offensive.

In France, however, the Protestant and prudish Salvation Army has organized protest demonstrations, particularly against *Hair*, a play in which actors appear naked on the stage and appear to give free rein to their instincts.

It must be acknowledged that, in France at least, the public tends to laugh at censors, and this is just as well, since the abscess must burst before the organism can be purged of its sickness.

In Turin, Italy, the police had to deal with black masses

in which naked girls, lying in coffins, sacrificed to Satan. A wave of uninhibited sexuality has broken over Germany. The first 'Sex Fair' was held in Copenhagen in 1969. There were live exhibitions and sadomasochistic accessories were offered for sale. The best customers of the fair were the Danes, sensible peoples in the world, peoples whose physical stamina and love of sport are clearly demonstrated in the Olympic Games!

'Mr Thestrup, the Danish Minister of Justice,' a reporter wrote in a large evening newspaper, 'a man as austere as a Lutheran pastor . . . does not hide his satisfaction with the results obtained: for the Danes, everything related to sex has lost the exciting taste of a forbidden fruit. It now takes so much to astonish them!'

Chemists have taken a decisive step in the domain of eroticism by discovering that serotonin, a substance found in the brain, has great influence on sexual behaviour. It will soon be manufactured in laboratories. It would seem that the mutant of the future will have to be the god Shiva himself!

It is undeniable that sex plays an important, even crucial part in human life and that for a long time bourgeois prudishness prevented a courageous and honest examination of the problem. As a result, women were often relegated to subordinate roles as childbreeders, housekeepers – slaves, in short. The growth of couples was stunted: two individualities remained separate, with no hope of fusion. Religions accentuated the discord still more, and ancient Oriental cults offered only ridiculous solutions to people subjugated by superstition and warped ideologies.

It was finally science that studied sex in its deep physiological nature, by means of the electromagnetic design it produces around each body: the electroaurogram.

16 The Electric Image of Sexuality

In 1968 the biologists Pavel Guliaev, Vladimir Jabotin, and Nina Schlippenbach, of the University of Leningrad, published an article in *Reports of the Soviet Academy of Science* (vol. CLXXX, no. 6) presenting the results of their work on 'the electric component of the electromagnetic field' created by the biocurrents (biological electric currents) of the cardiac muscle. They gave the name of electoaurogram (from the Greek *aura,* 'breath,' and *gramma,* 'picture,' hence 'aurogram': 'picture of breath or emanation') to the recording and measuring of the electric field around the human body, that is, in the space surrounding the body.

Their study showed that the activity of living tissues is related to that of biocurrents, which are produced naturally and can be detected by connecting the tissues to devices measuring electric tensions on the order of a millivolt.

The Soviet scientists, taking up the experiments of the American scientists Barr and Mauro, were able to study the electric field of the brain at a distance of twenty-five centimetres for several thousandths of a second, the time taken by impulses from the devices to traverse the organ. They were surprised to observe that *the shape of the field was conditioned by the environment,* that is, by the shape and especially the nature of the objects in that environment.

Adornments and Precious Stones

If a metal plate or any other kind of conductor is placed near the organ whose aurogram is being recorded, there is a screening effect. The opposite effect is produced by a nonconductor, such as ebonite, plastic, wood, etc.

To sum up, we can say that the activity of the living

tissue and organs of the body is influenced by the nature of the immediate environment, and the nerve impulses are dispersed by metals and concentrated by nonconductors.

Women who wear diadems, hairnets, combs, eyeglasses, necklaces, bracelets, etc., thus create an electric environment that conditions their physiological equilibrium.

Gold, steel, and copper disperse. Minerals, wood and plastic concentrate, and therefore become charged. Precious stones, being nonconductors, tend to become charged without screening our nerve impulses. Among the precious stones, the diamond (pure carbon), the opal (hydrated silicon dioxide), the agate, and the onyx (chalcedony) are in perfect harmony with our electromagnetic field. The amethyst (quartz coloured by manganese oxide) may cause slight perturbations, which are accentuated by stones richer in metallic salts, such as emeralds, rubies, sapphires, and topazes.

An Explanation of Telepathy

The scientists of the University of Leningrad were able to obtain photographic evidence of the main human electric fields. The electoaurogram thus produced shows that, after the brain, the knees and the heart have the largest fields. It is strange to note that the genitals are not the centre of an emission. Whatever the validity of the Soviet experiments may be, I am convinced that the two primordial human motor centres are the genitals and the brain.

The field of the human musculature has a complicated configuration which changes with the slightest movement of the body; that of the brain becomes larger with the mere thought of a movement to be performed, or with what are known as ideomotor dreams.

This provides a rational explanation of telepathy, and of divination by a very sensitive person of another person's real but unformulated desires, as with mediums of the calibre of Wolf Messing and Michael Kuni.

The currents detected by the electroaurogram act in the same way as the high-frequency waves of radar, giving an 'echo' when they strike an obstacle. This is what enables extremely sensitive individuals to sense the shapes of objects without seeing or touching them. At a higher level, these currents (and trains of electromagnetic waves) provide possibilities of choice for judging truth at a speed equal to that of a computer.

Theoretically, it is no longer impossible to record ideomotor acts and thoughts with the aid of electronic devices. Perhaps science will some day succeed in making robots that can be controlled from great distances by thought alone; they could be used, for example, to do work in such hostile environments as deserts, swamps, and interstellar space.

The electromagnetic field is propagated at the speed of light, and (still on the level of speculation) we may imagine that all the world's people will some day be closely connected with one another, not only by the impulses of their cardiac muscles, but especially by those of their brains.

Ideas that are 'in the air,' such as the phenomena of messianism and protest, are partially explained by this kind of telepathy.

According to the American scientist L. Falkington, homing pigeons find their way by *seeing the magnetic landscape of the earth.*

Feathers and Sound Waves

An astonishing experiment was recently performed in a laboratory. A 'microphone' made of a bird's wing or a piece of a bat's skin was fixed in place near an amplifier. A dynamoelectric motor was connected to a standard installation, parallel to an oscillograph. The experimenter spoke into the strange microphone and his voice, quite audible, came out of the dynamoelectric motor in another room. When the wing or the skin was removed, no sound was transmitted. The microphone, charged with electricity, gave rise to electromagnetic waves with the frequency of sound waves, and the dynamoelectric installation picked them up.

It is believed that living nature uses a system of this kind for transmitting information. A nightingale's song, for example, is probably heard by other nightingales before the sound reaches their hearing organs. The bird's feathers are responsible for the phenomenon: they act as a microphone and transform the singing into a train of electromagnetic waves which are propagated at the speed of light (and therefore much faster than sound), theoretically into all of cosmic space.

It was thus that the Soviet scientists recorded the electro-aurograms of bumblebees, honeybees, wasps, flies, mosquitoes, butterflies, and caterpillars.

In the Novgorod region a scientific expedition similarly recorded the natural electric environment: electric voices of insects, trees, grass, wind, and signals of disturbances from cosmic space. It also established that, like a bird's feathers, human hair (including whiskers and body hair) functions as a microphone and a transmitter.

These observations and experiments shed new light on the perceptions and apperceptions of mediums, clairvoyants, and initiates, and on a whole area of the Mysterious Unknown which seemed destined to defy the science of rationalists for a long time.

For the same reason of presonic or simply ideomotor transmission, sorcerers use costumes of animal skins or, more often, bird feathers, which enable them to communicate with someone hundreds or even thousands of miles away. The sorcerer speaks, writhes, and dances to charge his garments with electricity. The sound of his voice will never reach its destination, but the message will be received in the form of electromagnetic waves. Great initiates know this secret of telecommunication.

Necklaces are Condensers

The fact that metals have a screening effect in aurograms does not mean that they are biologically harmful.

Copper is one of the best of all conductors; its great conductivity enables it to carry off excess human electricity.

For reasons of biological equilibrium, it is necessary to establish a direct and nearly constant connection between our bodies and the mother-earth. The ideal connection exists when we walk barefoot. Even if they live in a country with an inadequate system of medical care, Africans who walk barefoot and wear copper jewellery resist disease very well. Those who abandon their ancestral costume usually become extremely vulnerable to diseases formerly unknown in Africa.

Among prehistoric peoples, necklaces worn by both men

and women were condensers.

By trial and error we can select the kinds of jewellery and other adornments most favourable to our electric and psychic equilibrium.

Sexual Harmony

Specialists at the University of Kazan have observed a strange phenomenon: when two individuals undergo aurography at the same time, the two aurograms are altered, being either in harmony with or in opposition to each one. It is thus possible to study compatibility or incompatibility between a man and a woman. This raises the possibility of finding the ideal 'soulmate' or sexual partner for each individual.

With regard to purely sexual affinity, it has been observed that if one centre is stronger than the other, it may cover it with its zone of influence. The first sphere succeeds in drawing the other one into a kind of electric exchange, which is contrary to the laws of conventional physics. This phenomenon may explain personal attraction and antipathy between individuals.

As a result of this observation, Soviet scientists believe that mate-swapping may be able to restore a couple's equilibrium by harmonizing their aurograms.

Mate-Swapping

The wave of eroticism that is now breaking over the urban world (rural areas are somewhat sheltered from it) originated in the Scandinavian countries, which are cold, socialistic, and relatively liberated from religious morality.

Eroticism or, more precisely, the need to break inhibitions and throw off the restraints of bourgeois decorum, is the logical outcome of a century of hypocrisy. This release of sexual forces to the point of obscenity will be followed by a period of prudishness, just as the licentiousness of the eighteenth century was followed by the Victorian morality of the nineteenth.

The fact is that husbands and wives have been deceiving

each other since the beginning of known time, which is why prostitution is called 'the oldest profession.'

I have no desire to preach a sermon on this subject; I want only to understand why so many couples are mismatched, why there are so many cases of sexual incompatibility which cause dissension, unhappiness, and even tragedy.

Briefly, three basic explanations can be proposed:

- There is no electric harmony between husband and wife.
- A thinking, intellectual person needs to restore his equilibrium.
- Human beings are naturally inclined toward a multiplicity of sexual experiences, that is, they have a need to change partners.

From here to the idea that mate-swapping is a kind of therapy, there is only one step. That step has been taken by the Swedes, Norwegians, and Danes, and swapping is already accepted by certain scientists in the Soviet Union. If it is adopted by the rest of the world, it will undoubtedly be responsible for a sexual, moral, and religious revolution.

The Unique Odour and the Aurogram

The aurogram represents the human electromagnetic field (something like the aura) and it seems that each individual's aurogram is closely related to the sense of smell.

When a couple finds each other's odours pleasant and even sexually exciting, and especially if each has a unique odour of his own, it can be observed that their aurograms are in harmony, which means that they are sexually compatible.

Is this odour simply a sensation with a material basis, or does it have a certain spherical organization? This question is being studied; it is thought that the field of emanation of the odorous particles takes the shape of the aurogram and may be carried by aurogram waves.

However, at the physiology convention held at Cannes in 1967, Knut Larsson of the University of Göteborg, Jacques Le Magnen of the Collège de France, and Dr Azémar of Avignon expressed the hypothesis that odours do not directly stimulate the sexual motor centres. Their stimulating effect would thus be the result of a conditioned reflex.

Odours and Animal Sexuality

The physiologists at Cannes confirmed something that has often been expressed by writers: the hairy parts of the human body, along with the smell of the breath, play the greatest part in arousing desire. In short, desire is directly related to the most animal features of a human being.

Perfume manufacturers are well aware of this; they always choose animal substances as the bases of their products: musk (a secretion of the Asian musk deer), civet (from the anal scent glands of the civet cat), ambergris (from the intestines of the sperm whale).

Some women naturally secrete sweat with a unique, aphrodisiac odour that is always strongly attractive to men.

R. Harari reports (in 'L'Odorat et la sexualité,' *Science et Vie,* January, 1968) that the science of odours was curiously associated with the construction of a mosque in Tabriz, Iran. Its builders mixed musk with their mortar, with the result that in hot sunlight the walls give off a strong musky smell which, according to legend, intoxicates lovers.

Women are much more sensitive than men to aphrodisiac odours, especially at the time of ovulation, and they have a veritable sexual attraction toward fur garments, which would seem to indicate that they are instinctively more animal than men.

But this is not the opinion of Jacques Marcireau, who writes in *Histoire des rites sexuels* (soon to be published by Robert Laffont), 'Attentive examination of the oldest rite, which is bestial copulation (Eve and the serpent), leads to a surprising hypothesis on the origin of humanity, namely, that women, the first non-animal creatures, had sexual relations with animals which produced hybrids, and that the progressive elimination of these monsters by natural selection gradually gave rise to our species, with its two sexes. The male sex would thus be physiologically posterior to the female sex.'

With regard to sexual rites, Marcireau says quite rightly

that 'sacred prostitution, the right of a feudal lord to de-
flower a female vassal on her wedding night, worship of the
lingam and the yoni, and circumcision are vestiges of mysterious practices which were once universal and played a
very important part in the formation of religions and
societies.'

The Noses of Prehistoric Men

It is interesting to note that even if a man can smell external
odours perfectly well, he is almost totally unable to smell
his own odours, especially his breath. Human beings are
not bothered by foul odours coming from themselves, even
if they can smell them to some extent.

This is a curiosity of nature which corresponds to an
ancient necessity: if a man could smell his own odour, it
would prevent him from smelling that of others, and there was
no doubt a time when smelling an enemy was a matter of life
or death.

If the hairs on a hunting dog's muzzle are cut off, he
can no longer follow the scent of game; if the same thing
is done to a cat, he becomes cowardly and unable to catch
rats.

To discourage attackers, the badger emits a foul odour,
but he himself does not smell it, or at least it has no unpleasant effect on him.

It seems that in prehistoric times men in backward
regions had noses, and particularly nostrils, more fully developed than those of modern man.

A drawing carved on a bone found in a cave at Isturitz,
France, shows a man crawling after a naked woman with
bands around her ankles. His hands are outstretched, as
though to seize her, and his large nose is pointed toward her,
as if he were sniffing her like a dog.

Specialists wonder whether the shrinking of the nose
and nostrils through the ages may not signify an appreciable
lessening of a faculty that once partially governed sexual
and social behaviour.

Interactions between odours and the human electromagnetic
field seem to have brought previously unknown elements to
the study of human equilibrium and erotic behaviour.

Part 6

THE SECRETS OF THE VATICAN

17 The Gospels Have Been Altered

A considerable number of gospels appeared in the first few centuries after Christ. The Church regards as canonical (in conformity with the rules of the Church) only those of Matthew, Mark, Luke, and John. The oldest of these is Matthew, which was directly inspired by the Gospel of the Hebrews.

One point must be stressed: the Apocrypha and the fifty or so Gospels that still exist, or existed before being destroyed by conspiracies, are unanimous in acknowledging that Jesus lived in the time of Pontius Pilate and Tiberius, but there is no known historical document attesting to his real existence.

It has been said to be proved by the *Acts of Pilate,* a series of reports supposedly sent to Emperor Tiberius by Pontius Pilate, Procurator of Judea, containing an account of Jesus's life and death, the crimes imputed to him by the Jews, his crucifixion, and even his resurrection. If these *Acts* ever existed, they must have been made out of whole cloth by Christians; in any case there is now no trace of them.

Many false reports, allegedly by Pilate, have been written with the same fraudulent intent, but none of them has been accredited by the Church.

No Authentic Documents

Although the Gospels are consistent with one another concerning the time when Jesus lived, there is less agreement on his acts and personality. Some Gospels attribute to him a doctrine and a frame of mind that are diametrically opposed to the accounts of Matthew, Mark, Luke, and John. Matthew and Luke are often in sharp disagreement with Mark and John, and sometimes contradict themselves. The vagueness and inconsistency of the four canonical Gospels explains why it was once forbidden for anyone but churchmen to read them.

Authentic documents have existed; there may still be some left in the Vatican Library.

Dr M. Spencer Lewis, Imperator of the Rosicrucians, has written that we know that the Fathers of the Church had access to secret documents because in the councils of the early Church there were references to parts of manuscripts and official documents dealing with the crucifixion and other events of Jesus's life. These documents, says Dr Lewis, are now either hidden or destroyed, and one of the main concerns of the Church Fathers between the seventh and twelfth centuries was to obtain manuscripts from collections in eastern countries which might contain information different from the version of the facts that had been officially accepted by the Church.

John the Apostle, who became Bishop of Ephesus, is said to be the author of the Fourth Gospel, but it is now acknowledged that this pseudo-Gospel was written later by clever theologians. It is certainly not by John, and moreover we have no historical proof that he ever even existed.

A Hundred Gospels

Somewhere between fifty and a hundred Gospels appeared in the second and third centuries. Among the better-known ones are the Gospels of the Hebrews, the Ebionites, Matthew, Mark, Luke, John, Thomas the Israelite, James the Minor, Nicodemus, Marcion, the Nativity of Mary and the Childhood of the Saviour, the Childhood, the People, the Twelve Apostles, Bartholomew, Barnabas, Cerinthus, Peter, Basilides, Truth, Eve, Perfection, Philip, the Egyptians, the Gnostics of Egypt, Judas, Paul.

For the sake of unity, the Christian communities adopted the Gospels of Matthew, Mark, Luke, and John, and considered them as equally sacred and truthful, despite their gaps and contradictions.

The Gospels, being books 'inspired' by the Holy Spirit, must not, in theory, be criticized, suspected, or disputed, but in our time this rule has been greatly softened. Theologians readily admit that the Gospels *must* be interpreted and even corrected, 'in the right direction.'

To bring the different stories into agreement, the Church often modified or even rewrote the Scriptures. Tatian, a disciple of Justin, tried to solve the problem by writing the *Diatessaron,* a composite of the stories of Matthew, Mark, Luke, and John.

But how are we not to be disconcerted by the different genealogies of Jesus, according to whether we read Matthew or Luke? Matthew says that Jesus was the son of Joseph and descended from Jacob, Matthan, Eleazar, Eliud, Achim, Zadok, Azor, and so on back to David and Abraham. (Matthew 1 : 1-16.) Luke also says that Jesus was the son of Joseph, but that he descended from Heli, Matthat, Levi, Melchi, Jannai, Joseph, Mattathiah, and so on back to Abraham, Shem, Noah, and Adam. (Luke 3 : 23-28.)

Strangely enough, considering their basic divergences, Matthew, Mark, and Luke are called the 'Synoptic Gospels' because of their supposedly close agreement with one another.

Saint Augustine Gives His Guarantee

We read in Saint Augustine, 'It is not permissible to say or even to think that any of the Evangelists might have lied.' Furthermore, says the good saint, if we encounter seemingly contradictory statements (such as the two genealogies of Jesus), we must believe that they are actually in agreement, even if we do not see how this can be true.

John, whose story must be suspected, is in total disagreement with Matthew, Luke, and Mark concerning the chronology of Passion Week, and all four of them give different dates for Easter. According to John, Jesus was crucified not on Friday, but on Saturday, the day before Easter.

The divergences are even greater with regard to the resurrection, or, more exactly, the reappearance of Jesus. Matthew says that both Mary and Mary Magdalene were present; Luke and John say that only Mary Magdalene was there.

There is no acceptable evidence from the authenticity of the Gospels. The Church prudently presents them as the

Gospels *according to* Matthew, Mark, Luke, and John.

In the second and third centuries, scholars and Doctors of the Church, such as Irenaeus, Clement of Alexandria, and the ardent Tertullian, believed that the Gospels had been written by the Apostles and that they were eye-witness accounts as well as being divinely inspired.

The Dubious Gospel of John

Polycarp, said to have been ordained Bishop of Smyrna by John the Evangelist in about the year 80, was the worthiest and most estimable of all the saints. Unlike the Apostles, who denied Jesus, he preferred death to the shame of denial. He was burned at the stake, but he was so effectively armoured by his faith that he died without uttering a sound and without suffering as Jesus did.

Polycarp is the author of a letter to the Philippians concerning the contested writings of Ignatius Theophorus (the first Saint Ignatius), who was falsely said to have been ordained by the Apostle Peter. (There was a rash of alleged ordinations by Apostles. There are no historical documents to support these claims; if there were, they would establish the authenticity of the Apostles and Jesus.) Polycarp speaks of the first three Gospels, but not of the fourth, because *the Gospel of John did not exist at the beginning of the second century*. It is mentioned *for the first time* by Theophilus of Antioch *in about the year* 180.

The Gospel of John is the most highly regarded, the most 'initiatic,' according to the ignorant, the one that was written by 'the eagle John,' who slept in the arms of Jesus and later, at Gethsemane, between Peter and James. Yet this Gospel is a notorious fraud perpetrated in the second century to make up for the lack of proper theological content in the other three. It is said to be a Gospel 'not of facts, but of ideas.'

The Curious Cerinthus

If we are to find our way through this imbroglio, we must have some idea of the climate of opinion that prevailed two thousand years ago in Egypt and Asia Minor.

Gnosticism was the basis of all religions and sects – as it is today with spiritualists, theosophists, and believers in divine revelations. Cerinthus was the head of a Christian sect, but he did not recognize the divine origin of Christ.

The following passage from the *Grand Dictionnaire du XIXe siècle* will help us to understand the outlook of men in the first century.

'Cerinthus accepted the existence of two opposing principles, not good and evil, but an essentially active principle, existing by itself: God; and a passive principle, imperfect and not existing by itself: matter. The author of the world was not God, who could not enter into a relation with matter; the creator belonged to one of the lowest classes of inferior spirits, called "forces" and "angels" by Theodore, but he nevertheless bore within himself something of the Divine Being. . . .'

The same was true of the *aeon*, creator of the Mosaic legislation. . . .

'Jesus was not the son of God; an *aeon* named Christ had united with him at the time of his baptism in the waters of the Jordan, and had abandoned him on the day of the crucifixion.

'Cerinth, a Jew by birth, believed in the obligatory Mosaic Law and in the future domination of the world by the Jewish people. . . . The Cerinthians used the Gospel of the Hebrews.'

Some exegetists believe that the so-called Revelation of John, the last book of the New Testament, was written by Cerinthus.

The Popes and Charlemagne Revise the Gospels

As my friend the writer Kronos reports in *Essai de méditations immatérielles*, under Popes Gregory VII and Innocent III, the Church judged it wise to publish, for the use of priests, a highly modified summary of the Gospels, with reminders of daily rites and prayers. It was, and still is, the breviary.

It must also be stressed that translations of the Gospels were formerly forbidden, supposedly for fear of misinterpretations or mistranslations. It is hard to forgive these pious misgivings in view of the fact that councils, popes, and Christian sovereigns shamelessly altered the 'Holy Scriptures,' including the translation done by Saint Jerome in the fourth century, that is, the Vulgate, which is the only one accredited by the Roman Catholic Church.

'The most radical alterations,' writes Kronos, 'date from the Nicene Council and were motivated by the understanding between Pope Damasus I and Emperor Constantine. It was on this occasion that the oldest Gospels, notably the Gospel of the Hebrews (the original Gospel of Matthew) were declared to be "hidden" (*apokruphos*=*apocryphal*).

'Furthermore, additions, omissions, and alterations were made in the four remaining Gospels. Saint Jerome, who had been commissioned to translate them into Latin, was surprised by this. He was all the more surprised because he had just translated the Gospel of the Hebrews into Latin, and he was now instructed to disregard it!

'Saint Victor, Bishop of Tumones (Africa) reports that at the end of the fifth century Pope Anastasius II again had the Holy Scriptures examined, criticized, expurgated, and amended. Charlemagne did the same, a few years before his death (Duchesne, *Historiae Francor Scriptores*), and he was imitated by Pope Sixtus V (1585-1590), who completed the work begun by his predecessors, to please Emperor Charles V. In this period the Church fabricated an Epistle of Saint Peter, later rejected by theologians. . . .

'Several thousand alterations were made. The Pope threatened terrible anathemas against anyone who might dare to tamper with the texts in the future, then he made a new revision which modified more than two hundred passages! A few years later, Pope Clement VIII (1592-1605) made more alterations, which fortunately were the last, for printing had been invented.[1]

[1] Each bishop and each college had Gospels copied with varying degrees of accuracy, arranged to suit the copyist's ideas, then revised by the bishop or the head of the college. The texts of the Archdiocese of Bordeaux were unlike those of the Archdiocese of Strasburg, those of Avignon differed from those of Cambrai. It was so easy to forget or falsify a text! But when printing with movable type was invented (in 1436), fraudulent changes became impossible and the Gospels had to be reproduced in conformity with an original.

'Why all those alterations? It was quite simple: since most dogmas were inconsistent with the holy books, the holy books had to be made consistent with the dogmas!

'Between God and man there had to be a Church to which man must submit beforehand, for otherwise he would not be allowed to have any contact with God. Christ had said, "God is everywhere," but this was dangerous pantheism! The Church could not run the risk of having man worship God in his creation. Only the Church transmitted God's will.

'And "will" in this sense is contrary to the free will that the creator gave us: the early Gospels spoke only of God's *wishes*, and held that he counted on all his creatures, particularly man, to help him in realizing them.'

18 The Old Testament Has Been Revised

The commandments were dictated to Moses on Mount Sinai and the Law was written by God himself: 'Moses turned and went down the mountain with the two tablets of the Tokens in his hands, inscribed on both sides; on the front and on the back they were inscribed. The tablets were the handiwork of God, and the writing was God's writing, engraved on the tablets.' (Exodus 32:15-16.)

It would seem inconceivable that believers would dare to contest and falsify what is most sacred and divine in the Law: God's Commandments. And yet . . .

The Fifteen Commandments

God's Commandments are stated in the twentieth chapter of Exodus (and also in the fifth chapter of Deuteronomy, with variations). In verses 4-6 we read: 'You shall not make a carved image for yourself nor the likeness of anything in the heavens above, or on the earth below, or in the waters under the earth. You shall not bow down to them or worship them; for I, the Lord your God, am a jealous god. I punish the children for the sins of the fathers to the third and fourth generations of those who hate me. But I keep faith with thousands, with those who love me and keep my commandments.'

The text is perfectly clear and precise: it is forbidden to draw, paint, or carve images of God, angels, saints, Jesus, Mary, Gabriel, etc., or even of anything on or under the earth or in the sky. Crucifixes are undeniably sacrilegious, as are statues of the Holy Family and the Apostles, pious images inserted in missals, illustrated Bibles, and illustrated publications of all kinds. Newspaper publishers, for example, can be assured of a place in hell, along with television producers.

Bearing in mind that *the Commandments are not numbered in the Bible,* we can make the following list of fifteen, taken from the twentieth chapter of Exodus:

1. 'You shall have no other god to set against me.' (Verse 3.)
2. 'You shall not make a carved image for yourself nor the likeness of anything in the heavens above, or on the earth below, or in the waters under the earth.' (Verse 4.)
3. 'You shall not bow down to them or worship them.' (Verse 5.)
4. 'You shall not make wrong use of the name of the Lord your God.' (Verse 7.)
5. 'Remember to keep the sabbath day holy.' (Verse 8.)
6. 'Honour your father and your mother.' (Verse 12.)
7. 'You shall not commit murder.' (Verse 13.)
8. 'You shall not commit adultery.' (Verse 14.)
9. 'You shall not steal.' (Verse 15.)
10. 'You shall not give false evidence against your neighbour.' (Verse 16.)
11. 'You shall not covet your neighbour's house; you shall not covet your neighbour's wife, his slave, his slave-girl, his ox, his ass, or anything that belongs to him.' (Verse 17.)
12. 'You shall not make gods of silver to be worshipped as well as me, nor shall you make yourself gods of gold.' (Verse 23.)
13. 'You shall make an altar of earth for me, and you shall sacrifice on it both your whole-offerings and your shared-offerings, your sheep, and your cattle.' (Verse 24).
14. 'If you make an altar of stones for me, you must not build it of hewn stones, for if you use a chisel on it, you will profane it.' (Verse 25.)
15. 'You must not mount up to my altar by steps, in case your private parts be exposed on it.' (Verse 26.)

God's Law is Flouted

It is appalling to realize that twelve of these fifteen commands are disobeyed by the Church, which truly respects only the first and the fourth. God himself is flouted, for it is not honouring him to disobey him, to kill, to steal, to build cathedrals!

Pope Alexander VI, to take only one example, went still further in sacrilege: he had five children, the most famous of whom were Caesar and Lucretia Borgia, by Rosa Vanozza, who was married. Having violated all fifteen commandments, he died in 1503, poisoned, it is said, because he inadvertently took a drink that he had prepared for a cardinal whose property he coveted.

It is not certain that God was completely wise in issuing all those orders; most of them are sound, but some, unfortunately, seem rather outdated. It was no doubt for this reason that men altered them and censored the Gospels, that is, revised the words of God and Christ.

God Is Excommunicated

At the second Nicene Council, held in 787, three hundred and sixty-seven bishops from Greece, Thrace, Sicily and Italy, assembled in the Saint Sophia church in Constantinople, decreed as follows against iconoclasts:

'We decree that holy images, made of paint, mosaic work, or other suitable material, are to be displayed on vessels, holy garments, and walls in churches, as well as in houses and on roads, for the more one sees images of Jesus Christ, his holy mother, and the saints, the more one is inclined to remember the originals and love them.

'Salutation and honorific worship is to be given to these images, but not true worship, which, according to our faith, is to be given only to the divine nature. One may, however, approach them with incense and lights, as one does with the Cross, the Gospels, and other sacred things, in accordance with the pious custom of the ancients, for the honour is rendered to the original depicted by the object.

'Such is the doctrine of the Holy Fathers and the tradi-

14 Statues, busts and heads from Tihuanaco. The eyes are round, oval or square, like those of the 'Giants of Tula' in Mexico. They are never slanted. Yet, according to official prehistory, the first peoples of America came from Mongolia. This is a groundless view that conflicts with clear evidence.

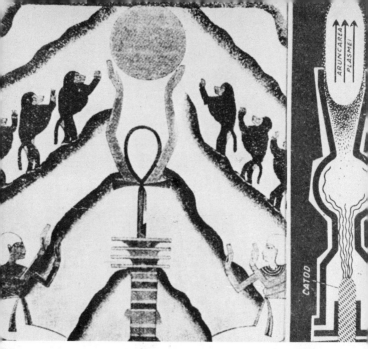

15 *Left:* Ancient Egyptian Fresco showing an invocation to the Sun
God.
Right: A plasma generator.

16 A dolmen and menhirs from San Augustin, Peru, similar to those at
Carnac in France.

17 The menhir of Cinturat, Brittany – 21 feet high and the best in France.

18 Giant heads on Easter Island. The eyes are not empty – the pupils are there, charged with magic *mana* which they radiate over the tribe to protect it and revitalise it.

19 Sculpture in the Devi Jagadamba temple at Kharjuraho.

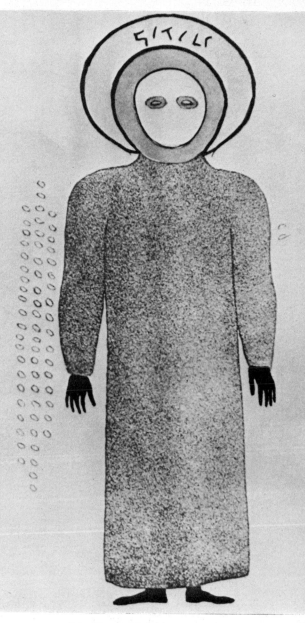

20 The cosmonaut of the Glenelg River cave in Australia.

21 The Petra Palace. Behind this artistically carved facade there is only an empty passage.

22 The Lake of the Seven Cities in the Azores. According to tradition, the seven cities of Atlantis lie under these green and blue waters.

23 According to Oriental tradition, this portrait of Jesus was painted
by Anan, secretary to King Abgar V of Edesse in Syria.

tion of the Catholic Church. We order that those who dare to think otherwise are to be deposed, if they are bishops or clerics, and excommunicated, if they are monks or laymen.'

This decision was undoubtedly the most important ever made by men, for *it either deposed or excommunicated God,* depending on whether he is regarded as a priest or a layman.

In his Commandments, God specifically forbade the making of images, and it was this prohibition that the second Nicene Council condemned.

The first Nicene Council was held in 325. It included two thousand and forty-eight bishops, most of whom had come to deny and oppose the divinity of Christ. Emperor Constantine I succeeded in imposing the divinity of Christ, threatening the dissidents with exile if they persisted in refusing to accept the judgment of the 'majority.' This 'majority' consisted of three hundred and eighteen Church Fathers. Threats finally reduced the number of dissidents to twenty-two, including Arius and Eusebius, Bishop of Caesarea. Artius's books were burned and the council decreed the death penalty against anyone who kept one of them.

The Bible is a Novel

We must not, of course, deny all value to the Bible, even if everything in it concerning the Hebrews and their privileges is false and groundless. Exodus, for example, is either a pure invention or an inordinately exaggerated account of something that happened to a nomadic tribe. No Egyptologist believes in that fantastic wandering. No trace of it is found in manuscripts or in the form of hieroglyphics.

During a French television programme on July 30, 1970, Jean Leclant, professor of Egyptology at the Sorbonne; Shafik Allam, lecturer at the University of Tübingen; Labib Habachi, director of the Department of Antiquities in Cairo, and André Caquot of the Ecole Pratique des Hautes Etudes, a Biblical scholar, all agreed in saying that the Bible was a novel.

Labib Habachi states that in the time of Moses there were only a few hundred *ancestors* of the Hebrews in Egypt, and they were nomads belonging to several different nations.

L.W.   G

According to André Caquot, the artificial creation of the Hebrew people goes back only three thousand years.

From the statements of these experts it appears that the story of the Hebrews' wandering in the desert until they entered the Promised Land is false and was probably written in the time of Solomon.

The famous crossing of the Red Sea is therefore also fictitious. The Egyptian record-keepers of the House of Scribes were always on the lookout for events in an empire where, usually, very little happened. They recorded the slightest incidents: the passing of migratory birds, punitive expeditions against thieves and pillagers, a small over-flowing of the Nile, unusually large or small crops, etc. They would certainly not have failed to record such events as the flight of the Hebrews from Egypt with soldiers in pursuit and the drowning of Pharaoh's entire army in the Red Sea. *But no mention of this can be found in any of the Egyptian historical and traditional archives.*

Although Professor Caquot does not believe that the story is literally true, he feels that it may be symbolic, representing the victory of God over the waters and of Israel over Egypt.

On this view Israel and the Bible are, in deep truth, only fabricated artificial emanations, like the writings of other peoples and other religions.

The god Yahweh himself is only a borrowing from the Bedouins of the desert.

Yahweh was not the God of the Hebrews

Here is what Professor Caquot says on the subject:

The lower parts of the pillars in the hypostyle hall of the Nubian temple of Soleb (built in the early four-teenth century B.C. by Amenhotep III) are covered with shields bearing the names of Asian and African peoples vanquished by the Egyptians. Each shield is surmounted by the bust of a man, in bas-relief, with his hands tied behind his back. Several shields begin with the formula 't3 s3-s-w,' 'land of the Shabus [Bedouins] of . . .' and one of them has 't3 s3-s-w y-h-w3-w,' in which 'w3-w' should probably be pronounced 'wo,' so that this shield speaks of the 'Bedouins of Yahwo.'

It is very tempting to see this as the same name as that of God in the Bible, for it has long been suspected that the original pronunciation of the Tetragrammaton must have been 'Yahwo,' rather than 'Yahweh.' But in this document 'y-h-w3-w' is not a divine name. Judging from the other shields, it is a place-name, indicating the land of those whom the Egyptians called Shasus, nomads living east of the Isthmus of Suez.

Thus Egyptologists as well qualified as S. Herrmann and J. Leclant do not hesitate to accept an identity between an Israelite divine name and the name of a place east of Egypt.

It may be that the name of the God of Israel came from the name of a place, perhaps a mountain in the region from which YHWH came, according to several passages in the Bible; Deuteronomy 33:2, for example: 'The Lord came from Sinai and shone forth from Seir,' and Judges 5:4 'O Lord, at thy setting forth from Seir, when thou camest marching out of the plains of Edom . . .'

The name of Israel does not appear at Soleb. It is attested later, by the stele of Pharaoh Merneptah (about 1230 B.C.), as the name of a people of Syria.

This name is surrounded with mystery. It is a personal name of a type that is well known in Semetic languages, containing a divine name, 'el (god), preceded by a verb in the present-future beginning with a verbal prefix indicating the third person masculine singular: y (i). The whole question is to know the meaning of the verb whose consonantal skeleton is s r (יִשְׂרֵאל).

G. A. Danell wrote a thesis on this subject, *Studies in the Name Israel in the O.T.*, published at Upsala in 1946. Since then, a *ysr'l* (Israel) has been found as the name of a person in the texts of Ras Shamra; it strongly resembles the one that concerns us, but we know little more than before . . .

This exposition is extremely important because Professor André Caquot is recognized all over the world as the most eminent specialist on the subject.

In the legends of Ras Shamra, related by tablets in cuneiform writing, El is the oldest and highest-ranking god of the eastern Semites, notably the Phoenicians. He is the

Beli of the pre-Celts, the Bel of the Assyro-Babylonians. In reality, these names are only masks of the unknown god, or at least of the Lord, whose real name is known only to initiates. He is the *El*ohim taken over by the Hebrews, who gave him a plural identity which foreshadows the Trinity.

But El is also the god of the Gaelic and Norse city of Ys, the Lord of the Arrow and the Waters, foreign to the Hebrews and typically *pelagos* (from the North Sea), like the ancient Aryans who, after the Deluge, wandered from the Iranian plateau to the Mediterranean basin.

Men are Wiser than God

God's Commandments have become a dead letter: not only is it now permitted to make images of anything in the sky, on earth, and in the water, but this is *approved* and *recommended*. So much so that for a thousand years the Christian Church monopolized and controlled the work of architects, stonecutters, sculptors, and painters.

More respectful of the real Law, religious Jews were for a long time reluctant to be architects, sculptors, painters, or, more recently, photographers.

Was the wrathful and bloodthirsty Jehovah, God of the Hebrews and Christians, right to forbid the arts that copy nature? By this prohibition did he intend to precipitate men toward the abstract and make them gain three thousand years of development? Did he want to direct history into a path diametrically opposed to the one that men were following?

If this had happenèd, what would our civilization have been like? What forms of thought and social life would it have achieved? I do not know, and it is hard even to imagine an answer.

Men deliberately decided to revise God's orders. It was a bold and adventurous decision, but it was also the result of mature reflection. I believe that the heretical popes, bishops, monks, and priests who made and applied it showed concern for the good of mankind, and probably wisdom.

The prohibition against copying nature, which amounts to an obligation to devote oneself to purely intellectual speculation, is comparable to the prohibition against reproducing and using the wheel that was imposed on the Mayas and Incas.

Generally speaking, they respected the taboo, and it led to forms of religious civilization that were devoured or died of languor and impotence.

The taboos placed on images among the Judeo-Christians and on the wheel among the Mayas and Incas were actually directed against the atomic bomb and the self-destruction that seems to be the inevitable, tragic end of any civilization like ours. These taboos prove the existence of Superior Ancestors who had already used images and the wheel and found that they led to punishment and the Deluge.

h
p

the
was
had
T

19 The Judas Affair

In the absence of any historical evidence, it is easy to
imagine Jesus and his Apostles in any way one chooses:
with light or dark hair, with white, brown, yellow, or black
skin. Historians have had a field day. According to their
various versions, the Man of Nazareth was a prophet, a
hippie, the leader of an armed band, a conspirator, or a
prince determined to take his rightful place on the throne.
Saint Augustine, like Matthew (who in my opinion is
least suspect of the Evangelists), was certain that Jesus
of royal as well as divine origin and that he should have
temporal, political power in Palestine.
This view rests only on articles of faith and accounts
that have no historical validity, since they date from several
centuries after the supposed existence of Jesus. They may
nevertheless be taken into consideration, but if Jesus really
had political aims it seems strange that no first-century historian ever mentioned them.

The Gospel of the Hebrews

The Old Testament has been revised as much as the Gospels,
but it still contains some poetic passages. It speaks of the
beauties of nature, of trees, flowers, women, and love, and
it even flirts with eroticism, as in the Song of Songs.
My colleague Kronos, author of *Essai de méditations
immatérielles,* writes as follows:

In the remaining Gospels the text is so dry that it con-
veys nothing of the splendour of Lake Tiberias, surrounded by oleanders, water lilies, and lotuses, or the
warm beauty of the ancient olive groves where Christ's

prayers, in the fragrance of countless aromatic plants, did not interrupt the singing of the cicadas.

What a difference between the Gospels that are left to us and the Gospel of the Hebrews, which is probably the original of Matthew!

Here are some passages of it, translated from the Latin version of Saint Jerome.

From Chapter 13:

'After saying these words, the angel stopped the beast because the time of childbirth had come, and he told Mary to descend from it and go into an underground cave in which there had never been light; it was always dark because daylight did not penetrate it. But when Mary entered it, the whole cave because resplendent with light, as if the sun were inside it, and the divine light illuminated it as if it were the sixth hour of the day; and as long as Mary remained in that cave, night and day, without interruption, it was illuminated by that divine light.'

From Chapter 35:

'And Jesus was eight years old, and he left Jericho and went toward the Jordan. And there was beside the road, near the bank of the Jordan, a cave in which a lioness was feeding her cubs; no one could take that road with safety. Now Jesus, coming from Jericho and having learned that a lioness had given birth in that cave, entered it within sight of everyone. But as soon as the lions saw him, they ran to meet him and worshipped him. And Jesus sat down in the cave, and the cubs ran this way and that around his feet, caressing him and playing with him. The old lions, however, remained at a distance with their heads bowed; they worshipped him and slowly wagged their tails before him. Then the people, standing far from the cave and not seeing Jesus, said, "If he or his parents had not committed great sins, he would not have offered himself to the lions." And while the people were having these thoughts and feeling overwhelmed with sadness, suddenly, in the presence of all, Jesus came out of the cave, with the lions preceding him and the cubs playing at his feet. His parents stood far off, because of the lions, and did not dare to join them. Then Jesus said to the people, "How much better than you are wild beasts, which recognize their Master and glorify him, while you, men, created in the image and knowledge of God, do not know him. Beasts recognize me and become meek; men see me and do not recognize me." '

From Chapter 36:

'After this, Jesus crossed the Jordan with the lions in the sight of all, and the water of the Jordan parted to the left and to the right. Then he said to the lions in such a way as to be heard by all, "Go in peace and do no harm to anyone; but let no one harm you until you have returned to the place from which you came." And the lions saluted him, not with their voices, but with the attitude of their bodies, and went back into the cave. And Jesus returned to his mother.'

From Chapter 39:

'For the first time, the Jews asked Mary and Joseph to take the child . . . to another master, to be educated. And Joseph and Mary, fearing the people, the insolence of the princes, and the threats of the priests, took him again to the school, knowing that he could learn nothing from a man, since he possessed perfect knowledge from God alone.

'Now when Jesus entered the school, guided by the Spirit of God, he took the book from the hand of the master who was teaching the Law, and in the presence of all the people, who saw and heard, he began reading not what was written in their book, but speaking in the spirit of the living God, as though a torrent of water were gushing forth from a spring, and as though the spring always remained full. And he taught the people the greatness of the living God so forcefully that the master himself fell to the ground and worshipped him. But the hearts of all those who were there and who had heard him speak were stricken with amazement. And when Joseph learned of this, he ran to Jesus, fearing that the master might die. When he saw him, the master said to him, "You have not given me a disciple, but a master, and a master who can support his words." '

In the Gospel According to Luke, this same event is related as follows (2:46-47): 'And after three days they found him sitting in the temple surrounded by the teachers, listening to them and putting questions; and all who

heard him were amazed at his intelligence and the answers
he gave.'

What dryness in the official Gospels! What sincere
emotion in the earlier Gospels! They are like freshly
plucked flowers, with all their colour and fragrance, whereas
the Churches have left us only a choice among dead,
desiccated plants that seem to have been taken from
a herbarium for a demonstration.

Blackout on the Apostles

Although he was of modest origin, Matthew must have
known how to read and write, since he was a publican. The
other Apostles were men of humble condition, mostly fishermen, illiterate, and with a very low intellectual level. Theologians believe that the writings attributed to them were
dictated.

This was also the opinion of Bossuet, who said, 'When
Jesus Christ was with the Apostles, their coarse understanding did not penetrate the mysteries.'

'Of a world of crimes, passions, and superstitions,' said
the theologian Pierre-Claude Frey de Neuville, 'the Apostles
made a world of faith and holiness.'

This is far from being true, but it is not completely
false, since two thousand years of civilization have flowed
from Operation Jesus-Apostles-Gospels. Whatever the authenticity of the characters and events in the Gospels, the history
of the West has taken place as if everything in them were
true. Even now, when the Christian Church is crumbling
away and collapsing beneath the weight of its own errors and
falsehoods, the question of whether or not its foundations are
authentic can be regarded as having no real importance.

We have no historical knowledge of Matthew or the
other Apostles. Their real existence is attested only by stories
in the Gospels and Christian traditions: the Acts of the
Apostles and the Epistles.

Paul is said to have lived approximately between the
years 11 and 66 and to have been Bishop of Ephesus, but
he too has left no conclusive historical evidence of his
existence. Only ecclesiastical history speaks of Saul, who

became Paul in the Christian religion. The miracles described in the Acts of the Apostles are not credible, and real history often belies the stories of Paul's life, particularly with regard to his conflicts with the magistrates of Jerusalem, the riot stirred up against him, the conversion of Seneca, and his travels, of which there is no trace in any chronicle.

All of Paul's adventures rest only on the Acts of the Apostles, of dubious authenticity and by an unknown author, and on the Epistles (of Paul, Peter, John, and Jude), some of which – two Epistles of John – are considered apocryphal by eminent theologians. The authenticity of the others is equally unsupported by evidence, though Renan believed in it. The Epistle of Paul to the Hebrews and the second Epistle of Paul to Timothy are certainly apocryphal.

The Gospels are far from being in agreement on the names and number of the Apostles and on the facts themselves.

Judas's alleged betrayal is an example.

The Judas Affair

If it is difficult to form an opinion regarding the real Jesus, what are we to say of the man presented as the most infamous traitor in history: Judas?

Poor Judas has been endlessly insulted and reviled, yet, contrary to the reports of false witnesses, there is good reason to believe that he played the part of a hero in the events with which his name is associated.

It has been said that the myth of his betrayal was invented in order to let Paul enter the circle of Jesus's twelve companions. One of them had to be excluded and a conspiracy was organized for that purpose. It failed so far as Paul was concerned, because the Judeo-Christian faction had Matthias chosen instead of him.

In support of this assertion, it is pointed out that Paul, in his writings, and John, in his Revelation, say nothing at all about there having been a traitor among the Apostles, which is very strange!

If the betrayal actually took place, one is tempted to believe that it had other motives, more political and more estimable.

Judas the Initiate

The role of Judas Iscariot – so named because he was said to have come from Kerioth, a village in Palestine – is extremely disturbing.

The tribe of Judah was the most renowned of the twelve Hebrew tribes and Judas was probably the best-educated and most intelligent of the disciples, since he was in charge of the group's receipts and expenditures.

John assures us that Judas was a thief, which does not speak well of Jesus's discernment, and the eleven other disciples were unanimous in denouncing him, even though *he was the only one who did not deny his master*.

Here is what we know about Judas Iscariot from the four canonical Gospels.

John 12:1-5:

'Six days before the Passover festival Jesus came to Bethany, where Lazarus lived whom he had raised from the dead. There a supper was given in his honour, at which Martha served, and Lazarus sat among the guests with Jesus. Then Mary brought a pound of very costly perfume, pure oil of nard, and anointed the feet of Jesus [Matthew 26:7 says, '. . . began to pour it over his head.'] and wiped them with her hair, till the house was filled with the fragrance. At this, Judas Iscariot, a disciple of his – the one who was to betray him – said, "Why was this perfume not sold for thirty pounds and given to the poor?"'

Matthew 26:8-9:

'The disciples were indignant when they saw it. "Why this waste?" they said, "it could have been sold for a good sum and the money given to the poor."'

Mark 14:4-5:

'Some of those present said to one another angrily, "Why this waste? The perfume might have been sold for thirty pounds and the money given to the poor."'

Luke does not speak of this meal.

John 12:6:

'He [Judas] said this, not out of any care for the poor, but because he was a thief; he used to pilfer the money put into the common purse, which was in his charge.'

The other Evangelists make no remarks on this subject.

What John says about Judas is malicious and rancorous, *as if he were jealous of him.*

John 12:7-8:

' "Leave her alone," said Jesus. "Let her keep it till the day when she prepares for my burial; for you have the poor among you always, but you will not always have me." '

Thus Jesus, in his extravagant pride, found it natural that his feet should be washed with expensive perfume and he let a woman wipe them with her hair. Was the upright Judas offended by this repulsive attitude and this contempt for women? It is quite possible, but there were many other complaints that could have been made against Jesus. He was always saying that he was the Son of God, claiming that no one could go to the Father except through him, predicting imitators and stating that he was the Christ: he disparaged Moses and David and announced that he would be immortal in the world's memory. In short, his megalomania made him tend to believe that he was as great as God himself, 'Jesus said, "Now the Son of Man is glorified, and in him God is glorified." ' (John 13:31.)

But he treated his disciples as fools and to the end he told them that they did not have faith and would deny him, especially the simple-minded Peter, who could not bear John.

Perhaps as a result of this painful situation, knowing that he was going to be arrested and put to death. *Jesus also seemed to have no faith in himself, in his courage, in his mission, in his God.*

When he came to Gethsemane with his disciples, he took the three best of them with him and told them to stay awake while he prayed. The prudent John does not relate this incident and it should be noted that his name is omitted from Mark's story when Jesus makes his reproaches. What strange Apostles, and what a strange Messiah to surround himself with men of that kind! For while their Lord was praying to prepare himself to meet his death, Peter, James, and John disobeyed his order and took advantage of his absence to take a little nap!

This detail, reported by Matthew, Mark, and Luke (but omitted by John), shows the low esteem that the pseudo-disciples had for their Master, one can even say the contempt in which they held him – if events took place as they are described!

Jesus Refused to be the Saviour

One man emerges from the singular association of the twelve Apostles. He belonged to the noblest of the Hebrew tribes. Judas was the only one capable of writing the true Gospel. He did write it, but it has *mysteriously disappeared.*

He was also the only one, according to John, who protested when the pseudo-Master let Mary wash his feet with an expensive perfume that was worth several times a worker's daily wage.

He saw Peter, John, James, and the others making strenuous but vain efforts to understand Jesus: he saw them eat a good meal, then lie down and sleep beneath the scornful gaze of the Master. He knew, since the prediction had been made, that these gluttons were all going to be traitors. Furthermore, he sensed that Jesus was weakening: perhaps he lacked the moral and mental capacity to be a Christ; perhaps he realized that he had failed with his disciples. In short, everything was about to collapse: there would be neither the Christ nor the Christian religion, and chaos would continue.

Disgusted and indignant, but still clear-headed, Judas decided to force the wavering Jesus to become the Saviour, but he refused to deny the man he knew so well, too well! For if we consider the matter honestly and take into account the indecent conduct of the disciples and the admissions by the Evangelists concerning their Master's reluctance to sacrifice himself, *it is very probable that, before going to Gethsemane, Jesus had already decided to avoid being crucified.*

On this hypothesis, it is easy to understand why Peter, James, and John let themselves fall asleep: they had nothing to fear for Jesus, since they knew that he had changed his mind, that he was afraid. He had admitted to himself, and perhaps even in public, that he was only a poor visionary, little better educated than his disciples, and no more the Son of God than they were.

It seemed that everything was lost, that the whole adventure was about to sink into oblivion. But since Jesus was a kind of initiate that the ancient world needed, Judas forced events to take another course, he went to bring soldiers and handed Jesus over to them, to be executed.

For money? Certainly not. Even the most firmly convinced Christians acknowledge that thirty pieces of silver (a tenth of the price of a bottle of perfume) was too insignificant a sum to be a temptation. And how can we doubt his disinterestedness when we are told that he was seized with remorse, testified that Jesus was innocent, threw down the cursed money in the temple, and then hanged himself?

Jesus, the Instrument of Providence

Analysis of what is claimed to be a betrayal shows that events were wrongly reported by the Evangelists.

Since Jesus had worked no miracles and had passed unnoticed in the history of Judea, he was unknown to Pontius Pilate, who consequently had no reason to arrest him. This is clearly apparent in the Gospels, since, to point out the man who was to be arrested, Judas designated him by kissing him. It is impossible to believe that if Jesus had been a troublemaker he would have been unknown in Jerusalem. It would be like saying that before Cohn-Bendit, Geismar, or any other modern agitator could be arrested, one of his fellow demonstrators would have to kiss him on the cheek to identify him to the police!

Jesus was unknown to the police, but the Jewish priests were acquainted with his revolutionary ideas. Pontius Pilate had nothing against him; it was the chief priests and elders who accused him of being a blasphemer, which was no doubt true from their point of view.

The Roman procurator was so convinced of Jesus's insignificance that he 'washed his hands in full view of the people' to show that he was not responsible for the crime that was about to be perpetrated. It was the outcome of a quarrel among religious sectarians which would have been unknown to history if initiates had not described it, perhaps fictitiously, a century later.

But, at the time, the primary initiate was Judas. Without him, Jesus would not have existed in history. In the second century, the Cainites and other Gnostics saw Judas as the instrument of Providence necessary for the redemption of men. A true hero of history, he forced Jesus to become the Saviour, consenting to assume the role of a traitor, a role that is belied by his words, his disinterestedness, his scruples, and his tragic death when his mission had been accomplished.

Such were the trial of Jesus and the real identity of Judas, according to a view that has won a certain amount of support.

But a revelation in the Dead Sea Scrolls throws convincing light on the pseudo-traitor of the Gospels: the Essenes were called Judases by their mortal enemies, the Hebrews, long before Jesus's birth. It is thus easy to understand the confusion that may have existed in the minds of Christians two centuries later. But this view implies that Judas did not exist and that his story was invented.

20 Sacrilegious Hypotheses

For exegetists, historians, and cultivated people who know the extent to which the Old and New Testaments have been altered, the historical existence of Jesus poses a delicate problem. If the Bible is suspect, as it certainly is, what are we to think of the man known as Jesus of Nazareth, an ordinary prophet to some, the Son of God to others?

The Opinion of Rationalists

There is no historical record of his existence. No writers of the period, such as Flavius Josephus, Seneca, and Philo of Alexandria, make any mention of him. Although he was always on the lookout for unusual political facts, Pliny the Elder (23-79) says nothing about the existence of Jesus; he does, however, speak of the Essenes, who wrote the Dead Sea Scrolls (*Historia Naturalis* V-17).

In his *Lives of the Caesars,* Suetonius (first century A.D.) says that during the reign of Claudius the Jews caused disorders in Rome, at the instigation of an agitator known as Chrestus, but this name (or epithet) cannot have designated Christ because the reign of Claudius began in 41 A.D., several years after Jesus's crucifixion.

'Jesus is a pure myth, analogous to those of Osiris, Adonis, Attis, Mithra, Hermes, and Apollo,' the rationalist Prosper Alfaric stated at the Sorbonne on December 17, 1946.

(Osiris was an Egyptian god, first of nature, then of the dead, similar to the Dionysus of the Greeks. Adonis was a Phoenician god, analogous to Osiris or the Adonai of the Hebrews. Attis was another Greek god analogous to Adonis; he was attached to Cybele, the Queen of Caverns. Mithra was a Persian god associated with Ahura Mazda. Hermes was the god of herds in Greece, and of knowledge, arts, and letters in Egypt, where he is identified with Thoth. Apollo was a Hyperborean god of the Greeks.)

In *La Fable de Jésus-Christ,* Guy Fau writes of 'the testimony of Don Diego Hurtado de Mendoza, a writer and ambassador of Spain to the Vatican, with regard to Pope Paul III (1534-1549): "He carried impiety to the point of affirming that Christ was none other than the sun worshipped by the Mithraic sect, or Zeus Ammon, represented in paganism in the form of a ram or a lamb. He explained the allegories of his incarnation and resurrection by the parallel (which he had read in Saint Justin) between Christ and Mithra. He said that the Adoration of the Magi was only the ceremony in which the priests of Zoroaster made an offering to their god consisting of gold, incense, and myrrh, the three things consecrated to the sun. He maintained that the constellation of Virgo, or rather of Isis, which corresponds to this solstice and presided at the birth of Mithra, had also been chosen as an allegory of the birth of Christ, which, according to the Pope, sufficed to demonstrate that Mithra and Jesus were the same god. He dared to say that there were no incontestably authentic documents proving the existence of Christ as a man, and that he personally was convinced that he had never existed."'

It is not at all certain that Paul III actually stated these heretical views, but since the version favourable to Jesus has been known and taught all over the world for two thousand years, often abusively, it is good to be also acquainted with the opinions of rationalists, theists, and historians in the opposing camp.

Unknown in his Time

Pliny the Younger (62-113) wrote that the Christians of Bithynia, in the year 112, worshipped a god named Christos, but there was no question of an earthly man named Jesus.

Juvenal (60-140), Tacitus (55-120), Plutarch (46-120), Cio Cassius (born c. 155) and Pausanias (second century A.D.) make no mention of Jesus.

The Platonic philosopher Celsus, an enemy of Christianity, did speak of Jesus, but in the second century, and he said that Jesus had been a magician and a bandit leader. (See Origen's *Contra Celsum*; and, for all refutations of a rationalistic nature, see Guy Fau's well-documented book *La Fable de Jésus-Christ*.)

The Dead Sea Scrolls, the most recent part of which dates from 69 A.D., contain no reference to anyone named Jesus, or to his pseudo-Apostles and the turmoil they are said to have caused in Judea.

Even the very Christian writer Daniel-Rops, in his *Jésus et son temps,* admits the tenuousness of the evidence for Jesus's existence: 'If we refer only to Roman documents, it cannot be rigorously demonstrated that Jesus really existed.' His reluctance to be categorical is understandable, but it would have been more logical to say simply that the real existence of Jesus is purely an article of faith.

Pious Inventions and False Evidence

This chapter could be filled out with the long list of pious insertions and false writings intended to distort authentic history by making it lend support to an episode for which there is no real evidence.

A false correspondence was fabricated between the philosopher Seneca, whose existence is certain, and the pseudo-Apostle Paul. A fifteenth-century monk falsified the work of the philosopher and consul Cornelius Tacitus by introducing into it a manuscript, probably apocryphal, of the erudite Italian humanist Poggio Bracciolini.

The *Acts of Pontius Pilate* give an idea of the clumsiness of certain falsifiers: these alleged reports of Pontius Pilate were addressed to Emperor Claudius, who, as Guy Fau points out, reigned from 41 to 54, whereas Pilate ceased to be Procurator of Judea in the year 36.

The letter of Lentulus, governor of Jerusalem, to the Senate and the Roman people would be clear evidence of Jesus's existence if it were not for the fact that the title of Governor of Jerusalem never existed, and neither did this Lentulus. The only historically known men of that name who lived during the period were C. C. Lentulus Getulicus, a consul under Tiberius, and his son Cneius Lentulus, a consul and conspirator, and neither of them ever held a position in Jerusalem.

Here, in an extremely condensed version, is the viewpoint of rationalists and historians on the general problem: we cannot conclude categorically that Jesus never existed, since history often forgets, sometimes unintentionally, events of the greatest importance; but in any case, whether or not he really lived two thousand years ago, Jesus exists now, because the *phenomenon* of Jesus is an established fact that has become part of history.

A Hippie Named Jesus

Examination of the hippie phenomenon of recent years may shed a certain amount of light on the mysteries and contradictions that we find in the Gospels.

The real Jesus must have been one of the countless mystics who abounded in the Near East two thousand years ago. It is easy to imagine him as a counterpart of the modern hippie: long hair, long beard, barefoot or wearing sandals, making speeches that are sometimes incendiary, sometimes filled with pacifism and flowers. He did not, of course, wear a big badge on his robe with an incisive slogan like 'I love you' written on it; instead, he used an oral password: 'Love one another.'

He must have lived with a group (his Apostles), like Cohn-Bendit and Alain Geismar. Perhaps he also made music and improvised dances.

Some Rather Strange Apostles

It is bewildering to examine the strange conduct of Jesus's favourite disciples when he had gone to the Mount of Olives to prepare himself to face death.

The Apostles showed indifference, even contempt, for Jesus. They all betrayed him, except perhaps for Judas, and even when the Master, his face bathed with sweat, was preparing to face death, they carried callousness to a point unknown in the savage history of mankind: they fell asleep! And it was not the obscure, subordinate, uncomprehending disciples, but the favourites, Peter and James, and

John, who had rested on Jesus's chest. They slept like logs,
not in ignorance of the danger that hung over Jesus, but,
according to the Gospels themselves, knowing very well that
he was about to die. Even after he had reprimanded them,
they fell asleep again as soon as he had turned away from
them, and as he prayed he must have heard their snoring
in the background. It is enough to make one doubt the Holy
Scriptures!

Such degradation is almost inconceivable. Would the
henchmen of a gangster, or followers of Hitler, Stalin, De
Gaulle, or Mussolini, have let themselves fall asleep if they
had known that their master was preparing to meet his death?
No. No gangster or bodyguard would sink so low. History
provides no example of such abjection.

A drug addict, however, would be capable of such a
vile betrayal of confidence, either because his will was
annihilated by his drug or because his moral deterioration
masked the horror of the situation.

The scene on the Mount of Olives irresistibly suggests
drug abuse among the Apostles, to explain their incredible
behaviour.

Jerusalem is on the route of the spice trade, and also,
in our time, on the route of marijuana and the paradises of
Benares, Kabul and Katmandu.

The Apostles: Drug Addicts

How are we not to make a connection between Jesus's
band of disciples and the hippies sprawled on the banks of
the Ganges at Benares? Especially since those disciples, who
lived in idleness and had no fixed abode, *had a strange propensity for sleeping.*

It is well known that in antiquity narcotics were used in
social life as well as in religion, prophecy, and the arts.
Were the Apostles drug addicts? One is inclined to think
so, if one believes the canonical Gospels. Those hippies, living
without working, were certainly not tired, yet Jesus found
it natural that they should be sleepy. He must therefore
have known the reason for it.

The idea of drugs is also suggested by the abjection, the
total lack of moral feeling, affection, and even pity shown

by Peter, James, and John.

Did they use the nepenthe that is spoken of in the Odyssey?

The Nepenthe of Homer

Here is a translation of the passage dealing with that narcotic:

'Yet the daughter of Zeus, the fair Helen, thought of something that was of great aid to her: in the wine that was served at table, she mixed a powder which stifled sorrow, calmed anger, and made one forget all ills. Anyone who had taken some of it in his drink would not have shed a single tear all day if his parents had died, or if his brother or his only son had been killed in his presence and he had seen it with his own eyes. Such was the power of this drug which had been given to her by Polydamna, wife of Thonis, King of Egypt, whose fertile soil produces countless good and bad plants and where all men are excellent physicians.'

According to the Bible and the Dead Sea Scrolls, Jerusalem had become the Great Prostitute. In its shadows flourished idolatry, licentiousness, pederasty, and therefore drug abuse.

As initiates and hippies, the Apostles must have tried to heighten their intellectual faculties and show their dissent by the use of hallusinogens. That is what is done by the hippies of Los Angeles, Paris, Amsterdam, and Katmandu, and it is also how seers, diviners, soothsayers, and prophets have always acquired their powers. It is not by chance that modern fortune tellers read the future in tea leaves: before reading it, they drink the cup of initiation, and not only once!

Indian hemp, nepenthe, opium, bugloss, borage, the *hyosciamus datura,* and many other plants or drugs unknown in our time (the species having died out) were widely used in antiquity. For the prophets and initiates of those times, there was no illumination without an initiatic drink.

In our own time, history has begun again, or rather is continuing and moving toward its end, under the sign of drugs and initiation, which signifies the apocalypse. And soon some authentic messiah will appear and say to the astonished world, 'Verily I say unto you, sacred history and classical history were not what you think . . .'

Jesus was not what he is thought to have been, and although the hippie hypothesis suggested by the altered Gospels should not be rejected without consideration, it is my own belief that the real Jesus was a highly admirable man who came from a dissident Jewish sect that we must now examine: the Essenes.

21 The Authentic Gospels

If one Gospel is to be considered authentic, at least in the eyes of honest exegetists, it is the Gospel of the Ebionites (perhaps from Ebion, the name of a Jewish Stoic, or, more likely, from *ebionim*, 'the humble, the poor'), also known as the Gospel of the Hebrews.

The Ebionites were purists and idealists convinced that only the poor could obtain salvation. They denied the divinity of Christ, regarded him simply as a prophet, still observed the Law of Moses and maintained that only the Gospel of the Hebrews expressed the truth.

The Baptism of Jesus

In this Gospel, the legend of Mary's miraculous conception, the coming of the Three Wise Men, miracles, and magic events were banished in favour of a logical, natural narrative. Yet the Ebionites acknowledged that Jesus had been penetrated by the Holy Spirit, that is, inspired by God, on the day when he was baptized by John in the Jordan.

Esoterically, to baptize, that is, to anoint with lustral water, means to be born. One takes life with the lustral water. And here is confirmation of this in the account of Jesus's baptism according to the Gospel of the Hebrews:

'When the people had been baptized, Jesus also came and was baptized by John. As he was coming out of the water, the heavens opened and he saw the Holy Spirit of God descend in the form of a dove and enter into him. A voice from the heavens said, "You are my beloved son, and in you I have placed my affection." The voice added, "I have engendered you today," and immediately a great light shone.'

It is interesting to compare the exoteric account of Jesus's baptism according to Matthew with the esoteric account according to the Gospel of the Hebrews. (Only Matthew and Mark give an approximate description of the baptism.)

The presumably authentic character of Jesus, the Teacher of Righteousness, is made clear in the book of the Ebionites. In Matthew 5:17 Jesus says, 'Do not suppose that I have come to abolish the Law and the prophets; I did not come to abolish, but to complete.' Since the Law included sacrifices, and since a sacrifice is a ritual murder, it is rather surprising to hear this from someone who is regarded as the God of love! But in the Gospel of the Hebrews Jesus says, 'I have come to abolish sacrifices; if you do not cease to sacrifice, the wrath of God will not cease to weigh upon you.'

It is obvious that the Jesus of the Christians, who approved of bloody sacrifices, was on a lower level than the Jesus of the Ebionites.

Ebionite = Essene

According to the erudite Michel Nicolas, a Protestant theologian whose books include *Etudes sur les Evangiles apocryphes,* (1865), *Des doctrines religieuses des Juifs pendant les deux siècles antérieurs à l'ère chrétienne* (1860) and *Histoire des croyances juives depuis et avant l'avènement du christianisme,* among others, the Ebionites were Essenes of Samaria and accepted nothing in the Old Testament except the Pentateuch.

They practised rules and rites derived from both early Christianity and Judaism: circumcision, baptism, strict observance of the Sabbath and ascetic disciplines, the eucharist, and the jubilee. Poor, sincere, and charitable, they can be regarded as representing the Jewish and Christian religions in all their purity. It is possible that they saw Jesus as the Teacher of Righteousness announced by ancient texts and by the Essenes. Their spirit of equity and their moral probity made them detested by both Jews and Christians, who finally declared them to be heretics. They had the same rules as the first Christians.

The fiery Paul fulminated against their gospel and those

who accepted it: 'I now repeat what I have said before: if anyone preaches a gospel at variance with the gospel which you received, let him be outcast!' (Galatians 1:9.)

The Gospel of the Hebrews sheds so much light on Jesus and his unknown life that it was withdrawn from the Bible, like the Book of Enoch, in the fourth century. Both these books, as well as the Essenian Dead Sea Scrolls discovered in 1947, were and still are severely censored. The truth was too dangerous to reveal.

The Gospel of the Hebrews and the Book of Enoch, which we now possess, are of great interest even though translators and monks deliberately altered their substance.

All the books of the Ebionite sect have mysteriously disappeared, like all first-century books of history. . . .

The Gospel of Khenoboskion

There are many 'Gospels according to Thomas,' Egyptian gospels and Gnostic gospels. The Gospel of Khenoboskion, however, is not identical with the 'Book of Thomas the Israelite, a philosopher who wrote on the things done by the Lord when he was still a child,' which has been known since the fifteenth century.

The writer and Egyptologist Jean Doresse (in *L'Evangile selon Thomas, ou les Paroles de Jésus*), Dr Pahor Labib, H. C. Puech, G. Garitte, and L. Cerfaux have given translations of the Gospel of Khenoboskion, which may have been altered but at least has the merit of having a physical existence, since the manuscript, written in Coptic on papyrus, can be seen and examined. Part of it is in the Jung institute in Zurich and the bulk of it is in the Coptic Museum in Cairo.

Jesus, an Essene

Taken from Jean Doresse's translation, here are some passages that may elucidate the true nature of Jesus:

(7) 'Jesus said, "Blessed is this lion which man will eat, so that the lion may become a man. But cursed is the man whom the lion will eat, so that the lion may become a man."'

(This is a veritable acknowledgment of reincarnation.)

(17) 'Assuredly, men think that I have come to cast peace over the world. They do not know that I have come to cast upon the earth disorder, fire, the sword, war. . . .'

(27) 'And if you make the male and the female in one, so that the male will no longer be male and the female will no longer be female . . . then you will enter the Kingdom.'

(29) 'He who has ears, let him hear! If a light exists within a luminous creature, it illuminates the whole world; but if it does not illuminate, it is a shadow.'

(30) 'Jesus said, "Love your brother as your soul; watch over him as over the apple of your eye." '

(42) 'When you strip yourselves without being ashamed, when you take off your clothes and lay them at your feet in the manner of little children, and when you trample on them, then you will be the sons of Him who is alive. . . .'

(60) 'Jesus said, "He who will not hate his father and mother cannot be my disciple; and if he does not hate his brother and sister and does not take up his cross as I do, he will not become worthy of me." '

(61) 'He who has known the world has fallen into a corpse; and the world is not worthy of him who has fallen into a corpse.'

(83) 'Happy is the belly that has not engendered, and happy are the breasts that have not suckled.'

(105) 'He who has not, like me, detested his father and mother, and he who has not loved his father and mother as [he loves?] me, cannot be my disciple. My mother in truth [lacuna in the text] because in truth she gave me life.'

(116) 'Woe to that flesh which depends on the soul, and woe to that soul which depends on the flesh!'

(117) 'The Kingdom of the Father is spread over the earth and men do not see it.'

(This statement implies belief in a paradise on earth, that

is, a possible life which would be a paradise. It seems to reject belief in an afterlife.)

(118) 'Simon Peter said to him, "Let Mary go out from among us, for women are not worthy of life." Jesus said, "Behold, I will draw her to me so that I may make her male, in order that she too may become a living spirit like you males. For every woman who has been made male will enter the Kingdom of Heaven." '

Translation of the Khenoboskion papyrus has not yet been completed, but what we know of it so far is edifying. It is a gospel similar to those of Matthew, Mark, and Luke, but more vigorous, which means that it has not been expurgated by the Church. The sentiments expressed in it, like those in the canonical Gospels, show a Jesus who is both a lover of justice, as the Essenes were, and monstrously inhuman.

22 The Real Jesus

Five or six hundred people in the world know who Jesus was and what should be thought of the Bible, but *they all remain silent*.

These Knowers are Christians, Jews, or eminent professors at secular universities. Some refrain from speaking for religious reasons, others do not dare to make revelations that would have disastrous effects on their careers or their everyday lives.

What I am publishing in this chapter is, in my opinion, the first serious and documented study ever made of the real Jesus. My thesis may not be an exact expression of a truth that we will never know, but it probably comes quite close to it.

Examined in the dubious light of the New Testament, the enigma could not have been given a reasonable solution. Translation of the Dead Sea Scrolls was begun in about 1960, and although not everything has been made public, they give an unquestionable insight into the real nature of Jesus.

Jesus the Incendiary

The contradictions in the Gospels make it easy to distinguish two Jesuses diametrically opposed to each other.

One is Jesus the God of love and peace: Love one another. We read in Matthew: 'How blest are the peacemakers; God shall call them his sons.' (5:9.) 'You have learned that they were told, "Eye for eye, tooth for tooth." But what I tell you is this: Do not set yourself against the man who wrongs you. If someone slaps you on the right cheek, turn and offer your left.' (5:38-39.) 'If a man in authority makes you go one mile, go with him two. Give when you are asked to give; and do not turn your back on a man who wants to borrow. You have learned that they were told, "Love your neighbours, hate your enemy." But what I tell you is this: Love your enemies and pray for your persecutors.' (5:41-44.) 'For God said, "Honour your father and mother," and, "The man who curses his father or mother must suffer death."' (15:4.)

The other Jesus is a Teacher of Righteousness.

Matthew 10:34-38:

'You must not think that I have come to bring peace to the earth; I have not come to bring peace, but a sword. I have come to set a man against his father, a daughter against her mother, a son's wife against her mother-in-law; and a man will find his enemies under his own roof. No man is worthy of me who cares more for father or mother than for me; no man is worthy of me who does not take up his cross and walk in my footsteps.'

In Luke, Jesus is still more severe:

'I have come to set fire to the earth, and how I wish it were already kindled! I have a baptism to undergo, and what constraint I am under until the ordeal is over! Do you suppose that I came to establish peace on earth? No indeed, I have come to bring division.' (12:49-51.)

'If anyone comes to me and does not hate his father and mother, wife and children, brothers and sisters, even his own life, he cannot be a disciple of mine.' (14:26.)

Which of the two Jesuses is an impostor: the one who tells us to love one another, or the one who says that he wants to set fire to the earth?

Thanks to the Dead Sea Scrolls and the true Gospels, from which I have given a few quotations, it is easy to recognize the real Jesus. He is not the one who preaches the dangerous philosophy of love, that is, of privilege, favouritism, and injustice. The real Jesus is the one who punishes crime, lets only the righteous subsist, and tells us that we must hate our parents, our family.

He is the real one because, in fact, the double Jesus of the Gospels detests his earthly mother, despises women, and abominates love. This Jesus is undoubtedly an Essene, righteous, perhaps, but also harsh, intractable, and pitiless.

Such was the real Jesus: he was hated by his Apostles,

and he hated them; he was hated by the Jews, and he stigmatized them; and he was finally crucified by them, as an exemplary punishment.

Love is unquestionably a bad notion, but is not justice more terrible? The Conspirators of the Year 1 gave preference to the concept of love because, detestable though it was, it could be applied and assimilated by the peoples of the time, within the first few centuries. The Jesus of the Gospels is thus an antichrist, and we begin to see the real secret history of Christianity.

The Dead Sea Scrolls

Only one document enlightens us with regard to the actual origin of Christianity: the Dead Sea Scrolls, discovered in 1947 by a Bedouin named Mohammed el-Dib in a cave near Qumrân, on the western shore of the Dead Sea.

It is now known that in the first century three sects contended for philosophical, religious, and social dominance in the Near East: the Essenes, the Christians, and the Biblical Hebrews. (The Essenes and the early Christians were also Hebrews, but for the sake of convenience I will call 'Biblical Hebrews,' or simply 'Hebrews,' those who in principle abided by the decisions of the Sanhedrin, the council of the Jewish elders in Jerusalem.)

Our ideas of the Hebrews and the Christians are derived from traditional writings, but their real character, previously hidden, is revealed by the Dead Sea Scrolls.

The Essenes were pure, incorruptible, and ascetic, enemies of sin, wealth, women, and even life. Prefiguring the Cathars, they wanted only the righteous, or the Children of Light, to subsist; the wicked must perish.

According to Pliny the Elder, their community was on the shore of the Dead Sea, precisely where the famous scrolls were found. (See *The Dead Sea Scrolls*, by Millar Burrows, and *Les écrits esséniens découverts près de la Mer Morte*, by André Dupont-Sommer.)

These scrolls include the St Mark's Scroll of Isaiah (second century B.C.), the Manual of Discipline (about 100 B.C.), the Habakkuk Commentary (20 A.D.), the Lamech Scroll (from which I quoted in *Le Livre des Secrets Trahis*), the War

Scroll (first century A.D.), and the Isaiah Scroll (first century A.D.)

Historians all agree in stating that none of the scrolls was written later than 70 A.D.

The True Elect, the Chosen People, the People with a Mission

The founder of the Essenian sect was an Unknown Superior called the Teacher of Righteousness.

The Essenes, enemies of the official priesthood, had broken with the 'congregation of perverse men' (the Hebrews) to form a sect of the True Elect in the midst of those who called themselves the Chosen People.

These fanatics were ready to go to any extremes, as is shown by the Scroll of the War of the Children of Light against the Children of Darkness. There was to be a 'vast slaughter of the Children of Darkness.' The True Elect would inevitably have to struggle against the Chosen People.

In this connection, it should be pointed out that peoples with a tendency toward domination claim that they have a special mission, sometimes one that has been assigned to them by God. This was the case, for example, with the Hebrews, the Japanese, and the Germans. But most other nations have shown the same racism or belligerent spirit: the Romans imposed the Pax Romana on the Middle East; the Spanish imposed their military and religious yoke on all of South America; the English feel that they are at home anywhere in the world; the French stupidly believe that they are the most intelligent people on earth. . . .

Two thousand years ago, while the Romans held the known world under their military domination, the future subjugation of humanity was contested among the True Elect (the Essenes), the Chosen people (the Hebrews), and the People with a Mission (the Christians).

The Essenes

The Essenes were perfectly acquainted with the Law. They accepted no women as members, but tolerated them in their community, where everything belonged to everyone. Their teachings involved stages of initiation; the great initiates were the *rabbim* (masters or perfect ones). To them, prayer was 'the offering of the lips,' and they had no worship in a temple because they had left Jerusalem when, in their opinion, Israel had defiled the sanctuary by its hypocrisy and perversities.

On the level of magic, they venerated three mysterious letters: aleph, men and, nun, which phonetically are singularly related to the AUM of the Hindus.

Like the Zend-Avesta, they divided mankind into two factions: the Children of Light (the righteous, or men of God) and the Children of Darkness (the wicked, or men of Belial). Their high priests were Teachers of Righteousness. The last one known to us was put to death at some time between 65 and 63 B.C.; the next one will come at the end of the world, as the Messiah.

According to a source whose authenticity is unproven (*The Death of Jesus,* supposedly written by an Essene who was a contemporary of Jesus), 'The Essenes are not of Jewish origin, but of Pythagorean [?] origin, and among the Hebrews they have taken on a particular and national form [*sic*].'

They made it a rule to cultivate the earth and not to be charitable and hospitable. They practised medicine, did not concern themselves with politics, had no servants, and did not marry among themselves. They led a communal life and their primary principle was to assist those in need.

Champions of Truth

The Book of Tobit, the Damascus Document, and the pseud-epigrapha give interesting details on the rules of the Essenian communities.

The Essenes advocated observance of the truth, no matter what the consequences. According to Professor Dupont-Sommer (*Extrait de l'Annuaire du Collège de France*; Résumé des cours de 1968-1969), their horror of lying came from the influence of the Persian and Hindu religions.

'The Persians,' wrote Herodotus (*History,* I, 36), 'teach their children only three essential things between the ages of five and twenty: to ride a horse, to shoot a bow and arrow, to tell the truth. . . . What is most shameful in their opinion is first of all to lie, and second, to incur debts; there are many reasons for this, but it is especially because when a man is in debt he necessarily lies.'

This intense reverence for truth permeates all of Mazdaist spirituality as well as the character of Zoroaster, who was the Jesus of the first millennium B.C.

This deep cultural sentiment was certainly one of the main reasons for the Essenes' hatred of the Hebrews, whom they regarded as unscrupulous: they distorted history to their own advantage, took over Adam and Eve, and honoured patriarchs such as Abram, who, in order to be well received by the Egyptians, whom he was going to solicit, 'presented his wife Sarai as his sister, thus abandoning her to her libidinous admirers,' as Dupont-Sommer writes, interpreting Genesis 12:10-20. Pharaoh finally reproached Abram for his devious conduct, but without depriving him of the possessions he had gained. A short time later, the 'noble patriarch' again presented his wife as his sister, this time to King Abimelech (Genesis 20:1-12).

Not to be outdone, the good Isaac did the same with his wife Rebecca when he went to Gerar (Genesis 26:7). Still worse was the abuse of confidence that Jacob and his mother Rebecca committed against Isaac – who did not care, it must be acknowledged – and Esau, who was robbed of his birthright by a wily hoax.

But the worst part of all these dark and immoral stories is that Jehovah, the God of the Hebrews, approved of such lies and frauds. 'I will make you into a great nation, I will bless you and make your name so great that it shall be used in blessings,' he said to Abram just before the affair of Egypt. (Genesis 12:2.) And it was by usurping his brother's birthright that Jacob became the leader of the Chosen People.

The Bible abounds in example of lying, injustice, and genocide regarded as justifiable means to an end. Appalled by this immorality, the Essenes broke with the Biblical Hebrews, whom they considered corrupt, impious, and untruthful.

The True Messiah: Melchizedek

A text in the Qumrân writings found in Cave 11 has permitted the Dutch Professor Van der Woude (in *Oudtestamentische Studien*, 1965) to write that Melchizedek, the mysterious personage mentioned several times in the Bible, may have been the Messiah with the mission of bringing the good news and salvation.

'In early Christianity,' writes Dupont-Sommer, 'the Letter to the Hebrews contains a long passage (in Chapter 7) in which the ministry of Jesus, the Messiah of the Christian faith, is related to the mysterious ministry of Melchizedek, that transcendent ministry whose superiority over the ministry of the Levites is proclaimed and demonstrated by the author of the Letter.' For the eminent professor of the Collège de France, Melchizedek was actually the Saviour, and this was also the opinion of the Essenes.

And we too are led to this astounding conclusion: the real Messiah, the Saviour, the Christ, was Melchizedek!

The Hebrews ignored this *khristos* (anointed one), forgotten in an old story, and the Christians resurrected him at a favourable time, giving the name of Jesus to the man who was to play the part of the Priest of Salem.

'The scarcity of information supplied by the Jewish Bible concerning Melchizedek,' says Dupont-Sommer, 'obliges us to assume that between the New Testament and the Jewish Bible, that is, the Old Testament, there were speculations in which the King-Priest of Salem (Jerusalem) was to be exalted to the point of becoming more or less, in the words of the Letter to the Hebrews (7:3), "like the Son of God."'

This opinion is shared by honest exegetists of the Bible and of the Dead Sea Scrolls. It lends new support to the view that the Bible was fundamentally altered and that the Gospels are actually only a revival of much older myths and facts, written for the purpose of accrediting a Messiah accepted by the Christians.

Philo of Alexandria wrote that the Teacher of Righteousness of the Essenes was influenced by the spiritual currents of the Greek Sages, the Persian Magi, and the Indian gymnosophists. (These last were devoted to asceticism, celibacy, vegetarianism, and nudism. Their spiritual influence extended into the Western world, passing by way of Arabia, Egypt, and Greece. Their doctrine was a kind of immaterialistic pantheism. They believed in metempsychosis.)

This remark shows once again that religions, in Europe as well as in the Middle East and Asia, have a common mythical foundation and that it would be futile to try to find any basically new, original, and well-grounded expression in them so far as their personal truths are concerned.

The Teacher of Righteousness

To struggle against the falsehood and impiety of the Hebrews and the privilege they claimed for themselves, a Teacher of Righteousness, who was a high priest, a lawgiver, and a prophet, brought about the Essenian schism toward the middle of the second century B.C., during the occupation of Palestine by the Romans.

The Sadducees of Aristobulus II and the Pharisees of Hyrcanus II, the latter supported by the mass of the Jewish people, were contending for royal power. The Essenian commentators called Aristobulus 'Manasseh' and Hyrcanus II 'Ephraim.'

The Sadducees and the Pharisees were in league against 'Judah,' that is, writes Professor Dupont-Sommer, 'against the Essenian sect (which, in the eyes of its adherents, represented the only authentic Judaism), and against its leader, the Teacher of Righteousness.'

The depiction of Judas's betrayal in the Gospels was no doubt inspired by this hatred of the Jews against the Essenes, that is, the 'Judahs.'

The Essenes wanted neither Aristobulus nor Hycarnus as King of the Jews. Diodorus Siculus reports that, according to them, 'the nation should not be ruled by a king, but by a very high priest.'

The Teacher of Righteousness was a high priest, and the Essenes felt that, as a champion of the republican ideal, he alone was worthy of ruling the Jews.

In about 63 B.C. terrible persecutions were launched against the democratic Essenes. They were all but annihilated. The Qumrân community, sheltered in caves, was probably the one that lasted longest: until about 80 A.D.

The Teacher of Righteousness, states the Habakkuk Commentary (XI, 4-8), was martyrized and put to death. 'At the end of the festival, on the resting of the Day of Atonement, he appeared in splendour unto them [his enemies, including the impious priest who had persecuted him] for the purpose of swallowing them up, and that they might stumble on that fast day, the sabbath of their resting.' The Teacher of Righteousness was thus the Prophet awaited by the Jews, the successor of Moses, 'God having revealed to him all the Mysteries of the words of His servants the Prophets.'

The Teacher of Righteousness was probably put to death by crucifixion, which singularly recalls Jesus's death.

This impression is strengthened by the fact that the Teacher of Righteousness had his gospel and, in the Dead Sea Scrolls, 'he presents himself as the preacher of the gospel, that is, the good news.' (*Annuaire du Collège de France*; Résumé des cours de 1965-1966.)

Woman: Creature of the Devil

The gospel of the Essenes was governed by the concept of sin and penitence. In the Psalms Scroll we read that it was the duty of the Teacher of Righteousness 'to denounce the conduct of the creature of clay and the misdeeds of him who is born of woman.' This same sentiment is expressed in the gospels of the Christians and the Egyptian Gnostics, in which Jesus shows, more than anywhere else, his repugnance for women, including even his mother.

Obsessed with the idea of sin and defilement, the Essenes judged all pleasures to be satanic, particularly sexual pleasure, though they did not categorically condemn marriage and procreation. For them, woman was the essence of perversion and a diabolical danger to all men, especially the Elect of Righteousness. Their intransigence and sectarianism even drove them to call women in general 'prostitutes.'

Since, for the most part, the Dead Sea Scrolls are much earlier than the canonical Gospels and the Revelation attributed to John, it is obvious that the latter are only a plagiarism containing certain dominant ideas of the Essenian precepts. This is notably the case with Jesus, an enemy of women, a protester, and a puritan on occasion, the leader of a community and a threatening preacher against the 'bourgeoisie' of his time. The 'great whore,' the woman 'clothed in purple and scarlet' (Revelation 17:1-4) was directly drawn from Essenian thought.

Like the Pythagoreans and the French republicans with their signs and passwords, the Essenes recognized one another by the fraternal greeting, 'Peace be with you,' which has led some exegetists to classify them among the ancestors of the Freemasons.

Jesus Revived

A document found in the nineteenth century by a member of the Société Française Commerciale in Abyssinia, in the library of an old building formerly occupied by Greek monks, casts new though dubious light on the role of the Essenes in the first century, and on the death of Jesus.

This undated parchment states that Jesus, born in Nazareth, was an Essene. He made himself recognized by signs: breaking bread, presentation of the chalice.

After the crucifixion, Joseph and Nicodemus went to the foot of the cross, where John was keeping his vigil. Nicodemus told Joseph that he was going to resuscitate Jesus, but that John was not to know it.

The law stated that a condemned man was not to remain attached to the cross all night and that his legs were to be broken to make sure of his death. Then he was to be buried. Pilate consented to give the body to Joseph; but Jesus was not dead.

'Nicodemus prepared long strips of byssus coated with fortifying ointments which he had brought with him and which belong to the secrets of our Order. He wrapped them around Jesus's body. . . . Jesus was taken to the nearby cave that belonged to Joseph. There, Nicodemus and Joseph burned aloes and other fortifying and stimulating substances.

'When the body had been laid down on a bed of moss, they closed the main entrance of the cave with a heavy stone barrier, called a *gotal*, in order to conserve the vapour of the fumigations.

'The earth trembled again that night.

'An Essenian brother, wearing his festive garments, as had been decided by the Community, then came toward the tomb. As he was approaching it through the thick, stifling morning mist, the servants of Caiaphas, who were keeping watch in the vicinity, believed that an angel had descended from the rocks, and they fled.'

Twenty-four Essenes soon arrived at the cave. Jesus had now revived. He was taken to the Community, but as soon as he was feeling better he insisted on leaving. A few days later he appeared before his disciples and his adepts, who believed that they were seeing a man who had risen from the dead.

'Then Jesus disappeared from Jerusalem and died from the efforts he had made.'

The Biblical Hebrews

It must be admitted that this account bears no convincing stamp of authenticity and that it only thickens the mystery that hangs over Jesus's life and death. It does, however, give us a complementary glimpse of the Essenes which does not differ appreciably from what we have learned from the Dead Sea Scrolls.

We now have a sketch, drawn from their own writings, of those Essenes whose influence in antiquity was so deep that it finally conditioned the whole history of the Western world.

The truth is that those intractable ascetics were dangerous men: sectarian, narrow-minded, hateful because of the inhumanity of their doctrine. If they had prevailed, the human race would have ceased to exist from lack of procreation, which makes it possible to say that they were most likely in error as well as being sacrilegious with regard to mankind, God, and the universe.

Scarcely more appealing were their relentless enemies the Biblical Hebrews, that is, those who were able to come to terms with the imponderables of life but professed ideas of megalomania that were detrimental to peace and morality.

The Hebrews observed the Law, at least in appearance, but in reality they fashioned it to their advantage. They were determined to impose their supremacy on the world. They unilaterally took over God-Jehovah-Yahweh, the only God, jealous and exclusive, who was to propel his people into the vanguard of all nations, provided they remained faithful to him. He was a God of love, that is, of privilege, wrathful and vindictive, as distinct from the real God, who is a Teacher of Righteousness and grants no unjust favours or exclusivities. Love, as a primary concept, is a hateful sentiment, the source of all perversions.

To attain their promised destiny, the Hebrews refused to let themselves be contaminated by other peoples; they practised a racist policy, marrying only among themselves. But when they were unmasked by their dissident co-religionists the Essenes, they finally chose a solution in the style of Joshua: they massacred their adversaries and destroyed their communities.

They had a single objective: to become the guiding light among nations, the one that would lead all others to salvation, in the name of the jealous God.

The Christians

While these two factions were bitterly hating each other, a new movement was born: Christianity. It arose from traditional Judaism, of course, but it opened the gates of heaven to all the world's peoples. By their faith and their noble human qualities, the early Christians upset the balance of forces, changed the face of the planet and altered the very essence of the Western world.

Because of them, admirable monuments would be built everywhere: churches, cathedrals, monasteries; morality would evolve toward less selfishness and barbarism; the arts would flourish; unknown continents would emerge from the dark seas; the poor, the disinherited, and the humble would see smiles and promises in the heaven that it had become possible for them to enter.

That was how Christianity appeared in the first century. Yet that whole admirable movement was based, if not at the beginning, at least by the second century, on falsification of texts and pure and simple invention of pseudo-historical persons and events.

When it built its structures, Christianity *knowingly* drew upon a falsified version of the occult, fabricated, spurious documents and 'sacred' writings, and appropriated the deeds of heroes borrowed from the old religious and mythical repertory. Two major arguments excused this strange policy: the God of the Christians was universal and merciful and the social situation of the time justified such procedures.

The Teacher of Righteousness was Named Jesus

It is now difficult to doubt that the Teacher of Righteousness either was the Christ announced by the Bible or aspired to become the Christ.

He was arrested, tried, and put to death; he arose from the dead, says the Habakkuk Commentary. But these events, which took place at some time between 56 and 63 B.C. according to Millar Burrows, were concealed. The Hebrews, out of religious hostility, and the Christians, because this crucified prophet resembled Jesus a little too closely, destroyed all records of his existence.

Just as the Hebrews had not seen the pyramids and temples in Egypt, where they supposedly lived for centuries, they seemed to be completely unaware of their sworn enemies, the Essenes.

Flavius Josephus, who never even mentioned Jesus, wrote at length about the three great Jewish sects: the Sadducees, enjoyers of life; the Pharisees, hypocritical and affected; the Essenes, pure and without weakness.

The Christians would have been able to impose their Jesus only with great difficulty if they had left any trace of the existence of the Teacher of Righteousness, from whom they borrowed many characteristics as well as the manner of his death.

Jesus and the Teacher of Righteousness are so closely connected that it is reasonable to conjecture that the man who was crucified in about 63 B.C. may have been named Jesus. It is, in fact, very probable.

Jesus, an Essenian Protester

There can no longer be any doubt about Jesus's membership in the Essenes. It is constantly apparent in the canonical Gospels and, still more, in apocryphal writings and the gospel of the Egyptian Gnostics.

Jesus was a protester when he promised 'hot summers' to those who took their religion complacently and when he stigmatized the rich and announced that the first would be the last. But his flights of democratic lyricism did not prevent him from remaining, in the depths of his heart, a harsh and misogynous Essene. He said that the last would become the first, but he did not raise women from their condition of servitude – far from it! His attitude was that they must 'become male,' which would be an annihilation rather than a liberation. He refused to see his mother and even declared that she was foreign to his blood. He let women wipe his feet with their hair.

This offensive attitude is incompatible with the spirit of protest that should have incited him to elevate women, to give them back the primacy they had possessed in the time of matriarchy. It is obvious that Jesus was not a worshipper of the Mater!

The Hermaphroditic Being

When Jesus says, according to the Gospel of Thomas, that women must become male, he seems to be expressing agreement with the view that the human race began with a hermaphroditic being, that is, a being that was both male and female. (In Matthew 19:4 he says, 'Have you never read that the Creator made them from the beginning male and female?' See also the creation of mankind before Adam, in Genesis 1:27.)

This concept of the creation of man rests on the idea that his original and fundamental nature is shown by the fact that he still has vestigial breasts and in some cases is born with both male and female genitals.

The fecundation of man by man is impossible in the present stage of evolution, but nature shows examples of productive hermaphroditism: in leeches, snails, acephalous mollusks, plants, etc.

Some human hermaphrodites have a vulva, a vagina, testicles, and a penis, but no uterus or ovaries. Others have a vulva, a vagina, a uterus, ovaries, and a penis, but no testicles, and the penis is only a highly developed clitoris. These phenomena are thought to represent one of the transitory phases of fetal development, or a hormonal and chromosomal disorder. It is nevertheless true that the cell has the possibility of developing in any direction and assuring any of the individual's biological functions; from this viewpont, hermaphroditism is a possible biological and human solution.

The Bible implies (and most sacred books present similar theories) that Adam was a hermaphrodite, since Eve was drawn from him.

In Genesis 2:21-22 we read: 'And so the Lord God put the man into a trance, and while he slept, he took one of his ribs and closed the flesh over the place. The Lord God then built up the rib, which he had taken out of the man, into a woman.'

Certain commentators maintain that there has been a mistake in translation and that the correct word is 'side' rather than 'rib.'

If we accept this version, the expression 'better half,' to indicate a man's wife, takes on literal meaning; we can then understand why a man always seeks a woman who will make him *one,* and why sexual dualities persist in some individuals. We also see greater plausibility in Etienne Serrès's theory that each animal body is formed of two symmetrical halves which, to some extent, develop *independently.* This would explain the arrangement of the sex organs in hermaphrodites: male organs on one side of the body, female organs on the other.

Knowledge of this fact, or more simply, I believe a narrow interpretation of the Biblical account of Creation, prompted the Essenes and Jesus to demand or seek the physical state of the hermaphrodite in order to resemble the original creature, shaped by the hands of the Lord, a creature that they imagined as being both male and female.

Initiation or Error

A number of spiritualists (or people who think they are spiritualists) and pseudo-initiates worship a Jesus whom they regard as a great initiate, and at the same time they worship the Mater, whose symbols are multiple and, in my opinion, bear the imprint of the deepest esotericism. It seems inconsistent, to say the least, to honour two concepts that are fundamentally opposed and mutually destructive.

If Jesus had been an initiate (which is highly unlikely: he was only a harsh, bitter, misogynous Essene, with little subtlety of mind), he would have been close to the truth in believing in original hermaphroditism, disapproving of the evolution of animal species and advocating a return to the first state.

It is not impossible that original man may have been a reproducing hermaphrodite, but recent work in biology gives us to understand that the creation of species was more a matter of chance cellular structures than of logical and closely controlled evolution.

The idea of a return to the first state, presumed to be a state of purity because it was directly created by God, is an absurdity. God is always creating not the beginning of a species, but all its links. He is always present in an always-present time. This is an irrevocable initiatic dogma.

Moreover, evolution pertains to an unknowable design of Providence and a universal necessity: nothing remains intact, everything degenerates and evolves. The cloud of original time did not remain motionless in the sky: it dissolved into rain, which was transformed into fertilizing elements, plants, animals that eat plants, men who eat animals, and so on in an endless cycle.

If Jesus had been right, worship of the Mater (mother of humanity) would not belong to real initiation, and the same would be true of the symbols of the cave, the Virgin Mother, the Black Virgin, Isis, the cup, cave water, the Mystic Almond, the vulva, the scars of Gaea, and the Mother Goddess, the basis of all pagan religions. It would be sacrilegious to adorn the Mater, who would not have engendered, with a halo that would not belong to her. Worship would have to be devoted to Hermaphroditus and perhaps to the Phoenician Aphrodite, closely related to the bearded Aphrodite who was venerated in Cyprus.

This view, which necessarily rests on the myth that Jesus was an initiate, is unacceptable and I categorically reject it, that is, *I do not consent to regard Jesus as a Knower.*

I believe in the deep meanings suggested by the Mater, the cave, the Great Goddess of the Celts and, finally, mother water, the Mater of cellular life or, I am tempted to write, of all life. The concept of the Essenes and the misogynous Jesus contradicts the universal principle of life and the command of the Bible: Increase and multiply.

For an initiate worthy of the name, the Mater is virgin, primordial, original water, symbolized by baptism and the sacral spring; virgin and yet pregnant with all cellular life, with all possible lives. And it is because this virgin water is pregnant that it is identified with the Virgin Mother.

Jesus had an instinctive repugnance for the Virgin Mother (Mary), for women in general, and there are those who see this as a sign that he belonged to a world of error, if not of darkness. With regard to initiation and the origin of life, the Essenes and Jesus represent superstition and ignorance, but they must be granted the excuse of faith and good intentions. Jesus could no doubt have found revelation through Mary Magdalene, but he deliberately refused to make that advance.

Like the Essenes and a few other ascetic sects, the Cathars denied women their primordial and magnificent role: engendering the life of humanity.

Two thousand years ago, considering the selfishness of the megalomaniac Hebrews and the barbarous asceticism of the Essenes, a group of initiates, or a Jewish sect of initiates, decided that it was necessary and beneficial to stage Operation Jesus.

Operation Jesus

This conspiracy had a high ideal. I believe that its three main goals were as follows: to recast the rules of morality, to give all men a universal God, to spread democratic social ideas favourable to the disinherited.

The original sect probably had a secret name that has

not come down to us, but when it expanded to the scale of the entire Western world its philosophy grew prodigiously and became Christianity.

The Christians, or catholic (*katholikos,* 'universal') initiates, were not rigorous, intractable, or exaggeratedly ascetic, like the Essenes, or impious and racist, like the Biblical Hebrews. They wanted the world to continue and they preached a God for all men.

Three Gods contended for the favour of mankind: the implacable God of the Essenes, the jealous God of the Biblical Hebrews, the universal God of the Christians.

At that time, after the decline of Greek influence, systematic thought was essentially Jewish. Jewish initiates set out to reshape the world and give it its universal religion. The movement had several things in its favour: the Biblical Hebrews were slaughtering the Essenes, the conspiracy used an Essenian Jesus converted into a God of love, the early Christians were willing to face self-sacrifice and death. The time was also extremely propitious for a renewal; the Egyptian gods were dead and had been replaced by the half-human, half-divine Greco-Roman gods, in whom everyone had ceased to believe. The world of the Mediterranean basin was therefore ready to accept the only god who could satisfy its aspirations: the universal, merciful Lord is needed.

Thus was born Operation Jesus, with, perhaps, an authentic Teacher of Righteousness whom the Biblical Hebrews crucified because he was an Essene and a catholic reformer.

The Substitution of Jesus

We know nothing of that Jesus; the Conspiracy did everything in its power to disguise his true identity. Was he really a Teacher of Righteousness, an Essenian prophet? There is reason to think so, because even though he had been transmuted into an apostle of love, the Jesus of the Gospels constantly reveals his Essenian nature.

He converted the jealous God of his co-religionists into a universal God, he considerably softened their inhuman morality; but he never succeeded in ridding himself of his mistrust, even contempt, of women. In many passages of the Gospels his ascetic temperament explodes, overwhelming his Christian good will, and then we see the Jesus who was armed with a sword and a firebrand, the Jesus who reviled women, whether his own mother or a prostitute, with Essenian monstrousness. The contradictions in the Gospels are thus explained clearly and logically.

We can imagine this Jesus preaching in Judea, perhaps working miracles or apparent miracles, but only within a restricted circle. If he had worked miracles before large crowds, or if he had simply succeeded in standing out above the other prophets of his time, Tacitus, Flavius Josephus, Pliny the Elder, and Suetonius would not have failed to speak of him.

Then he was crucified by the Biblical Hebrews – to the great relief of anyone concerned.

Afterward, as time went by, the Christians transformed this inconstant Jesus, ill-adapted to his role, sometimes gentle and sometimes fiery, into a Christ who blessed, radiated, and preached the gospel of a compassionate God. A Teacher of Love was substituted for the wayward Teacher of Righteousness.

The Gospels were edited accordingly. It must have been no easy matter, a hundred years later, to give a decent and flattering biography of someone who had actually attracted so little attention! To round off the sharp angles, add good precepts and expunge those who had become bad or outdated, the Christians revised Matthew, Luke, Mark, and the pseudo-John, always placing the accent on the Jesus of love at the expense of the protesting and misogynous Essene.

The Pope – adorned with gold and precious stones, seated on his golden throne in his luxurious Vatican palace, receiving, blessing, and rewarding the great, the rich, and the powerful of this world – is a perfect representation of what Jesus denounced as impious and satanic.

With the exception of China and the Soviet Union, Christians and Jews hold most of the world's wealth and the power to destroy, reconstruct, and repress, and they claim a monopoly on dispensing blessings in the names of Jehovah and Jesus.

In the Orient, a Teacher of Righteousness prepares for a new adventure.

Mao Tse-tung the Messiah

Every thousand years, concepts of values become outmoded and must be changed. (History is accelerating, however: the values of the year 2000 will probably be outmoded by 2500.) Jesus succeeded Moses, the second God succeeded the first, and in our time Judeo-Christian civilization, having accomplished its task, has reached its end. A third God will come with the disappearance of the Christian Church.

Protest on all levels – students, politicians, workers, peasants, intellectuals – announces the dawn of a new cycle, a new era that will witness the triumph of a truer, more abstract God, a more universal justice, and a concept of love that will no longer be based on exclusivity and privilege.

A child is not naturally good; his selfishness yields only to justice. When he becomes an adult, his emotional reactions and intellectual speculations make him inclined to give a predominant place to love and privilege. Later he enters his 'second childhood' and again gives primacy to the notion of justice.

It is the same with peoples and societies. China is now in the period of juvenile and implacable justice. Before disappearing, she will pass through a phase of love and then return to justice.

It is good for a man to love his father if he has equal love for the stranger at the other end of the world, his black brother, his yellow brother, his animal brother, his tree brother, and the grain of sand in the desert. Universal love, as taught by Buddha, must be substituted for the concept of love extending, in decreasing order, to God, then to one's family, then to one's friends, then to one's social group, and finally to everyone else in the world.

This notion of justice and universality, misunderstood by the Christians and misapplied by the Marxists and the Nazis, may find a prophet in China's Mao Tse-tung. The deterioration of the white reign, pointed up by the revolution of 1968 – which was infinitely more profound than many like to imagine – is the forerunner of the advent of the yellow peoples.

Maoist doctrine, however monstrous it may seem to be, has remarkable points of similarity with that of the Essenian Jesus of Thomas, and even with that of the Christians.

Matthew 12:46-50: 'He was still speaking to the crowd when his mother and brother appeared; they stood outside, wanting to speak to him. Someone said, "Your mother and your brothers are here outside; they want to speak to you." Jesus turned to the man who brought the message, and said, "Who is my mother? Who are my brothers?"; and pointing to the disciples, he said, "Here are my mother and my brothers. Whoever does the will of my heavenly Father is my brother, my sister, my mother." '

This is the pure doctrine of Mao Tse-tung and the Red Guards.

We are unprepared to analyze and accept it, too corrupt to adopt it, but a new cycle is appearing above the horizon, frightening, horrifying in its implacable purity.

It would be insane not to meditate and try to recognize that, for a billion people, Mao Tse-tung may be the announced Messiah.

God

The only valid worship of God is a determination to live one's life naturally, without letting the hereditary legacy deteriorate. Any other practice is masochism and devotion to the devil.

Such is the certainty of real spiritualists. It is opposed to that of materialists who waste their time, strength, and dignity in genuflections, rogations, prayers, litanies, and other vain pretences, and give lip service to childish dogmas and a morality that is never observed.

The man who lives in harmony with God is healthy, cheerful, happy, and just; he has children to perpetuate life and honour universal Nature.

When a man does not waste his time devoting himself to a God of his imagination, faith, or fear, he can think of devoting himself to other men.

The right religion consists in respecting first of all the God who exists in our fellow men and in the whole universe.

It would be amusing to imagine one of our cells establishing worship of our human self! But we do not expect that, and neither does our biological complex or the universal complex. If the cell fulfills its cellular function, and man his human function, the universe-God will be content.

Part 7

ODDITIES

23 Crimes and Curiosities

A chapter of the Talmud entitled 'Tradition of the School of Elijah' says that the world will last six thousand years. There will be two thousand years of confusion, the Law will be imposed for another two thousand years, and then will come the 'Days of the Messiah.'

The ancients may have wanted to live that time; in any case, they resorted to magic for the purpose of prolonging their lives.

Longevity Recipes

In his *Histoire des personnes qui ont vécu plusieurs siècles, et qui ont rajeuni* (1753), Monsieur de Longueville Harcouet presented several cases of extraordinary longevity.

'Thomas Parke was an Englishman who died without pain at the age of a hundred and sixty-nine. When he was a hundred and one, he had to perform public penance at the door of the church for having impregnated a girl, which shows his strong temperament at such an advanced age.

'In eastern India, according to Pliny and Solinus, there are people who live four hundred years because they eat vipers.

'In the Hebrides Islands, west of Scotland, the people are so long-lived that, it is said, there is the cruel custom of putting to death those who, after a hundred and fifty or two hundred years, have become so decrepit that they are considered useless.

'It is well known how the famous Paracelsus boasted that with his "Mercury of Life" he could change an old woman into a young one as easily as changing iron into gold; he himself, however, after promising others the years of the Sibyls, the long life of the stag, or at least the three hundred years of Nestor, died shortly after his thirty-seventh birthday.'

An Air Ministry in 1740

In about 1740 the Duke d'Argenson conceived the idea of an Air Ministry long before the airplane had been invented. Here is a passage from his memoirs:

'This is another idea that will be called madness: I am convinced that the next great discovery that will be made, perhaps in our century, is the art of flying. People will then be able to travel rapidly and comfortably, and even merchandise will be transported in great flying vessels. There will be aerial armies. Our present fortifications will become useless. Treasures, and the honour of women and girls, will be exposed to danger until an aerial police force has been established. Artillerymen, however, will learn to shoot the vessels in flight, and the kingdom will require a new office of Secretary of State for the aerial forces.'

Leonardo Da Vinci's Perfect Crime

According to Catherine Deshayes, known as La Voisin, a murderess who was burned alive for her crimes in 1680, the playwright Racine poisoned the beautiful actress Thérèse de Gloria, known as La Duparc. It is quite possible; Racine stole lines, glory, and women, and he robbed poor Molière by taking La Duparc away from him to install her in the Théâtre de l'Hôtel de Bourgogne. Since he was often guilty of intrigue and abuse of confidence, I am inclined to accept La Voisin's accusation.

It is less well known that Leonardo da Vinci was also an expert on poisoning, if not sorcery. Here is what has been said on the subject.

The great painter was skilled in making poisons. He anticipated the technique of 'passages,' in which an animal is killed by an injection of poison and the essential organs that have been impregnated with the poison, such as the liver, spleen, and lungs, are then removed. An extract is prepared from these organs and administered to another animal, and the process is repeated. With each 'passage,' the strength of the poison increases.

Da Vinci studied the procedure in plants. He injected potassium cyanide under the bark of fruit trees in increasingly large doses. The fruit – pears, peaches, cherries, apples – was, of course, poisonous, but contained only small amounts of cyanide. It had to be eaten for weeks before it could cause death.

At a banquet in the house of Lodovico Il Moro, fruit from Leonardo da Vinci's garden was presented to Giangaleazzo Sforza, who was fighting for Italian unity. More fruit was sent to him during the following days, until he yielded his soul to God.

This anecdote is also related by the Russian writer Merezhkovski in his biography of Leonardo da Vinci.

The River under Paris

Geologists know that a great underground river passes under Paris. Its volume of water is much greater than that of the Seine. It flows about three thousand feet below the surface and is fed by underground water from the nine parallel spurs of the Jura Mountains, hence its name: the Jura River.

It empties into the ocean between northern Ireland and Scotland, near the Sound of Jura, which separates the Scottish island of Jura from the Kintyre Peninsula.

After passing below the Morvan region of France, it passes below the Morven region of Scotland, near Inverness and Loch Ness, famous for its monster.

I do not know if the Loch Ness monster really exists, or if it is an inhabitant of the Jura River, which may be connected to Loch Ness, but it is interesting to note that the animal hero of the Jura region in France is also a fabulous serpent: the Vouivre. Another coincidence: etymologically, the name Jura means 'wild beast.' It may well be that the French and Scottish legends have a common and authentic source.

The Footprint Rock

To see the strangest rock in France, one must climb to an altitude of nearly ten thousand feet, near Lanslevillard in Savoy. This rock, reports the magazine *Phénomène inconnus,* was transported from its original resting place by a glacier. It is now on the edge of the glacial basin between the Grand Roc Noir and the Roc de Pisselerand.

Like the Celtic rock at Poiré-sur-Vie, it is covered with little cup-shaped depressions and footprints sunk into the stone, apparently the imprints of female feet, since they are between six and ten inches long. There are about fifty of them and they have a depth of a little less than an inch. It is as if they had been made before the rock had hardened.

In the vicinity of the large rock are smaller ones, also bearing footprints, arranged in such a way as to indicate its direction. The place was apparently marked by people from a civilization other than ours. Were they women or small men? The enigma will probably never be solved.

There are also rocks of the same type near Lanslevillard and near Susa, Italy. There are imprints of hands on a stone at Amélie-les-Bains, France.

The Left is Obscene

The ancient Aryans – Celts, Etruscans, Phoenicians, etc. – had what we now judge to be an extremely empirical faith in the interpretation of signs, omens, and events. Whatever was manifested to the right was regarded as a good omen, and the opposite was true for the left.

It is interesting to note that the word 'obscene' comes from that ancient belief.

The following study is borrowed from the great Swiss linguist Adolphe Pictet (1799-1875). He gives a detailed explanation of the bad reputation attached to the left, or obscene, hand. The word 'obscene' comes from *ob*, 'to go, move,' and *scaevinus,* 'left.' In ancient times, a certain physiological necessity presented 'perils' (now eliminated by toilet paper) to the hand that was used. To obviate this difficulty the Code of Manu prescribed the use of three lumps of earth, corresponding to the three handfuls of sand now used in Arab countries. In the arid land of the Greeks, the lumps of earth were replaced by three rough stones or four smooth ones.

The ancient Aryans, aware of the natural inferiority of the left hand, assigned this necessary but inglorious task to it. The Code of Manu specified that to purify the left hand it had to be cleaned with ten lumps of earth held in the right, and then the right hand had to be cleaned with seven more lumps of earth, to purify it after it had cleaned the left hand.

The Code of Manu, imported into the West long before the Sumerians and Greeks had developed their civilizations, was the direct cause of the bad reputation attached to omens involving the left hand.

Among the peoples of Guinea, the right hand is devoted to noble tasks and the left to dirty ones.

In ancient times it was considered discourteous to present the left hand in greeting. It had to be hidden behind the back, in fact, while the right hand was held out as a sign of honour and welcome.

In our time, left-handed people are proliferating at an abnormal rate, which indicates a disorder affecting the very source of our biological system.

The Wise Solomon was a Magician

Solomon, son of David and Bathsheba, King of Israel about three thousand years ago, is renowned for his great wisdom and knowledge. His virtue, however, leaves room for doubt. To protect his right to the throne he had his brother Adonijah put to death and expelled Abiathar from the priesthood. According to legend, he sacrificed nearly a thousand horses to the Lord, who, honoured by this slaughter, granted him the privilege of wisdom. As we read in 1 Kings 11:3-6, 'He had seven hundred wives, who were princesses, and three hundred concubines, and they turned his heart from truth.'

According to Moslem legend, eight angels of God gave Solomon a precious stone which, when he turned it toward the sky, gave him power over angels and the winds. Four other angels gave him a stone which, when placed on his head, enabled him to command all living creatures on land and in the water. Another divine messenger brought him a third stone that enabled him to flatten mountains and dry up seas and rivers to transform them into fertile land, while what had previously been dry land became seas and lakes. Finally, a fourth stone gave him command of all the good and evil spirits that live between heaven and earth.

With these four wondrous talismans, Solomon made a ring by means of which he could constantly exercise his power over the whole world.

He used it to mobilize the building genies when he decided to construct a temple dedicated to Jehovah. The genies' wives prepared meals and served them on tables that occupied an area of a square mile. All the people in Jerusalem were invited to these huge banquets.

The genies made such a great noise by hammering, sawing, and cutting stone and metal that the king, exasperated, asked if there was some way to make the work quieter.

'Only the powerful genie Sachz could satisfy you,' replied a genie, 'but he has succeeded in eluding your authority.'

Sachz was captured, however, near a spring in the land of Hidjs, and the fourth stone in the royal ring forced him to obey.

'You have been misinformed concerning my powers, Your Majesty,' he said, 'but the raven can solve your problem. Take the eggs from his nest, place them under a crystal vase, and you will see what he will do to break that barrier.'

This was done; the raven flew away and returned with a stone called *samur* in his beak.[1] When he touched the crystal with it, it split in two without the slightest sound. Solomon immediately sent some genies to bring *samur* stones from 'a western mountain.' The temple builders were then able to continue their work in silence.

While the temple was being built, Solomon made a journey to Damascus, riding on the backs of genies, but this mode of travel tired him so much that for the return journey he

---

[1] One tradition says that the raven brought herbs that had the power to make stone malleable. Another says that Asmodeus, the Prince of Demons, constrained Solomon to build the temple without hammers, saws, or any other iron tools, only with a certain stone that could cut any other stone as a diamond cuts glass.

had the genies weave strong silken carpets, large enough for him and all his attendants. He then ordered the wind, by the power of his magic ring, to lift the carpets and make them fly. Seated on his throne, he directed the flight like a coachman driving horses. Birds flying above him protected him from the sun with their wings.

This was the first legendary experience of aerial travel which gave rise to the mysteries of flying carpets in Arab literature.

But the magic ring that made the miracle possible was not destined to remain in Solomon's possession. It was his custom to leave it with one of his wives when he went to the bath. One day a genie took it and sat on the throne in the king's place. Deprived of his extraordinary powers, Solomon lost his kingdom and was obliged to wander from country to country.

Fortunately for him, a fisherman found the magic ring in the sea, where the genie had imprudently thrown it. Solomon was thus able to regain his authority, his throne, and his kingdom.

The Death of Solomon

After a reign that lasted nearly a century, the King of Israel saw the Angel of Death, who had six faces.

A legend reported by the German Orientalist Gustav Weil relates the last moments of the fabulous king as follows:

'"With my right face," said the angel, "I gather the souls of inhabitants of the East; with my left one, the souls of inhabitants of the West; with the one on my head, the souls of inhabitants of the sky; with my lower face, I take genies in the bowels of the earth; with the one at the back, the souls of the peoples of Jadjudi and Madjudi; with the one in front, the souls of believers, and yours is among their number."

'"Let me live until my temple is finished," begged Solomon, "for after my death the genies will stop working."

'"Your time has come; it is not in my power to postpone it for even a second."

'"Very well, then, come with me into my crystal room."

'The angel consented. Solomon said his prayers, then leaning on his staff, asked the messenger of God to take his soul while he stood in that posture.

'Thus he died, and his death was kept secret for a year. The genies did not learn of it until the temple was finished when the staff, now worm-eaten, fell to the crystal floor with the body it had been supporting.

'Angels took Solomon's body, with the magic ring, to a secret cave. They will keep it there until the Day of the Last Judgment.'

Part 8

SORCERY

24 Sorcerers of the Lands of Wonders

It is easy to lose sight of the thin line that separates sorcery and magic from phenomena that are supranormal and therefore inexplicable.

In a Bavarian village, two pretty peasant women have an evil reputation as witches: most of the men who approach them commit suicide for no apparent reason.

The Village of the Two Witches

The village is Oberbucha, near Straubing, and the first names of the two sisters are Therese and Anna. They are hospitable in the fullest sense of the word, and therefore attract a great deal of attention from the men of the region.

One of these men, Joseph X., age twenty-eight, was Therese's lover. One morning he was found dead in his barn; he had hanged himself.

Wilhelm X., fifty-five, took Joseph's place with Therese; he hanged himself a few days later.

Young Karl, twenty-one, frequented one of the sisters, or perhaps both, and he committed suicide by fire, after dousing himself with gasoline.

Max, thirty-three, hanged himself after having had the misfortune of falling in love with Anna. Konrad, forty-five, drowned himself after an amorous adventure with her.

This was enough to make the villagers regard the two sisters as formidable witches, and I must admit that an explanation in terms of coincidence seems a little strained. Yet how and why would they have exercised witchcraft? The police have been unable to bring any charges against them because there is no evidence of crime.

Here is one fact that should be included in the background of this shadowy but probably not diabolical affair: in 1435 Duke Albrecht of Bavaria fell in love with a beautiful commoner, Agnes Bernauer, who also had a reputation for making assignations with Satan. The duke's father, outraged by his association with a girl so far below his rank, had Agnes tried and convicted of being a witch. She was thrown into the Danube.

Black Spots on the Earth

In these tragedies, one fact holds the attention of occultists: the Straubing region seems to bring misfortune to its inhabitants. It is as if the 'poison veins of the Dragon' emerged at this place, causing a perturbation between its electromagnetic field and that of the sky.

It is certain that telluric currents condition the behaviour of individuals and, according to their nature and their interaction with the earth's magnetic field, may either be beneficial or cause terrible nervous disorders.

No matter what may be done, Italy will always be a land of good taste, art, and murder; France will be devoted to frivolity, art, and protest; Spain will be ardent, dramatic, and tragic; Germany will be scientific and orderly; Russia will be submissive and lavish; the United States will be authoritarian and generous; China will be cruel and brilliant.

At Straubing, there will always be suicides and unhappy love affairs.

On the highway that passes through Courtenay, near Montargis, France, there is a 'black spot' where cars have a terrible propensity for overturning. The road is straight and in good condition, but in February, 1968, Patrick Dautreau was killed there, along with seven other people, and on June 23, 1969, five more people were killed at exactly the same spot. If this is a coincidence, it is a strange one!

The Telluric Magic of Nanterre

Magic and sorcery appear most often in what are known as underdeveloped countries and in the most backward regions of technologically advanced countries.

At Lagos, Nigeria, a sorcerer killed a little girl from the village of Keffi because she had transformed herself into a snake. He argued that killing snakes was not against the law; the court seems to have partially accepted this argument, because it sentenced him to only three years and eight months in prison.

In September, 1969, a man was sacrificed in New Delhi by a Hindu who wanted to exorcise his wife in this manner.

In the Compiègne region of France there was a rash of deaths and cases of insanity in 1969 because of a 'magus' who was actually a bad sorcerer. The columnist Médicus, writing in a large Paris newspaper, stigmatized this case of possession, which could also be said to involve a collective madness, since the whole region came to the defence of the sorcerer.

'The amazing part of the Compiègne affair,' wrote Médicus, 'is not the fact that beetle-browed stupidity, donkey-eared idiocy, and blind superstition are manifested fifty miles from Paris; what is bewildering and intolerable is that these things also flourish within our capital itself, as well as in New York, London, and Moscow.'

Médicus is quite right, and he does not even mention that black spot of the Paris suburbs, Nanterre, where, for reasons that are mysterious to rationalists, and magic to empirics, there exist side by side a slaughterhouse, a home for the aged, and a university that is a hotbed of student protest.

In the past, this place was consecrated to Druidic worship, but was later Christianized. Since that fateful conversion, Nanterre has been the scene of atrocious cruelties between the Armagnacs and the Burgundians in 1411, between the French and the Prussians in 1815; and the story of the riots that took place there between 1968 and 1970 is well known.

Spells for Binding a Heart

Explain it as you will, the phenomenon is used successfully in French rural areas by hunters, horse dealers, butchers, in short, all those who know how to 'handle' animals: there are 'spells' which attract and hold affection. Any dog, for example, will go with you and be 'yours,' even if he adores his rightful owners, if he immediately consents to eat a piece of Swiss cheese that you have kept against the skin of your armpit for at least ten minutes. Unscrupulous hunters often use this method to gain the services of a dog that has a reputation of having a good nose, but happens to belong to someone else.

Vicious bulls and cows will become gentle and friendly – but only to you – if you succeed in making them eat a handful of salt while your other hand remains on their nostrils.

When a bull comes into the arena, he usually charges furiously, then stops at a certain spot. The bullfighter carefully notes this spot because he must never provoke the bull when he is there. He must lead him to the opposite side of the arena to do his most dangerous work and must give him the final thrust halfway between those two places.

You will master a balky horse if you feed him hay on which you have urinated. The process must be repeated several times, never using enough urine to make the horse sick.

In equatorial Africa, women use a spell similar to the one with Swiss cheese described above, but for the purpose of making a husband remain faithful. They manage to keep a piece of meat between their thighs for twenty-four hours, then they cook it in a stew; after eating it, their husbands stop even looking at other women.

Let us not be mistaken: these spells are effective often enough to deserve a certain credence.

In the arena, the bull traces his magic circle and his 'control stone.' It is up to the bullfighter to determine the location of the altar for the sacrifice.

Never confront an employer or a businessman when he is sitting at his desk, or a rebellious woman when the place does not suit you.

A piece of food that has been soaked in sweat, and is thus impregnated with a person's unique odour, undeniably has the power of a spell on certain individuals if they smell or eat it.

Sorcerer's Herb

It is easy to become a sorcerer. The best means seems to be the use of stramonium, a plant that is common in France, where it is known as 'sorcerer's herb' or 'devil's herb.'

A very weak decoction of stramonium must be carefully prepared: an overdose is fatal. A properly prepared decoction causes a slight feeling of intoxication and a blurring of consciousness. The drinker enters a languid state in which he is inclined to believe anything that is suggested to him. He also has pleasant hallucinations, often erotic in nature.

In the past, a sorcerer would give this decoction to someone who wanted to go to a witches' sabbath. He could then let the neophyte's imagination produce scenes that were usually a reflection of stereotyped stories, but it was more advantageous to his reputation if he verbally suggested events that he could later claim to have witnessed also: 'Did you see Satan order the woman next door to give herself to him on an altar draped with red cloth? And when her sister flew off on a broomstick, you saw her, didn't you?' The poor victim was then ready to swear that these things had really happened.

A husband or lover could attach his wife or mistress to him by persuading her that Satan would take her to hell if she broke the pact they had signed in front of him with their blood.

The 'enchanters' of the Middle Ages used the same method: after giving a stramonium decoction to a pair of consenting lovers, they gave them marvellous, ineffable pleasures that were only partially imaginary. An enchanter could also make a couple travel in a land of dreams for a time that he presented as very long by dividing it into days, nights, months, and even years. The lovers were then convinced that they had visited Venice and Naples, crossed deserts and stormy seas, escaped shipwrecks and ruled as the sovereigns of paradisiac countries. They became so entranced that they paid large sums of money for a continuation of that parallel life, so different from the commonplace world around them.

How could they not have believed in sorcery? This kind of 'magic' deceived gullible and superstitious people for centuries.

The Crocodile Doctor

Nevertheless, we must not believe that sorcery and magic are unreal. Chemists, biologists, and physicists may some day give a rational explanation, but for the moment the phenomena are largely beyond their knowledge. They remain perplexed, for example, by the incredible but true case of Dr Babor.

During World War II, Dr Babor was attached to a concentration camp, where one of his tasks was to hasten the deaths of seriously ill prisoners by giving them injections of carbolic acid in the heart region. After the war, not caring to confront justice in his country, he took refuge in Ethiopia, where he practised his profession.

One of his former companions met him one day and noticed – a little late, it would seem – that Dr Babor had a cruel, even sadistic nature. The only place where his soul felt at peace was at the edge of a pond infested with crocodiles. He liked them and played with them as if they were his pets.

When he was summoned to return to his country to answer for his acts during the war, Babor decided to commit suicide. He went to the pond with a pistol in his hand, waded into the water up to his waist, patted the crocodiles that thronged around him with no intention of attacking him, and shot himself in the head. His body remained unscathed for several days; none of the crocodiles had tried to eat it.

It is thought that, on a biological level, there had been a sympathetic relationship between him and the crocodiles, an alliance between a cruel man and creatures of the same temperament.

The Blood Rite

It appears that enmity between two individuals is controlled by the feeling that they are 'foreign' to each other.

There is then a phenomenon of rejection, repulsion.

Human relations are usually based on reactions of sympathy or antipathy: 'Either you are of my blood or you are not!'

The purpose of the ritual exchange of blood that was practised in the past was to establish a biological bond.

If a king's son did not succeed him, the throne went to a 'prince of the blood.'

There were many matrimonial alliances among France, Italy, and Spain in order to produce a consanguinity that created a climate favourable to good relationships among the sovereigns of the three countries.

A School of Black Magic in Paris

Saemund Sigfusson, once credited with being the author of the Norse poetic work known as the *Elder Edda*, is thought to have been an Icelandic scholar. At the beginning of the twelfth century he was priest of the parish of Oddi, the first to be established on his island.

He is said to have come to Paris to study in a school of black magic, but there is good reason to suspect that this is a false story spread by Christian priests to discredit a writer and a mythology unequalled anywhere in the world, with the exception, perhaps, of the stories of the Knights of the Round Table, written in French verse by the Norman Robert Wace in 1155, under the title of *Roman de Brut*.

Nevertheless, this legend of the Parisian school of black magic is worth recounting.

Courses in sorcery, lasting from three to seven years, were given in a crypt so deep that daylight never penetrated it. During the whole period of their studies, pupils were not allowed to go above ground. They received their food every day from a 'black, hairy hand' and 'acquired magic from books written in letters of fire.'

The teacher, who was the devil in person, never appeared. His lessons were presented magically. The only profit he derived from them was the right to take the body and soul of the disciple who was the last to leave the crypt after each annual examination.

On the day when Saemund Sigfusson finished his studies,

he decided to be the last to leave in order to save his companions, counting on his speed and cunning to enable him to escape from the devil. He wore a large white cape draped over his shoulders and manoeuvred so cleverly that the devil was left holding only the cape. But the iron door of the crypt closed so quickly behind him that it tore the skin off his heel.

According to another tradition, when he left the school the sun was shining so brightly that the devil, blinded by its glare, captured only Saemund's shadow, thus depriving him of it for the rest of his life.

Saemund the Magician

In the legend as reported by Dr Konrad Mauser, Saemund was taught real magic by an astrologer who lived in 'the southern lands of Europe.' Wishing to return to Iceland even though he had been forbidden to do so, he fled one night with the complicity of a bishop. But the astrologer's knowledge was great. He looked at the sky and knew where the fugitive was from the position of his star. Saemund, however, had profited from his teaching: he too looked at the stars, and read in them the danger that was threatening him.

'My master knows where we are,' he said to the bishop, 'and he is on his way. Take my shoe, fill it with water, and place it on my head.'

This magic was immediately effective: the astrologer stopped his pursuit and said to his companions, 'Bad news, my friends! The man we are pursuing has just been drowned, for I see the sign of water on his star. Let us turn back.'

The fugitives continued on their way, but the astrologer again looked at the sky and was amazed to see that Saemund's star was shining with its full brightness. He therefore decided to resume the chase.

Saemund saw that he was still in great peril.

'The astrologer is again coming after us,' he said to the bishop. 'Quickly, take your knife, stab me in the thigh, fill my shoe with blood, and place it on my head.'

The astrologer, who had continued to look at the sky, stopped and said, 'This time I see blood on the star of the man

we are seeking. He has surely been killed by the bishop
who accompanied him in his flight. He is now punished for
having abandoned me.'

He and his companions returned home. But when he
took one last look at the sky, from the top of his tower,
he saw that his pupil's star was again shining brightly. He
then realized that Saemund was his equal in understanding
and that it was just to let him lead his own life with the great
knowledge he had acquired.

The Infamous Column

The plague that ravaged Italy in 1630 supplied the history
of sorcery with one of its most horrible chapters, in which,
as usual, the 'sorcerer' was innocent and the inquisitor was
a disciple of Satan.

The plague attacked Milan and soon spread to the surrounding countryside, where the land ceased to be cultivated for lack of able-bodied workers. There was famine,
then terror, and finally atrocities: starving people were said
to have eaten human flesh.

'Anyone who had a tumour in his groin or his armpit
was lost,' wrote a chronicler.

Priests, terrified by the contagion, no longer even dared
to give extreme unction to the dying.

There were evocations of the Black Plague that had
killed more than twenty-five million people in the fourteenth
century (the figure has also been set at a hundred million),
and a psychosis of death, contagion, and finally diabolical
malediction took possession of all minds. Quarrelling neighbours and political or religious enemies took advantage of the
chaos to satisfy their thirst for vengeance. Finally, superstition
led to the belief that evil sorcerers called *untori* ('greasers')
were coating walls with an infected ointment to hasten the
spread of the plague.

A vicious shrew accused a poor man named Piazza of
having put contaminated grease on the walls of her house.
The accusation was, of course, stupid and groundless, but it
was taken seriously by the judges of the Milanese Senate
and by the religious authorities, always quick to see the hand
of the devil in the ills that overwhelm mankind. The abomin-

able practices of the Inquisition were employed.

Yielding to pain and a promise of pardon, Piazza in turn accused a barber named Mora, who confessed under torture. He denounced a third man, who, to save himself, accused a large number of people, including a Spanish captain, a fencing teacher, and a young man who persistently protested their innocence under the most atrocious torture; they were released after two years in prison. The others were executed.

The Milanese judges were so convinced of their wisdom and justice that they decided to perpetuate the memory of it by erecting a column on the place where the poor barber Mora's house had stood before it was demolished. This monument was called the 'Infamous Column.'

'Our Holy Mother the Church,' wrote a chronicler, 'had the evil sorcerers put to torture, and, more than the ordeal of the boot or of molten lead poured into their ears, was the will of our Lord that made those infamous wretches confess their crimes.'

Once again, in that seventeenth century dishonoured by religious persecutions and wars of superstition, Satan had taken the face of an angel, and the innocent had been transformed into diabolical criminals.

The story of the Infamous Column has been related by the Italian writers Manzoni (*Storia della Colonna Infame*), Ripamonti, Nani, Muratori, Parini, and Verri.

The whole history of sorcery is based on a fundamental error. The sorcerer or witch is either innocent or sick, and those who judge and punish in the name of the Lord or of justice are in reality evil beings inhabited by demons. For demons really exist, but not in those to whom they are imputed with such treacherous self-assurance!

Part 9

MYSTERIES OF THE SKY

25 Strangers from the Sky

It is nearly certain that our planet is the only one in the solar system inhabited by intelligent beings. It is unlikely that men *identical* to us exist in our galaxy or elsewhere in the universe, but there may be beings *similar* to earthly men.

Since 1968 the vogue of UFOs (unidentified flying objects) and flying saucers has died down considerably, as though a kind of lassitude had come over those who have a habit of scanning the skies at night.

The Rationalistic Viewpoint

Although they have not triumphed, rationalists are solidly entrenched in positions with which we should be acquainted.

In the opinion of Professor François Le Lionnais, the flying-saucer phenomenon is not a hallucination, but a collective illusion. The astronomer Paul Muller believes that most supposed UFOs are actually lens-shaped clouds. Dr René Held, a psychiatrist, judges in accordance with rigorous logic: 'In the three thousand years during which strange things have been seen in the sky, not one advance has been made; the situation is the same as at the beginning. In a science, however, even if we make mistakes, go backward, surge forward again, try new directions, or start over from the beginning, there is always something worth keeping, an addition is always made.' But there have been no such additions in the phenomena of UFOs, ghosts, God, elves, etc.

It is easy to draw a conclusion from these considerations. Sceptics believe that there is an intense subjective participation in the observation of singular objects. To understand the problem thoroughly, one would have to study the depth psychology of those who report sighting UFOs. Some of their observations are probably the result of projecting childhood fantasies into the sky.

No More Flying Saucers in Israel

In Israel, where radar and the whole population are constantly on the alert and where vigilance is a matter of life and death, each citizen must immediately notify the proper authorities if he sees an unidentified object in the sky.

If a report proves to be groundless, no action is taken, but if the same person makes a second groundless report of a flying object, he is given a warning. If he sees a third one and fighter pilots again find nothing, he may find himself committed to a psychiatric institution.

The result of this policy is striking: the number of flying saucers sighted in Israel from 1966 to 1969 is zero.

In the Republic of Chad there was a time when no one had ever seen a flying saucer or an extraterrestrial. Then, with the coming of radio, the people learned that every day, all over the world, watchmen, farmers, and motorists saw hundreds of flying saucers and dozens of Martians. Chadians now see flying saucers like everyone else, along with the usual extraterriestrial dwarfs or giants, and sometimes both at once.

Strangers from the Sky

These remarks are, to a large extent, honest and well justified, but the problem still persists because of traditions and exaggerated coincidences that cannot be dismissed out of hand.

The Fathers of the Church believed that the Angels of God were *pilots* of 'luminous vessels' that moved in the sky.

We read in the New Testament: 'All these persons died in faith. They were not yet in possession of the things promised, but had seen them far ahead and hailed them, and confessed themselves no more than strangers or passing travellers on earth.' (Hebrews 11:13.)

In the First Letter of Paul to the Corinthians there is this curious passage (15:45-47): 'It is in this sense that Scripture says, "The first man, Adam, became an animate being," whereas the last Adam has become a life-giving spirit. Observe, the spiritual does not come first; the animal body comes first, and then the spiritual. The first man was made "of the dust of the earth": the second man is from heaven.'

There are indeed two creations of man in the Old Testament (Genesis 1:27 and 2:7), but, contrary to what Paul says, the second one is stated to have been *earthly*: 'from the dust of the ground.'

Interpreting these texts in the light of the theory of the plurality of inhabited worlds, we may say that there was a native human race and another race that came from another planet, besides the angels who descended from the sky to marry earthly women.

According to the Koran, Adam was not born on earth, but elsewhere. In heaven, God says to the angels (Sura II, Verse 28), 'I shall establish a vicar on earth.' The angels protest, but God presents this vicar to them: Adam, who is capable of naming all creatures. The angels, with the exception of Eblis, then worship Adam. (It is specifically mentioned that this scene takes place elsewhere than on earth.) Adam and his wife 'inhabit the garden' and approach the forbidden tree. They are punished for it *and condemned to go and live on earth*. Verse 34: 'Descend from this place; you shall be enemies of each other, and the earth shall serve as your dwelling and your temporary possession.'

One of my correspondents, Gérard Guillet, has pointed out that in Sanskrit the words 'Mars' and 'Mongol' are written in the same way, which is very interesting, applied to the Sons of Heaven.

Stories of interplanetary relations are even more numerous in the East than in the West.

The Vimanas of the Samarangana Sutradhara

In *Essais de méditations immatérielles* Kronos-Paul Fisch quotes a passage by Louis Dubreucq, member of the Association Astronomique, concerning a Vedic manuscript: 'The Samarangana Sutradhara gives a vivid description of flying machines used by civilized peoples for communication between continents, maintaining order, and even great interplanetary expeditions.

'This manuscript,' continues Paul Fisch, 'devotes two hundred and thirty pages to the construction and use of *vimanas* (flying vehicles). They rose vertically, flew thousands of miles and were so fast that they could not be seen from the ground. . . .

'The Samarangana states that *vimanas* were not a product of poetic imagination, but machines functioning by means of the latent power of heated mercury when they were in space. They had no wings and were supported solely by the force emitted. There were forty-nine types of propulsive fire, related to electrical or magnetic phenomena.

'*Vimanas* could escape detection and silently transport perfectly protected crews. Each craft had its own name. The Vedic tablets speak of a *vimana agnihotra* with two propulsive fires.

'Men of that time were apparently accustomed to receiving visitors from other planets.

'Certain specially constructed *vimanas* could rise to the solar regions (*surymandala*), others to the stars (*nahsatramandala*). These were of enormous size, to enable them to go beyond the solar system. . . .

'The Tantjur and Kantjur of the Tibetans describe these wondrous spacecraft with long, tapered shapes, orbiting the earth while awaiting a departure with more than a thousand passengers.'

The Mahabharata, the Drona Parva, and the Ramayana give similar descriptions, as I have pointed out in *One Hundred Thousand Years of Man's Unknown History*.

Irish traditions speak of ancient times when 'everyone danced in the air like leaves dancing in the autumn wind.'

A legend of Saint Vincent Island says that the wise men of the past could easily fly without wings; they struck golden trays and rose into the air by the effect of sound. Another Caribbean legend says that people in ancient times did not go up and down stairs: they struck a cymbal, sang a certain song, and went where they wanted to go.

Paul Fisch gives a certain credence to these traditions and relates them to Superior Ancestors from Atlantis or Mu. 'A whole part of prehistory,' he writes, 'took place on land that is now submerged.'

Astronauts in Australian Caves

In 1838, in a cave near Glenelg River in the Kimberleys region of Australia, the explorer George Grey discovered a strange painting of what we would now be tempted to call an astronaut. The head of the figure is surrounded by bright red circles, perhaps symbolizing the sun; the body and hands are painted red.

In the same cave, Grey saw four heads with cowls or haloes, painted dark blue. One of these 'astronauts' was wearing a necklace. From the gentle expression of the face, Grey decided that it represented a woman.

In another cave he found a painting of a man ten feet tall, with a shapeless pink garment covering his whole body; it makes us think of a diving suit or a high-altitude flying suit. A double circle, pink and gold, surrounds the head, and on the pink part there are six letters or numerals of an unknown alphabet resembling that of Glozel. It is possible that the pink circle represents a Plexiglas helmet.

According to 'experts' and the anthropologist A. P. Elkin, these paintings were made by aboriginal artists and portray Wandpina, the rain god, but this interpretation does not seem convincing. There are many who believe that the Australian aborigines intended to depict astronauts wearing space suits.

The Venusian Aeroplane of Olbia

It is becoming increasingly obvious that official services or conspiracies are doing their best to hide something related to mysterious celestial objects.

My friend Professor Jean Villegoureix, of Limoges, will not disagree with this after what happened to him at Olbia.

'In August, 1968,' he writes, 'I went to Olbia, an attractive coastal town in the Var region, where for years the local archaeological society has been making excavations in great secrecy. On my first visit I was very badly received by a horrible shrew who, without even opening the door, ordered me to go away. . . .

'A few days later I came back with my wife Rosette.

This time I encountered a more obliging concierge and was able to go inside. At first sight, the ruins revealed three superimposed types of civilization: Greek, Latin, and Christian. The interesting objects had been taken away, but there was still a splendid tombstone with a carving of something that bore *an astonishing resemblance to a jet aeroplane*. I tried to take a picture of it, but the guide would not let me.

'I came back to Olbia two days later, and at nightfall I quickly went to the place where I had admired the tombstone, which, I cannot say why, made me think of the planet Venus. The tombstone had disappeared. . . .'

Despite all their efforts, Jean Villegoureix and my friend Philippe Lenglet, who are fascinated by the matter, have not been able to find any trace of the tombstone and its mysterious carving.

Adoniesis, Extraterrestrial Scientist

There is a 'Centre of Cosmic Brotherhood Studies' at 15 Avenue E. Pittard in Geneva, which says it is directed by extraterrestrials and their vicars on earth. The extraterrestrials call themselves 'sons of the divine Creative Flame,' and their spokesman is known as 'Adoniesis, Extraterrestrial Scientist.' The centre publishes messages whose general purpose is to warn the human race against its bad instincts, and also to glorify Jesus Christ, son of God, and the blessed Virgin Mary.

All this would scarcely be worthy of attention if the centre did not sometimes publish things like this:

'From Heaven to Earth, and from Earth to medical scientists and civil and religious authorities – by Adoniesis, Extraterrestrial Scientist:

'The Boniface serum could save millions of people afflicted with the deadly disease of cancer.'

After giving thanks to Jesus, 'the greatest genius,' the message continues:

'Boniface is the name of the doctor who discovered, prepared, and secretly experimented with a serum which can make cancer disappear or regress and, in hopeless cases, has the merit of abolishing pain. The result is never negative.

'Dr Boniface is not a great professor, but a humble

veterinarian who lives in Agropoli, Italy. He noted that goats never have cancer, and it was on the basis of this observation that he made his serum, which is currently being tested in the University Hospital of Heidelberg, Germany.'

Extraterrestrials Operate on an Egyptian Woman

Nasra Abdallah El-Kami, an Egyptian woman of thirty-six who had been suffering from a 'chronic hæmorrhage' for eight years, was cured by an operation performed by surgeons who arrived in a flying saucer.

I am not presenting this statement as factual: I am only repeating what was written in an article published by the Italian newspaper *La Sicilia* on August 15, 1970.

Nasra Abdalla El-Kami had been unsuccessfully treated at the hospital of the University of Alexandria. At the end of July, when she was staying with her sister at Kafr El-Dawar, a small industrial town thirty miles from Alexandria, she underwent an operation one night in the kitchen of the apartment. It was here that members of her family found her, having heard her sobbing.

She told them that three men and a woman had descended from 'an enormous round thing, white and flat' that had come from the sky. She did not remember very clearly what had happened afterward because she had lost consciousness, but the celestial visitors had come into the room and operated on her, removing a rusty nail from her abdomen. To support what she said, she showed the nail, which had been attached to the palm of her right hand with a piece of adhesive tape.

Doctors were summoned from Alexandria. They were astounded by the suture of the incision; it had been made 'with special thread, by a very modern method.' The hæmorrhage had stopped completely.

'The following night, Nasra awakened with a start and began screaming. To those who came running to her, she said that the three men and the woman had returned, this time by way of the ceiling, and had changed the dressing of her incision. One of them had patted her on the cheek and said a word that sounded like "okay." '

This story, which abounds in foolishness and improbabilities, is obviously a hoax. It is regrettable that 'the extraterrestrials Aller, Arkos, Karthos, and Mesek, four Children of the Cosmic Light who descended to earth [through a ceiling!] with infinite Christlike love' should have lent their names to it!

According to Countess Roland d'Oultrement, of Likebeek Belgium, the real 'Leader of the Extraterrestrials is Ashtar, who also speaks in God's name and has the appearance of a handsome adolescent boy.

I am willing to give all assertions and hypotheses the benefit of the doubt, but when I am confronted with Adoniesis, Ashtar, and the four or five other extraterrestrial leaders who have been brought to my attention, I would like to know which is the real one and which are the impostors!

The magazine *Phénomènes spatiaux,* in a special issue of 1969, condemns 'cultists' who glibly report contacts with spacecraft from Venus, Mars, Saturn, or Jupiter, and tell of Space Brothers who have cities on Venus with streets and factories, surrounded by fields with farms and rivers.

Such stories undoubtedly do great harm to the honest and sensible study of the UFO phenomenon.

The Aerial Vessel of Cloera

The Irish manuscript known as Konungs Skiggsa, dated at about 950 A.D., relates this extraordinary story, reported by Alexander Gorbovski:

'A miracle occurred in the little town of Cloera, on a Sunday, when all the inhabitants were attending Mass. A large metal anchor, attached to a rope, descended from the sky. One of its sharply pointed arms caught in the wooden door of the church.

'The congregation immediately came out. In the sky at the other end of the rope, they saw a ship that seemed to be floating on an imaginary ocean. Aboard it, men and women were leaning over the railing, as though watching what was happening at the bottom of the water.

'The people of Cloera then saw a sailor jump overboard and dive into the air, which must have been water for him and around him there was what seemed to be a splash of fire. It was obvious that he wanted to dive down and release the anchor.

'When he reached the ground, the people surrounded him to capture him, but the priest forbade them to touch him, for fear of a crime or a sacrilege. The diver did not seem to notice them. He tried to disengage the anchor but his efforts were unsuccessful. He then rose toward his ship, as though swimming upward. The crew cut the anchor line and the aerial vessel, liberated, sailed out of sight.

'But the anchor remained fixed in the door for centuries, bearing witness to the miracle.'

26 Flying Supermen and the
Mystery of Dolphins

One thing is certain: no one can produce the wreckage o
a flying saucer, or the body of an extraterrestrial, or
living extraterrestrial.

Yet *something is happening in the sky,* something extremel
mysterious which defies our logic, our intelligence, and ou
senses. It is as though celestial phenomena did not belon
to our three-dimensional universe! That is why I believ
that an exploration of what I call parallel universes migh
contribute to a solution of the UFO problem.

Mesmer's Tub

André Castou of Saint-Aignan believes that this problen
is related to that of 'Mesmer's tub,' which was the talk o
Paris in 1788, after the Austrian physician Franz Mesmer ha
discovered the astonishing properties of animal magnetism

This brilliant scientist (called a charlatan by some) invente
a device for producing collective magnetism. It consiste
of an oak tub six feet in diameter and eighteen inche
high, filled two-thirds full of water and containing a mixtur
of iron filings and ground glass. On these substances la
bottles full of water, with their necks pointing toward th
centre of the tub. Other bottles of the same kind lay pointin
in the opposite direction. A lid with holes in it covered th
tub. Metal rods were inserted in these holes. One end o
each rod was in the water; the end that emerged was pointe
and bent. The whole apparatus constituted a kind of batter
or accumulator of electricity.

Patients applied the pointed ends of the rods to the sic
parts of their body. Some of them, especially women, wer
into acute crises that often degenerated into collective hy

teria. To hasten the phenomenon, the patients either held each other by the thumbs or were bound loosely together with a thick rope.

At the peak of their excitement, they detached themselves from each other, ran, jumped *with extreme lightness,* laughed, took off their clothes, chased each other, and sometimes engaged in uninhibited revels.

Mesmer then had them taken into a room called the 'crisis room' or the 'inferno of convulsions.' It had padded walls to prevent them from hurting themselves, especially since some of them *seemed to be projected into the air as if they were in levitation.*

The patients finally passed through a state of languor and depression. Most of them later declared that they had been cured of their ills.

Was this therapy really effective? Did the animal magnetism generated by the tub really give relief? Opinion is divided on these questions.

Mesmer's tub was first tested in a mansion on the Place Vendôme, then in the Hôtel Bullion, on the Rue Jean-Jacques Rousseau. It became so renowned that tubs 'for the poor' were made available on the boulevard, at the end of the Rue de Bondy. It is reported that the 'tub' on the Rue de Bondy was simply a tree to which thousands of patients came to attach themselves with the faith that often works miracles.

The tub mania gripped the population of Paris for seven years, then the fad passed away and Mesmer had to leave the city: his animal magnetism no longer produced cures or relief, and he was accused of having chiefly relieved fools of their money, to his great profit.

A Step Toward Levitation

To a specialist such as André Castou, Mesmer's tub shows singular points in common with UFOs: 'Circular shape, chain formed by human beings, supranormal effects . . . the only difference being that at the Hôtel Bullion the individuals were outside the device, whereas they are inside a flying saucer.' 'I am convinced,' continues André Caston, 'that by using the means now available to science, in combination with the previously untapped powers of our cerebral electricity, we could obtain a new Mesmer's tub with effects multiplied by a hundred, and *there would be levitation of the tub and the individuals attached to it.*'

This hypothesis was attractive in itself, but it took on even greater interest when one of my correspondents, a fervent 'saucerite,' declared that it was also his, and integrated it into a strange thesis concerning the enigma of mysterious celestial objects.

The Terrible Confession of B.D.

This correspondent, whom I will designate by the initials B.D., has devoted more than twenty-three hundred hours of his life to nocturnal observation of mysterious celestial objects. He has no doubt given his last vital forces to it, which makes his confession all the more deeply moving.

'For years,' he writes, 'I have been losing my memory, having had lethargic encephalitis combined with meningitis that has become chronic, for I also have spontaneous hypoglycemia, which explains my difficulties: auras, trances, comas, ataxia, larvate epilepsy, split personality, hallucinations, drowsiness, and so on; I have a dozen other symptoms: torpor, Babinski's reflex, myoclonic contractions . . . but why list them all? I am severely handicapped, physically diminished, and I can barely drag myself through my daily life.

'During the time when I spent my nights scanning the sky, I became, very much in spite of myself, a kind of fakir or medium, capable of doubling myself, with many hallucinations of all five senses after each doubling.

'In a state of trance, I see phantoms and emit ectoplasm from my mouth, which is very unpleasant. Sometimes, especially at night, I also have tactile, auditory, olfactory, gustatory, and visual hallucinations.

'Eight doctors have said that I must have cerebral lesions that have become chronic. My disorders, contracted during my work, have no doubt been aggravated by the fact that I have spent hundreds of nights outdoors, even in winter, observing saucers.'

This sincere and tragic confession first arouses a feeling of pity, then a conviction that B.D. is completely unbalanced.

Does he not admit that he has trances, crises, and comas, that he sees phantoms and flying saucers, that he has hallucinations, and that eight doctors believe he must have cerebral lesions?

No. He does not *admit* anything: he *states,* with calm and precision, with terrifying lucidity.

He is, of course, seriously ill, but while it is this state that causes our doubt concerning the soundness of his judgment, he maintains that, on the contrary, *it facilitates genuine perception of phenomena which usually escape people not attuned to them, that is, normal people.* One would have to be mad to think that a normal mind could analyze and understand the abnormal and the supranormal!

We perceive only one of these three worlds; the normal, the abnormal, and the supranormal; we perceive the one to which we belong.

In which universe do flying saucers exist? In several, says B.D., and that is why nearly everyone can see some of them, but the reality of the phenomenon, or, more accurately, its most total manifestation, occurs in all three universes. Therefore only people who are simultaneously normal, abnormal, and supranormal, from different standpoints, can perceive the fantastic manoeuvres of flying saucers and their landings.

People are often officially classified as either normal (integrated into ordinary life) or abnormal (insane, that is, not integrated, unsubmissive to conventional norms), but never as supranormal. Yet this category exists: it includes people, such as mediums, who are highly sensitive to manifestations.

Schizophrenic or Superman?

The line between reason and madness, falsehood and truth, is so thin that it has always deceived us. A man is said to be sane if he is able to integrate himself into the conventional rules of our social system, even if he is full of cholesterol, believes all the propaganda he has absorbed from television, drives his car at ninety miles an hour, and has killed several pedestrians or motorists. Outside this conventional norm, a person shows disquieting signs of physical and mental imbalance.

B.D., who vomits ectoplasm and sees flying saucers and phantoms, is abnormal; yet this diagnosis would probably not be accepted without reserve by a neurologist. B.D. is seriously ill, but he remains largely integrated into our perceptible world, with this particularity or anomaly: he is *also* able to integrate himself into a universe to which we do not have access. In short, he has genuine psychic powers and his visions, his 'hallucinations,' may very well apply to genuine phenomena, invisible to normal men, but perceptible in the supranormal.

Although this is only a hypothesis, it would be wrong to believe that a man called sane (in relation to our norms) could understand and perceive by his five ordinary senses the objective reality that unfolds in the total universe.

For a neurologist as well as for a spiritualist, B.D.'s visions are not necessarily unreal; they may represent awareness of a superior reality, and actual contact with it.

This is what B.D. claims and explains with a logic that is all the more disturbing because the phenomena he witnesses are incontestably related to a domain forbidden to normal men: the Mysterious Unknown.

Flying Supermen and Mesmer's Tub

B.D. attempts to find hypothetical explanations of his observations. One of them identifies UFOs and luminous objects seen in the sky at night with flying supermen combining the natures of human beings, interstellar spacecraft, and materializations of desire-images.

Having originated on earth, these flying supermen left it in antediluvian times so that they could evolve in cosmic space. Their physical bodies have degenerated, but they have enormous and highly developed brains; they are physical dwarfs and mental giants.

They live at the extreme limits of our universe. They sometimes carry out experiments. A number of them, for example, have united in a kind of living physical conglomeration which serves as a gigantic artificial body. This complex of energy and matter constitutes what may be called an interstellar spacecraft, though B.D. calls it an 'artificial common sarcosoma.' It forms a 'flying saucer,' which is actually an accumulator of brains, a condenser of neuronal or cerebral energy.

As in Mesmer's tub, the brains are connected in series to increase their power. This is also related to the 'chain system' of spiritualists, who join the little fingers of their outspread hands. When the flying supermen are in a trance, their complex develops great energy which causes them to levitate and enables them to travel in space. The state of trance is natural for them, automatic and involuntary, as dreams are for us during sleep.

B.D. gives no precise explanation of the goal of these experimental journeys. Perhaps it is a natural evolution or an attempt to repopulate the earth, if the flying supermen think that the human race was annihilated by the Deluge. This might explain why some 'artificial common sarcosomas' are composed of the bodies and brains of animals – monkeys, snakes, dogs, lions, etc. – which, having left their universe before the Deluge, have gradually acquired an enormous brain and greatly increased intelligence.

B.D., no doubt thinking of his terrors, visions, and materializations, feels that these space monsters, invisible to people who are too normal and not sensitive enough, have always existed, and that they sometimes terrify human beings in the form of doubles, ghosts, astral bodies, souls, or spirits, perhaps unintentionally.

But it is also possible that the goal of these monsters is to be materialized by flying supermen so that they can contend with us for supremacy on earth.

It is obvious that for B.D., who always judges in relation to his psychic and physical states, life is a constant struggle between the normal men of the earth and the 'supranormal,' or spirits that inhabit the invisible superworld.

Let me state clearly that in my opinion these neuroses or psychoses which engender nightmarish visions are more closely connected with the problem of B.D.'s personality than with that of UFOs. Yet the kind of collusion that exists between phantoms and visions on the one hand, and UFOs and flying saucers on the other, may be one of the keys to the enigma that concerns us.

I believe it is important for us to be acquainted with

B.D.'s thesis. Its possible interpretations range from schizophrenia to the supranormal, passing by way of the golden mean, which, according to the great Rabelais, is a clinical sign of common sense.

Flying Supermen: Desire-Images

Besides these bizarre views, B.D. presents another version, related to a truth that is difficult to apprehend. It is less sombre and more fascinating, and it, too, is based on flying supermen.

Flying supermen exist in another universe, let us say a universe parallel to ours, in which they have superior perception of dimensions and no physical bodies. They are thus spirits with vast possibilities, since their system of life involves only manifestations of thought.

They left the earth at a remote time when they had physical bodies. They are now integrated into their superior universe, but they still have a nostalgia for their homeland, as though they were bound to it by their memory chromosomes.

In earthly man the return to his sources, which may be called a pilgrimage, is an unconscious desire that is fulfilled in dreams. In dead sleep, the sleeper identifies himself with the stone, dust, and clay from which he was made, or with the nothingness from which he emerged. In living sleep, he renews his ties with a mysterious past or projects himself into an unknown future, which, in reality, he may already have lived.

Similarly, in the powerful dreams of what may be called their gigantic brains, flying supermen emit desire-forces which, when they pass into our universe, are materialized in the form of images, luminous phantasms, or sometimes spontaneous, fleeting material creations: UFOs and flying saucers.

The lights and flying shapes observed in our skies at night are, on this hypothesis, desire-images, cinematographic projections from another world, a universal television; more precisely, they are the mental wanderings of flying supermen, having no specific purpose of contact, without meaning for earthlings.

'I have watched those televised projections,' writes B.D., 'as one looks at the Medusa or the truth, face to face.

have remained thunderstruck by the experience, and I know that no one will ever believe me.'

Aside from these metaphysical speculations, possibilities closer to the technology of our time must be studied in the hope of advancing our understanding of the problem.

Conquest of the Stars in 2050

Russian and American space scientists have calculated that by the year 2050 it will be possible to send agravitational spacecraft, propelled by magnetic forces or forces drawn directly from the cosmos, to planets inhabited by intelligent creatures.

Such planets necessarily exist in our galaxy, but not in our solar system, unless Mars and Venus have surprises in store for explorers, a possibility which now seems extremely slight.

At this point I will again clarify my view concerning the arrival of 'Venusians' on earth five thousand years ago. Their arrival coincided with that of the planet Venus in our solar system. I have called them Venusians because of this coincidence and because the ancients themselves said that they had originated on Venus, though they may actually have come from another planet.

An inhabited planet, as we conceive it on earth, is a planet that has water, an atmosphere, vegetation, and inhabitants endowed with intelligence, consciousness, and means of expression. Our galaxy undoubtedly contains such a planet, but it is unlikely that it is *identical* to ours, with the same size, density, rotation, magnetic field, and atmosphere. It is probably only similar, with an appreciably different atmosphere which conditions a human race biologically different from us. Furthermore, the distribution of dry land and oceans is surely different from ours.

Astrophysicists therefore expect, in the future, to encounter intelligent creatures whose nature they cannot yet even guess.

Be that as it may, astronauts will seek to contact physical creatures living on a planet with continents and oceans, made of limestone, carbon, hydrogen, nitrogen, oxygen, and all the other components of our globe. Astrophysicists are therefore preparing to communicate with physical creatures constituted like earthly animals or plants.

Analysis of matter taken from the moon seems to indicate that all heavenly bodies are made of the same elements.

Marine Space People

Before anyone had landed on the moon, many people believed that it had a certain microbic and perhaps even plant life, although no human beings lived on it and probably never had. Some writers had announced that it was inhabited and held the key to our protohistory, but this was generally regarded as esoteric nonsense.

The idea that the moon once served as a relay for space travellers is not an incredible hypothesis, but it is obvious that for thousands of years, at least, it has had no appreciable atmosphere and no population in the usual sense of the word.

In their present geophysical state, Mars, Venus, and Mercury probably have no human life, though they surely have forms of cellular life (except perhaps for Mercury, which must be radioactive and scorched like the moon).

Farther away from our orbit, it seems certain that Jupiter Saturn, Uranus, and Neptune are unsuited to human life because of their nature, density, and extremely low temperatures: between a hundred and fifty and two hundred and seventy degrees below zero Centigrade.

According to the American astronomer Kuiper, the rings of Saturn are solid ammonia whose temperature is about two hundred degrees below zero Centigrade. Jupiter is also said to be partially composed of solid ammonia, which calls for a remark on the miraculous nature of the names given to this planet and to ammonia. The word 'ammonia comes from 'Ammon,' because ammonia was once prepared near the temple of Jupiter Ammon in Libya. When earthlings land on Mercury, it will be interesting to know whether the metal mercury is abundant there, as was believed by alchemists. They maintained that the metal was generated by this little planet.

The first 'inhabited' planet discovered by astronauts – if they discover one – will be outside the solar system. I

may be either mostly dry land or completely covered by an
ocean. In the latter case, if it has any intelligent creatures
they can only be marine or amphibious in the sense of living
in both water and air.

How could we make contact with such creatures? Physicists,
biologists, and chemists have already considered all the
problems and possibilities involved in attracting the attention of those space cousins, making them understand our
intentions and adjusting ourselves to their way of life.

The first step would be to communicate with them by
signs, sound, drawings, writing, or even telepathy. If this
proved to be successful, scientists would next study the
possibilities of either adapting the space creatures to our
land and atmospheric conditions or creating earthlings with
gills.

Homo Aquaticus, capable of living in water for extended
periods, is now in an advanced stage of development. He
will be used by our astronauts for making contact with space
creatures if they are found on an 'oceanic' planet, that is,
one which is totally or mostly covered with water.

Extraterrestrials may therefore have their first contact with
earthlings in the form of a kind of sea monster. If they
are only relatively highly evolved, they may imagine that
all the inhabitants of Earth are fish-men.

Orejona, Oannes, Venus, and Homo Aquaticus

Logically, since American and Russian astronauts will most
likely succeed in reaching other planets, we must accept the
possibility that extraterrestrial astronauts have already succeeded in reaching ours.

There is no proof of such visitors in our time, but it is
highly probable that extraterrestrials came to our planet
in past geological eras, and even in protohistorical times.

Although a certain unscrupulous author, having arrogated
the idea to himself, likes to write 'my gods' in reference
to those cosmic travellers, I discussed them long before
he did (in 1962) and explained at length that they were
Initiators who had been deified by the ancients.

Although it is believed that most of those extraterrestrials
– for example the 'angels' of the Bible and the Book of

Enoch – were physically similar to us, some of them are described as having features that seem to indicate aquatic life. (See my book *Le Livre des Secrets Trahis,* Chapter VI-IX.)

Orejona, the mother and Initiator of the Incas, had only four fingers on each hand and four toes on each foot, and they were *webbed*.

Oannes, god of the Chaldeans, was, according to their traditions, the original civilizer of men. He taught them writing, the sciences, the arts, and agriculture, and his name means 'stranger' in Syriac. Berossus wrote that he was a monster, half man and half fish, who came from the Erythrean Sea.

Venus, a Greek and Roman divinity of Olympus, was born of the foam of the sea, which is in harmony with the modern biological view that all life arose in the sea.

It is not a good experiment to try, but it has been observed that a human baby can swim without having been taught to do so, or can at least adapt himself naturally to swimming.

To sum up, our time of scientific research, and no doubt of apocalypse, is witnessing the beginning of two phenomena that are connected by a fantastic bond:

– Men are preparing to go to other planets, and perhaps to those from which their ancestors came.

– Scientists are working toward the creation of men capable of living in water and even breathing oxygen directly from it: *Homo Aquaticus.*

It is as if earthlings had a premonition that *Homo Aquaticus* would soon serve to acclimatize a hybrid human species on a planet nearly or entirely covered with water.

The Dolphin, Ancestor of Man

No other animal shows as much disinterested friendship for us as the dolphin.

When a holiday-maker killed a dolphin off the Ile du Levant in 1969, his glorious exploit earned him the contempt of all the naturists on the island. Such acts of savagery are rare, but the law should protect the lives of dolphins as well as those of men.

The dolphin never attacks human beings; he always

swims toward them with obvious confidence and affection.
These touching sentiments suggest that in the past the dolphin
must have been a faithful companion of men, and may even
have been a kind of parallel man endowed with great intelligence and the power of speech.

According to the initiate Marcel Sourbieu, author of
Infernale Mission (soon to be published), insemination experiments were once performed by the Kerubim (angels) and
resulted in a human foetal monster: the dolphin. The germs,
unable to evolve otherwise, adopted amphibious life. Hence
the almost human faculties of the dolphin, and his possibility
of evolving toward humanity under certain favourable conditions of hybridation.

The ancestor of the dolphin was the creodont, which lived
a hundred million years ago on land and in the sea. From
that remote forebear his skeleton has preserved vestiges of
legs, pointed toes, hips, and vertebrae.

Like man, the dolphin lives in an organized society, with
rules, rites, and customs. He is subject to such human ills
as infarcts, cerebral congestion, and stomach ailments. His
foetus is so similar to a human foetus that physiologists have
serious reasons for believing that the two species may be
descended from a common ancestor. This is in agreement with
traditions which state that dolphins were once human and
still have a nostalgic yearning for that remote golden age. They
may be in the process of returning to it, judging from experiments that have been successfully performed in America.

The oceans now cover seventy per cent of the earth's surface and it is nearly certain that they covered much more of
it in earlier geological eras. It is therefore not unreasonable
to think that the first intelligent creature may have been a
marine animal: the dolphin.

In millions of years, mutants of this intelligent animal,
endowed with a large brain, may have evolved first toward
an amphibious form, then a specifically terrestrial one, as
the continents emerged from the oceans. If so, man is the
finished product of that evolution and the present dolphin is
either the original type or a retrograde species, conditioned
by having remained in the water.

This is only a hypothesis, but it would explain the dolphin's
extraordinary affection for man, since they would both
be of the same blood.

The Dolphin: an Experiment by Extraterrestrials

This human genealogy is not satisfactory, however, if we take into account a traditional datum, more fantastic and yet more likely: man in his present form is a descendant of extraterrestrials. The dolphin and the native form of man may have had a common origin, but other hypotheses must be considered. The problem of our origin is only pushed farther back in time: extraterrestrial man may himself be a mutated descendant of extraterrestrial dolphins.

If our astronauts land on an 'oceanic' planet, will *Homo Aquaticus* be able to make contact with the marine creatures of that planet? If not, Russian and American biologists will consider adapting the dolphin to extraterrestrial life. This would be the first stage of colonization, the second being the adaptation of *Homo Aquaticus*.

What is being considered in the space programme of the twentieth century may actually have happened thousands or even millions of years ago.

The theory of probability gives very little chance to the co-existence of two advanced civilizations in our restricted universe, unless superior extraterrestrials had solved the problem of time. If extraterrestrials visited our planet in the distant past, let us say in the Tertiary, they found it more than three-quarters submerged by the oceans. No intelligent creature is thought to have existed at that time, but the most highly evolved animal may have been a marine species.

If astronauts came here a million years ago, what did they do? We may assume that they made adaptation experiments with prototypes brought from their planet: the yeti on land, the dolphin in the sea. Perhaps they tried to adapt a species of man who was the only completely successful experiment, the only one with a perfect adaptation and a valid intellect. In that case, modern man is similar to his progenitors, but appreciably smaller. Traditions report that the Initiators, the original gods, were giants. (On the reign of the giants, see *Kobor Tigan't,* by Sylf, Editions Robert Laffont, Paris.)

They must also have tried other implantations: monsters that were half human and half snake, for example, or half human and half horse, or sphinxes and other hybrid animals that have vanished without a trace except for the memory of the struggle between men and monsters for supremacy on earth.

Then thousands of years went by; the Initiators either left our planet or abandoned their experiments; man established his superiority while the dolphin gradually lost his intellectual faculties. There was, however, the period described by tradition, when the two species were at about the same level, when men and dolphins conversed with each other.

After the Deluge, man descended to the lowest stage of his intelligent condition. It is possible that radiation, or a survival of their original faculties, then enabled mutant dolphins to play the part of Oannes. This is a hypothesis that should not be completely rejected.

Orejona came from an 'Oceanic' Planet

The legend of Orejona gives rise to a much more rational explanation. According to Incan traditions, a spacecraft that shone more brightly than the sun once landed at the edge of Lake Titicaca. From it came a beautiful young woman. She was from the planet Venus and she became the mother of the earthly human race.

Her name, Orejona, was given to her because, like many gods and beings of illustrious origin – Buddha, the gods of Easter Island, Tiahuanaco and Tula, the sphinx of Giza – she had *big ears*. Her skull was long and pointed and there were only *four webbed fingers or toes* on each of her hands and feet.

Was Orejona really from Venus? It cannot be proved, but we may believe it because this story has so many points in common with the Initiators of the Magi, the Chaldeans, and the Phoenicians that it seems impossible for them to be coincidences. Furthermore, the mysterious personages carved on the Puerta del Sol at Tiahuanaco, on whose heads are drawn strange flying machines and *a kind of diving suit,* also have only four fingers on each hand!

Are we to regard all these things as coincidences: the webbed hands, the diving suit, the Venusian significance that is attributed to the Puerta del Sol, the Venusian identity of Orejona, Oannes the fish-Initiator living in the same period,

and the ancients' constantly repeated assertion that Venus
was the *goddess of the waters*?

However fantastic may be belief in the authenticity of
Orejona's arrival on earth, it is much more reasonable than
rejection of traditions that are repeated countless times in
chronicles all over the world. We must therefore acknowledge
that Orejona belonged to an amphibious human race and
came from what I have called an 'oceanic' planet.

If space travellers of that period had the same concerns
as twentieth-century astrophysicists, they must have tried to
adapt an animal to life on earth. I have already examined
this hypothesis, but, viewed from another angle, it leads to
the conclusion that the messenger from an 'oceanic' planet
could only have been the dolphin, intelligent and able to
speak, scientifically conditioned – and here we come back to
brain transplants – to love man and respond to the magic,
melodious charm of his speech.

The Mystery of the Mermaid and Melusina

Another marine creature, legendary but perhaps real, is
the mermaid of the ancients, which has sometimes been identified as the manatee, the dugong, or the sea cow. The mermaid described by Homer as tempting the wily Ulysses never
existed, as such, except in the imagination of the Greeks,
but it is still interesting to note that they had a magic song
and a language. Are we to establish a correlation between
them and the dolphins, whose ancestors they may have been
in prehistoric times, if not the link between them and a species
of extraterrestrial *Homo Aquaticus*?

Three thousand years ago, Homer attributed a human
form to mermaids, as to goddesses and nymphs. It was not
until much later that they came to be regarded as marine
creatures with women's breasts.

Ovid says that they had wings, which shows the deterioration of the legend, and consequently the possibility of an
original reality.

Like Orejona and Oannes the fish-man, the mermaids
were Initiators and Knowers. In the Odyssey they call out to
Ulysses, 'Come, generous Ulysses . . . to admire the sweet
harmony of our singing and learn many things from us . . .

for nothing that takes place in this vast universe is hidden from us.' They were silent, says tradition, when they encountered the Argonauts, who were also great Initiators. Orpheus charmed them with his lyre and, out of resentment, they plunged into the sea and changed themselves into rocks.

The mystery of fish-gods, dolphins, and mermaids leads us into the realm of initiation and to the last of the Celtic mermaids: Melusina, the snake-woman who sang so melodiously or tragically, and whose den was the Fountain of Sé (Knowledge) at Coulombiers, in the Poitou region of France.

Whatever may be the mystery of the dolphin and of Initiators who were half human and half fish (or half snake), it draws our attention toward a Mysterious Unknown that seems to be related to extraterrestrial Initiators.

We do not know what UFOs are, but on the hypothesis that the universe is a vast living organism and that each planet is a part of that organism, we may assume that man has a great and unknown function, perhaps similar to that of DNA, the *messenger* of cellular life. Our mission is no doubt to go some day to the stars, just as the mission of other intelligent beings in the cosmos is to come to our planet to bring new germs of life and a beneficial hybridation.

But these exchanges, connections, and interactions probably do not take place as we imagine, because our understanding and our powers of conception are limited by our dimensional system. Yet already, to a small extent, physicists are detecting and studying certain messengers from other worlds: neutrinos and cosmic particles. This proves that all universes are able to communicate and exchange visitors.

Soon, perhaps, a real scientist, whether he be an astrophysicist, a chemist, or a great initiate, will find the golden key that will enable us to give a convincing meaning to those messages or messengers that we cannot now decipher or see because the time has not yet come.

Index